MATA HARI

The True Story

Russell Warren Howe

MATA HARI

The True Story

DODD, MEAD & COMPANY
New York

Designed by Claire Counihan

First Edition

1 2 3 4 5 6 7 8 9 10

Library of Congress Cataloging in Publication Data

Howe, Russell Warren, 1925–
Mata Hari, the true story.

Includes index.
1. Mata Hari, 1876–1917.   2. World War, 1914–1918—
Secret Service—Germany.   3. Spies—France—Biography.
4. Spies—Germany—Biography.   I. Title.
D639.S8Z454   1986   940.4'87'43   85-27527
ISBN 0-396-08717-5

As for myself, I have been sincere.
My life and my self-interest are the guarantee
of that. Today, around me, everything is
collapsing, everyone turns his back, even he for
whom I would have gone through fire. Never would
I have believed in so much human cowardice. Well,
so be it. I am alone. I will defend myself and
if I must fall it will be with a smile of
profound contempt.

MATA HARI
May 31, 1917

Contents

CONTENTS

Author's Note

W. Somerset Maugham once advised this writer to leave journalism "lest you lose the ability to create your own characters." The master was right: After two books of fiction, I produced eight books of history and politics. What Maugham could not know, when he spoke to me thirty-three years ago, was that after four decades of journalism, the high clowns of politics and the shrill crises that are soon forgotten all seem to a reporter to be more fictional than fiction itself. An author in search of a character tends to look to the past. I wanted to do a biography of an historical figure who had not tried to run a country. I never found a subject, but a subject found me.

In the January 1984 issue of *The Smithsonian*, there was a very readable article on the Orient Express, illustrated by pictures of some of the famous passengers of that famous train. One of the photographs was of Mata Hari in all her splendor—an hourglass corset and a turn-of-the-century ballroom dress. So far as I could recall, hers was a mystery that had never been solved.

Hers was also the best-known spy name in the world. She had slept with lovers on an almost industrial scale while managing to perform her given vocation of courtesan with a certain class. She was, in short, an intriguing subject. I decided to see what existed in the literature, then forgot about it.

About six months later, while in the library of American University, near my home, I remembered the lady and found that she was not listed, either under subject or author, in the card catalog; but in the *Encyclopaedia Britannica* I discovered that opinion was indeed still divided as to her guilt or innocence and that her judicial file in Paris was sealed.

Nothing fascinates a reporter more than a story to which his colleagues have been denied access. The encyclopaedia recommended two books for further reading: Major Thomas Coulson's, which concluded that she was guilty, and Sam Waagenaar's, which sought to prove her innocence. The article noted, however, that Waagenaar had been stymied by his inability to get a waiver on the dossier seal.

I put my name on a waiting list for both books at the Martin Luther King central municipal library in Washington. Coulson's arrived. Any reporter, even one attacking a subject for the first time, can tell when a book is hogwash. This was a potboiler that cited no sources. The King library never sent the Waagenaar book until I had almost finished my own. The Library of Congress had lost its copy, but it loaned me the French translation, which had the advantage of untranslated quotes.

Having now read the files that were withheld from Waagenaar (he did, however, get some surprisingly accurate excerpts by devious means), I can say that his work was the only serious book written on this subject hitherto. His thirty years of on-and-off research paid off in a book that contains surprisingly few inaccuracies or wrong guesses, even though it inevitably lacks nearly all the facts to prove his thesis. At the Bibliothèque Nationale in Paris, where there seem to be almost as many books on Mata Hari as on Napoleon, I learned why the *Encyclopaedia Britannica* had not bothered to mention any of them. It is hard to conceive of a subject that has been so badly reported, despite the lady's enormous fame.

I was also intrigued to learn from Waagenaar's own Author's Note that he had been a colleague of my father's and that both had been involved in the promotion of the Greta Garbo movie on Mata Hari in 1931 (which I never saw—I had a free pass to all MGM movies, but my mother thought *Mata Hari* would be unsuitable for a five-year-old).

Charles Hernu, the French minister of national defense, was persuaded to let me break the hundred-year seal on the Mata Hari dossier in spite of the fact that only sixty-eight years had passed. What I read did not conform to anything that I had expected or to any of the theories propounded by Mata Hari's defenders and detractors.

The papers were marked "secret," so the seat next to mine in the military archives reading room at Vincennes was left empty, lest any French general writing his memoirs be tempted to look over my shoulder. Since the material was classified, I was not allowed to make photocopies and, since it was a reading room, I could not talk into a tape recorder. (I was later permitted, however, to reproduce two of her letters and the snapshots, from her purse, of the lady with the love of her life.)

While I was reading through my approximately five hundred pages of handwritten notes, I naturally came across discrepancies and possible errors, along with some things that were not clear. I returned to Vincennes on a checking mission. This was fortunate, because I discovered that some of the most sensitive files had been withheld during my first visit and had been put in a large manila envelope marked "not to be communicated." This envelope was now in the files with an annotation saying that I had been authorized to read everything. The envelope contained key material that solved the discrepancies that I had found while reading my notes; but I would never have known about this material or about the bureaucratic minuet that had taken it out and put it back had I not returned to Vincennes on a routine fact-checking trip.

I would like to express my thanks to everyone in France who helped me to unearth this trove, notably to Professor Marie-Claire Pasquier-Doumer, and my gratitude for the cooperation of General Delmas, the director of the Historical Service of the Armies, and his cheerful and hospitable staff at the Château de Vincennes.

For the author of a book like this, it was an added and moving advantage to be able to look from the castle windows at the spot where Mata Hari was executed, and to reflect that, if the office of a general seemed too large for his desk, it was because these were royal quarters—and incidentally the ones from which Louis XVI and Marie-Antoinette went to their own executions.

The Ladoux and Lenoir files referred to in the narrative remain sealed, so this book is not the very last word on the fate of Mata Hari; but it does, I hope, destroy the myths. It responds to nearly all the questions; for the answers, the reader must read on.

Since I have a distaste for footnotes and appendices, I have made a point of quoting sources in the text. I have avoided all psychodrama; there are absolutely no events or conversations in this book for which there is not an historical record. I remain a reporter, despite Mr. Maugham's wise and well-intended advice.

RUSSELL WARREN HOWE
Paris, Washington, and Seoul, 1985

MATA
HARI

The True Story

I

THE GUNS OF VINCENNES

October 1917

IT WAS THE EARLY HOURS of October 15, 1917, in Paris. Mist hung in the yellow gaslight of the streets and the unseasonable temperature was just above freezing point as a military chauffeur drove his Salmson coupé to an old apartment building on the boulevard Péreire. The driver pulled his watch from a breast pocket, glanced at it and put it back, then waited a few minutes.

Promptly at four A.M., he opened his door, stepped onto the running board and down to the cobbled street. He closed the door and adjusted his cap. He looked up at a lighted window and saw a silhouette in officer's uniform signal to him that he was coming down. The chauffeur waited in the cold, clapping his arms briskly across his woolen *vareuse*.

A few minutes later, Captain Pierre Bouchardon, a forty-six-year-old lawyer who was serving in the French army's military justice section, emerged from the building, slamming the heavy door of the *porte-cochère* behind him. As he stepped across the empty street, the driver opened a rear door and saluted. Bouchardon, a thin, moustached figure, touched his *képi* and climbed wearily into the car, edging over to the right seat to have a forward view. The driver closed the door and took his place in the uncovered section in the front. He had left the engine running so as not to have to crank it again in the cold. With his left foot, he stretched all his weight against the heavy clutch pedal and moved the long gear lever into first speed. With his right foot, he pressed lightly on the throttle, watching the revolution-counter, then eased the clutch in gently so as not to stall; he drove away slowly, rubbing moisture from the upright windshield with his bare hand.

"Saint-Lazare," said Bouchardon.

"Understood, Captain."

They were not headed for the railroad station but for the women's prison of the same name. The streets were almost empty, and at four-fifteen they arrived. The driver stepped down and hurried around the car to let out his passenger. Once again, perfunctory salutes were exchanged, and the door was closed. The private trotted ahead of the captain to bang his fist on the small door in the prison wall. Soon Bouchardon was in the office of the prison director, Jean Estachy, and the two men exchanged brief amenities. Estachy poured bowls of coffee from a tall military thermos flask; the slim examining magistrate in uniform warmed his hands on the bowl and yawned. He sat down in a stiff, ugly wooden chair, his *képi* on his knees, his nervous eyes contemplating his coffee from their bony orbits. He took a sip, then glanced at his fingernails: one seemed a little longer than the others and, in what was his most noted tic, he began to bite it down to conformity.

Dr. Léon Bizard, the prison's visiting physician, and his intern assistant, Jean Bralez, arrived a few minutes later. Estachy's mean-featured male chief warder, Piétri, who had brought them in, poured more coffee; there was superficial conversation. Next came Lieutenant André Mornet, commissioner of the government—prosecuting attorney—of the Third Council of War, or military court; Lieutenant-Colonel Albert-Ernest Somprou, the middle-aged Republican Guard officer who had presided at the trial, and the other six judges; Captain Thibaud, the chief military court clerk; Major Jullien, the chief military prosecutor; Dr. Socquet, an army physician; General Wattine, chief legal counsel of the French army; and the defendant's seventy-four-year-old lawyer, Edouard Clunet. The officers discussed the uncertain news from the Front. Would the Americans, whose green soldiers were beginning to be shipped in from the plains and cities across the sea, make a real difference? Clunet, sleepless and haggard, stood apart, peering through a grim, dirty window at the darkness outside and wishing the prison coffee were stronger and not so sweet. He looked and felt older than his years.

They were waiting for Major Emile Massard, the representative of the military governor of Paris. Massard did not get there until four-forty-five. His driver had had trouble cranking his car. The major reported that the news of the execution had evidently leaked: a small crowd was forming outside for a glimpse of the condemned spy. He would estimate later, in his memoirs, that the crowd included "about a dozen" journalists, their hands and notebooks thrust into the pockets of their overcoats.

It was time to awaken the prisoner.

"Gentlemen, if you are ready, let's go," said Estachy, who would lead the way.

Clunet, who was aware that he had proved to be a cat among tigers as defense attorney, put his veined hand on Somprou's arm. Somprou had handled the distinguished corporate lawyer with great courtesy during the proceedings, and Clunet felt he was the most gentlemanly person there. He told Somprou that he would wait downstairs; he asked the colonel to tell his client that he had arrived. Somprou said gruffly that he was not the defense's messenger and that Clunet should go up to the cell with the rest of them. The crumpled old man looked startled at Somprou's manner but agreed.

During the time when capital punishment existed in France, prisoners were never notified of the date of their execution. The reasoning given was that it was less cruel to inform them at the last minute, but mostly it was to make them easier to handle in the final days. However, awakening someone in what is almost the middle of the night with the news that he or she is about to be put to death would often produce a harrowing scene; it was therefore traditional for the vast party which the law required to witness the macabre rite to make as much noise as possible, stamping down the corridor, so that the condemned person was at least awake and more or less prepared when they arrived.

The nuns who did most of the warder duties at Saint-Lazare had always found the stamping of male feet disquieting, and they had distributed muffling blankets along the rat-infested corridor the night before. As the chief warder went ahead, lighting the thin gaslights on the wall with a wax taper, the rodents scuttled away, and it was in relative silence that the group arrived at the door of cell number twelve.

Sister Léonide, who had spent forty-seven years of service inside the jail, since the age of nineteen, and who would stay there ten years longer, had invented an excuse to pass the night in the cell without telling the prisoner that the execution had been set for the following dawn. Also sleeping in the grim room were two prostitutes. One was in for theft, the other for murdering her baby.

Once a defendant had been condemned to death, it was standard practice to move in two other prisoners as companions. Their main role was to prevent suicide.

Sister Léonide, who had been on her knees in prayer for most of the night, came to the door and threw the bolt. While the party waited at the entrance, she struck a long sulfur match against the stone wall and lit the single gaslight in the cell.

Captain Bouchardon peered into the lifting gloom and asked: "Which bed?"

"The one in the middle."

The light and the voices had awoken the two prostitutes, who began to whimper.

"Put your clothes on and go to the refectory," Sister Léonide said to them.

With an imperious finger, she cautioned the official party to stay where it was, in the doorway. She went to the middle cot and put her arm around the prisoner's shoulders. Dr. Bizard had secretly doubled the dose of chloral, a sedative, in her glass of water the night before, and the invasion of her cell had not awoken her.

Mata Hari stirred and leaned on one arm. Her face, swollen by eight months of confinement, made her now appear older than her forty-one years. She did not look, any longer, like one of the most famous courtesans of the Belle Epoque. As her eyes opened on the scene, Bizard recalled later, they seemed full of fear. But she quickly composed her features and became almost disarmingly calm.

Her glance sought Clunet, but the old man, lost in a womb of despair, was too distraught to speak. It was Bouchardon who said, gently but firmly: "Have courage! Your request for clemency has been rejected by the President of the Republic. The time for expiation has come."

The request had been rejected two days before, but Clunet had lacked the courage to tell her.

Still leaning on one arm on her iron cot, she blinked her eyes and said: "It's not possible! It's not possible!"

Sister Léonide clasped her shoulders again, maternally. A younger nun who was also charged with guarding Mata Hari, Sister Marie, appeared.

"Don't be afraid, sister," Mata Hari said to Léonide. "I shall know how to die."

The nun stood up and signaled the men to leave the cell so that the prisoner could dress. Only Dr. Bizard remained behind. Mata Hari, who had been in simple clothes for the past eight months, had one question:

"May I wear a corset?" Bizard said yes.

The faded courtesan sat on the edge of the cot to pull on her silk stockings, saved for the occasion. As she put one foot on the thin mattress, revealing her loins, the nun quickly stood between her and Bizard.

"Don't worry, sister," Bizard later recalled Mata Hari saying. "This isn't the moment to be prudish."

When she stood up, Bizard offered her smelling salts, the equivalent then of an "upper."

"No, thanks, you will see that I have no need for that." The actress who had trod the boards in Monte Carlo, Milan, and Paris was entering her final role.

From the limited wardrobe that had been restored to her in the final weeks and that lay in a trunk, she chose her clothes carefully: a pearl-gray dress with a wide skirt, a lace *cache-corset* at the bosom, a tricorn felt hat. She could not wear the veil that fashion required to go with it, because hatpins were forbidden in prison. Her jewelry had been taken from her and would later be sold to pay the expenses of the trial; but she wore, all the memoirs say, "very elegant shoes." She had always had a penchant for expensive shoes, buttoned to the ankles in the style of the day.

Before putting on the hat, she asked for Pastor Jules Arboux, the gray, ascetic Baptist chaplain who had tried to comfort her over the endless months and who would clearly be consoled himself if she converted back from Hinduism to Protestantism. This would be a disappointment to Sister Léonide, who would have liked her to die a Catholic, with a ticket to grace, so Mata Hari asked Bizard and the nuns to leave her alone with the minister. When they returned a few moments later, she had beads of water on her brow; Arboux had apparently baptized her from a *fer-blanc* prison mug.

Arboux left the cell silently, in tears. The execution party returned and found Mata Hari calm.

"What's the weather like?" she asked. She seemed to be trying to ease their tension. Bralez, the intern assistant, said it was fine.

The others exchanged glances. It was still cold and misty outside, and the drivers had said there was fog in the suburbs, where they were headed. Mata Hari caught the glances and lifted a blue coat from a nail in the wall.

She put on her hat, using the remaining water in the mug as a mirror. She primped her wavy, graying black hair, cut short according to prison rules, and drew on long gloves, buttoning them to the elbow and frisking them to make them straight. She thanked Dr. Bizard for his services; she could have been checking out of a hotel. Sister Marie began to cry. The prisoner pinched her cheek and told her gently not to worry.

"Imagine that I'm leaving on a long journey, that I will return, and that we will find each other again," she said. Had Arboux remained, he might have been puzzled. It was a typical farewell from a member of the Hindu faith about to die, but trusting in reincarnation after forty days.

Bizard had one more formality to perform. He asked her if she was pregnant. Under Chapter I, Article 27, of the Criminal Code, a pregnant woman could not be executed until after the birth of her child, so as not to put an innocent to death as well.

Mata Hari seemed, not unnaturally, startled. She had lived for eight months under guard. She gaped at them without answering.

Dr. Socquet, of the army, repeated the question: "Have you any reason to believe that you are pregnant?"

"No reason at all."

This fruitless ritual was to give rise to one of the hundreds of myths that grew up around Mata Hari's death—that Clunet had pretended that she was pregnant by him in an effort to stay the execution. He had in fact written a letter the day before saying that there was a "rumor in the theatrical world" that his client was expecting a child and suggesting a delay of execution pending determination of the facts. It was clearly a desperate subterfuge. The letter, now in the military justice files, begins "Commandant" (Major), so it was presumably addressed to Massard, the representative of the military governor of Paris, General Dubail, who had ordered the execution.

It was time to go. She threw the blue coat over her shoulders like a cape. In the gaslit corridor, Piétri, the chief warder, moved to take her arm. She brushed him away.

"I am not a thief, a criminal!"

She took the arm of Sister Marie, who seemed broken by grief and in need of comfort; the whole party walked down steps to an office on the ground floor. Here took place the *levée d'écrou*—the lifting of the bolt—which signals release for a prisoner. In this case, it simply marked the passing of the captive from civil authority into the hands of the military, who would perform the execution.

She asked for a little time to write three letters. Confident of clemency, she had written no farewells before. One letter was to her daughter in Holland, another to her last lover, Vadim de Masloff, and the third to the Baron de Marguérie, the senior diplomat who had risked his reputation by testifying for her in person. None arrived at their destinations, and none are in the French military justice files. They were given to Arboux, who may have given them to Clunet, who would have known to which addresses to send them. Perhaps the shattered lawyer left them in a taxi.

It was then about ten to six. She gave a last glance at a wall mirror.

"I am ready, gentlemen," she said.

The drivers started to crank the cars, and the crowd outside the prison gate fell silent as the party emerged, with all eyes fixed on the tall woman. A gendarme led the way for Mata Hari and Sister Léonide to a large sedan, where they took their places on the back seat. Pastor Arboux and Sister Marie sat on the strap-seats facing them. The gendarme drew the blinds of the back windows, then took his place in the front beside the driver. Somprou and the other six judges crowded into a big car in front, with the sole noncommissioned judge sitting on the floor. The rest of the party took three cars that were parked behind. The convoy moved off, driving fast through the gray-lit streets, now becoming busy with horse-drawn carts and occasional cars. They were headed for the old castle-palace of Vincennes, where Louis XVI and Marie-Antoinette had spent their last night well over a century before.

Several taxis hired by journalists fell in behind. Bouchardon, whose memory is notorious for hyperbole, was to estimate the number at "twenty." The press cars soon overtook the vehicles of the officers; but, approaching Vincennes, the reporters' taxis turned toward the shooting range, only to find that the official cars were not following. They turned back, but by the time the press reached the castle, the execution party had driven swiftly in and the gates were closed.

The suburban fog had begun to lift and was now no more than the solemn mist of the capital. There was a hint of predawn on the horizon. The cars drove slowly over the cobbles of the central alley inside the palace grounds, stopping briefly to pick up another official at the fourteenth-century fortress well within the *enceinte*; then they continued to trundle on to the Caponnière, a broad field usually reserved for cavalry displays; it is now outside the castle grounds, and is used partly as a parking lot. This had been chosen in preference to the shooting range, from which it was harder to keep out the curious. The cars bumped across the muddy hummocks to a point where Mata Hari and Sister Léonide could see troops assembled.

A bugle call alerted the soldiery, who began straightening their uniforms and forming up in lines of three. They had been on call since two A.M.

Mata Hari helped the shaking Sister Léonide, who was sixty-six, down from the car.

"Don't cry, sister. I don't want to cry. I'm not going to cry."

Arboux followed, his frail legs, Bouchardon tells us, almost buckling under him. He turned to help Sister Marie. The gendarme closed the doors and fell in behind. Now Sister Léonide was finding strength by chanting in a loud voice.

"Mary, Mother of God, pray for us, now and at the hour of our death. . . ."

The stake was clearly visible, the limb of a young tree thrust into the ground. They could see the backs of the firing squad, twelve soldiers of the 4th Zouave Regiment in two lines of six, with the rear line facing between the shoulders of the six in front.

With Mata Hari and Sister Léonide in front, Arboux, Sister Marie, and the gendarme just behind, and the flock of officers following, the entire party walked before a battalion of troops standing stiffly to attention.

The command rang out: *"Sabre—main!"*

Then: *"Présentez—armes!"*

The sabers flashed, pointing at the somber sky.

It was a heterogeneous guard of honor. There was a unit brought

from the Front for such purposes (to see that the people at headquarters in Paris were doing their bit, capturing spies), some troops
from an artillery squadron without their cannon and, behind them,
some mounted soldiers from the cavalry company garrisoned at
the castle. Other cavalry were patrolling the perimeter to keep the
press and public out.

The captive walked briskly past, literally reviewing the troops,
with one gloved hand hustling the elderly, chanting nun to keep
pace on the muddy grass. Sister Marie walked behind, sobbing,
praying.

As they drew level with the Zouaves, Mata Hari said half-jokingly:
"I don't think it's safe for you to accompany me any further, sister."

She kissed the nun, gave her the coat from her shoulders, kissed
Sister Marie, and shook hands with Arboux, telling them all to
walk behind the Zouaves and "stand over there to the right. I'll
look at you."

She could have been telling some friends where to sit in the
orchestra stalls. She looked beyond the three religious to Clunet,
who could only shake his head helplessly. He had not said a word
since his brief exchange with Somprou.

A sergeant-major appeared to lead her to the stake, bearing a
cord and blindfold. Once again, it was beneath Margaretha Geertruida Zelle MacLeod's dignity to be handled by a trooper. She
turned her back on him and walked firmly to the stake alone. She
swung gracefully and faced the Zouaves. There were troops lined
up on all three sides. It was quite a parade.

Captain Thibaud, the chief of the military court clerks, had fol-
lowed. He had a formality to perform: to read the sentence. Wheel-
ing around to face the assembly, he said: "In the name of the
People of France, by order of the Third War Council, Marguérite-
Gertrude Zelle, unanimously condemned to death for espionage."
He marched away.

The sergeant-major looped the cord around her waist. He was
about to bind her wrists, then tie her to the stake.

"That will not be necessary," she ordered. The long, looped rope
hung to the ground like a monkish belt. The sergeant-major pulled
the blindfold from his lanyard. Mata Hari shook her head impe-
riously, indicating that that wouldn't be needed either.

The sergeant-major marched off, muttering gruffly to the *aspir-*

ant, or junior sublieutenant, in charge of the Zouaves: "By blue, this lady knows how to die."

The pale young officer looked at his men. He had received the assignment at Rosny-sous-bois the night before and had been told to choose four sergeants, four corporals, and four privates, so that enlisted men of all ranks should have the pleasure of shooting a German spy. But he was uncertain how the battle-shocked young conscripts would react to the order to shoot a woman, so he had selected twelve beribboned sergeants, ordering four to strip off one stripe each and pretend to be corporals and four others to take off their badges of rank altogether and pose as privates.

He raised his saber.

"Joue!"

The Zouaves lifted their rifles to their stubbled cheeks. The sub-lieutenant turned his face reflexively toward the target. The captive returned his frightened glance and said clearly, in a voice which all around could hear: "Thank you, sir."

She lifted her hands and blew a kiss to the firing party, then turned her head slightly, remembering to give one of her rare smiles to Sister Léonide and Sister Marie and Pastor Arboux. The two nuns were on their knees in the wet grass. Arboux saw nothing: he was standing, head in hand, praying in a piping, imploring voice. It was six-twelve.

As the saber came down, one of the Zouave sergeants fainted; eleven shots rang out. The prisoner crumpled. From where he stood, Bouchardon could see only "what looked like a heap of skirts."

II

THE LIGHT
OF DAY

1876—1916

1. *M'greet*

IT WAS August 7, 1882. As the summer sun rose over the peaceful Dutch hamlet of Leeuwarden, in Frisia province, Margaretha Geertruida Zelle awoke to her sixth birthday. These were the days when the daughters of poor families, if their birthdays were remembered at all, would revel in being given an orange from sunny Spain, or a handmade rag doll, or some article of clothing knitted by Mother. Children of the petite bourgeoisie, such as Margaretha, might receive a purse or a semiprecious trinket. But Adam Zelle, the flamboyant village hatter, had always spoiled his children and his only daughter most of all.

''M'greet, look outside!'' he called.

What gift could be so big that it had to be left outside the house?

She drew the curtains and peered out at the grassy lane. There stood a miniature carriage in which four small children could ride, made by Adam Zelle with his own hands; it had two tall goats in harness.

M'greet, who knew how to ride and had often held the reins of her father's jitney, couldn't dress fast enough to take her carriage and pick up her friends—fellow pupils from Miss Buys' local college for very young ladies.

The *bokkenwaagen*—goat carriage—was still remembered by many people in Leeuwarden, with its 27,000 inhabitants, thirty-five years later; this was when Dutch journalists came to the hamlet to start reconstructing the biography of the village's most notorious citizen, just shot at the stake. One of the visiting writers reported that the carriage had been the envy of her little friends and noted that stimulating envy is not the best way to conserve friendship.

Her father was controversial, with an overweening ego. He was often seen standing in front of his shop on the Kelders, a main street, wearing a top hat, his thumbs tucked into an embroidered vest. He had married a poor member of the petty gentry, Antje van der Meulen. By the time of M'greet's sixth birthday, she had twin younger brothers, Ari Anne and Cornelis Coenraad; another brother, Johannes Henderikus, would arrive later. Local lore, which does not remember Adam kindly, concedes that he doted on all of them and that his daughter appeared to be the light of his life.

The woman who was later to claim, at times, that she had been born in the Dutch East Indies—now Indonesia—and at other times in India, and that her mother had been a native, was actually a pure product of Holland's southernmost province. The "artist" who enthralled the French press of the day with tales of having been raised as a sacred dancer in a Hindu temple on the Ganges spent her childhood cocooned in a straitlaced northern European rural society, beside which Paris and Vienna were as exotic as Benares or Bali.

But from infancy she had one distinguishing feature, upon which she built the myth that fueled her brief years of fame: unlike Adam and Antje, who were pale, apple-cheeked Frisians, she had black hair, dark brown eyes, and a tanned complexion. Local lore explained this by saying that Adam, a member of the Dutch Reformed Church like everyone else in Leeuwarden except for a few Catholics, had some ancestors who were Sephardic Jews who had fled to the Low Countries from the Inquisition.

Sam Waagenaar, the most scrupulous investigator of Margaretha's early life, says that her traits actually came from the genteel van der Meulen family, who were of partly Woudker descent. He describes the Woudkers as a tribe from Asia whose descendants, like those of North African immigrants into Scotland and Ireland, have relatively swarthy features. Adam Zelle, for his part, was a descendant of Herman Otto Zelle of Westphalia, in Germany, who had arrived in Holland and settled in Leeuwarden in 1770.

Zelle, in a day when all men wore hats, was a highly successful shopkeeper at first; Waagenaar claims that in 1877, the year after Margaretha's birth, he earned 3,500 guilders, which he estimated to be the equivalent of twenty-five thousand dollars in 1965— about seventy thousand dollars today. He invested some of his profits in oil exploration. Although this would prove to be a disaster, it shows considerable perspicacity and his unquestioned confidence in his judgment: nearly two generations later, the wealthy financier Basil Zaharoff was to encounter great difficulty in convincing a British prime minister, David Lloyd George, that oil would one day replace coal.

A portrait of the bearded, slightly plump hatter hangs in the Frisian Museum. It shows him as one of the village's mounted guard of honor in 1873, for the visit of King Willem III. He is carrying a standard, wearing his perpetual top hat, and his white jodhpurs and black boots are set firmly in gleaming stirrups. When he was married later that year and moved from his apartment over the shop to a fine house at 28 Groote Kerkstraat, the oil painting must have been one of the first items of furniture installed in the new Zelle home.

The village gentry, local lore recalls, found him vulgar, and M'greet's famous *bokkenwaagen* was cited to journalists as an example of the hatter's inability to accept his station in life as a shopkeeper. Those less fortunate than the Zelles nicknamed him, with scorn, "the Baron."

M'greet was to inherit many of her father's traits, particularly his pretentiousness. She frequently claimed that her father was a real baron, for instance. The woman who invented the striptease could command servants as though raised in a royal palace. She would pretend to have been born in a local mansion, Amelands, also called The Caminghastate, which was visible from the Zelle house and was inhabited by an authentic noble family, the Caminghas. Like her father, she believed that—as W. Somerset Maugham expressed it in one of his notebooks—money is a sixth sense without which it is difficult to enjoy the other five completely. All this she clearly got from Adam. In the most successful of her careers, that of courtesan, she calls to mind a slightly blasphemous nineteenth-century English pun: She dearly loved a lord.

Whether the *bokkenwaagen* started it, we do not know, but the villagers who were questioned in the years after her execution recalled that she had not been very popular with the other girls. In her childhood, however, she was admired for her prettiness. One middle-aged village matron, a Buys School contemporary of the dancer, remembered in the 1920s that she had once written a poem comparing the Zelle child to "an orchid among dande-lions."

Like her father, she sought all her life to impress. She accorded herself the noble privilege of defying convention. Encouraged by Adam from the early years, she adored fine clothes. At high school, she would amaze or appall her fellow students in their trim black or blue attire by arriving in a dress of red and yellow stripes that she had made herself. On one memorable occasion, she swept into class in a robe of expensive crimson velvet.

Such whims could be indulged in her early childhood by her father, an affluent man by Leeuwarden standards. But Zelle's oil shares went down at the worst possible moment for the village hatter: another hatter had opened up in town. Apart from his oil investments, the shopkeeper always seems to have spent all he had on his and his family's appearances, and the arrival of a com-petitor was fatal to his commerce. In 1889, when M'greet was thirteen, he declared bankruptcy. The disgrace and the new poverty raised the "Baron's" temper. The marriage began to fall apart. The family had to move to a more modest home—an upstairs apart-ment on the Willemskade—and Adam went off to The Hague to find a job. Unsuccessful in the capital, he returned home the fol-lowing year, but the quarrels with Antje became more violent. He became tempestuous with his children, even with his once-spoiled daughter. That same year, 1890, Adam and Antje were legally separated.

Eight months later, on May 10, 1891, a few weeks before M'greet's fifteenth birthday, her mother was dead. Neighbors took the chil-dren in briefly, then they were dispersed. By then, Adam was living in Amsterdam with another woman. M'greet's world had fallen apart. All she had to take away from the family home, when she went to live with a staid uncle and aunt in nearby Sneek, was an album containing her mother's earlier love poems to her father. When she later divorced, she gave the album to her husband, presumably to indicate that she felt similarly betrayed.

Her uncle, a Mr. Visser, who was also her godfather, decided that since she had no dowry to bring to a marriage, she would have to earn a living. At that time, there were virtually only two occupations open to women apart from marriage—domestic ser-vice and teaching. He sent her at his own expense to an exclusive kindergarten-teachers' training college in the beautiful university city of Leyden.

The fifteen-year-old who had never much enjoyed big-sistering her younger brothers—whom she hardly ever spoke to again—was clearly not marked out by nature for such a maternal profession. Moreover, at Leyden it was now her turn to be envious of her contemporaries, most of whom were better off and had warm family situations; worst of all, many of them were more attractive.

The prettiness of the young M'greet had not endured. She still had the exotic dark looks and the sensuous mouth, but her face had become handsome rather than beautiful. She was a typical Frisian girl with big shoulders and ample hips, but there were two major problems.

She had grown to a height of five feet nine inches. This was taller than most Dutchmen in the late nineteenth century and was comparable to a girl being six feet tall today. Since most men, across the centuries and across the globe, prefer women smaller than themselves, and women are usually embarrassed by short male escorts, this limited her marriage chances. Still worse, this Amazon in Rubens country had almost no breasts. After her downfall, Dutch journalists found contemporaries from Leyden who recalled that this had been her prime obsession in her brief college years. Had she been petite, this vagary of nature would have been easier to carry off; but she was a giant with no dowry who had to stuff stockings into her camisole, with sometimes unfortunate results: the brassiere had not yet been invented, and she was too young to wear a corset.

But with her sense of dress and audacity, she was unquestionably sexy, as we would say today. She largely distrusted other girls and looked back at life with father before the crash as a brief paradise. It was, indeed, at the kindergarten-teachers' college at Leyden that she discovered her real vocation: the principal, a gray-bearded intellectual called Wybrandus Haanstra, fell in love with her. He was daddy and lover in one, and she responded.

He would ask her to stay behind after classes, and the two would go on long walks together. Given the mores of the time, it is quite possible that they never got beyond holding hands. Her choleric future husband, who later mustered every argument against her, never complained that she was not a virgin when he seduced her. But the principal's infatuation soon became known, and Mr. Visser withdrew his ward from the college.

After a while back in Sneek, the bored, moody maiden went off in March 1895 to stay with another uncle, a Mr. Taconis, in The Hague, and the Vedantic wheel of destiny began to turn.

2. Greta

WE ARE IN THE MONTH OF March 1895, and it says something about the frame of mind of the eighteen-year-old M'greet Zelle that she should be reading the equivalent of the "personals" in the *Het Nieuwes van den Dag*. Perhaps it was because in those days such advertisements, complete with box number for a response, were inserted as fillers among the news items.

The paragraph read: "Captain in the Army of the Indies, on leave in Holland, seeks wife with a character to his taste, preferably with means. Write to . . ."

The man behind the box number was Captain Rudolf MacLeod, always known as John. But he was not the author of the advertisement.

MacLeod was a Dutchman whose Scottish ancestors had emigrated to Holland nearly two hundred years before. The family had always been associated with the military. One cousin was a vice-admiral. His great-uncle, a retired general, had been an aide-de-camp to Willem III. His father, who had married the penniless Baroness Diana-Luisa Sweerts van Landas, John's mother, had been less successful, retiring as an army captain.

John had become an army private at sixteen and had been commissioned from the ranks. He had transferred to the colonial army—then the only Dutch force to see any action. At thirty-nine, he had fulfilled seventeen years of service in the Dutch East Indies without home leave. That he was still only a captain at that age does not reflect poorly on his performance. Promotion was not the quasi-automatic process it has become today, and in the Dutch East Indies, a captain was often in charge of all the military on a sprawling island. Everything indicates that he had a distinguished record as an officer, including two decorations for bravery on Sumatra. His ambition, he confided once, was to reach the rank of lieutenant-colonel so that he could wear the respected title of "colonel" in retirement. He was too much of a rough diamond to make general.

The advertisement had been inserted by one of the paper's reporters, J.T.C. de Balbian Verster, whose duties included writing about colonial affairs. To pick up stories, Verster made a point of drinking with officers on leave from the Indies, and he had been one of a group of men sipping schnapps one day at Amsterdam's American Café with MacLeod, who was recovering from a bout of malaria and seemed depressed. Someone suggested that it was time the veteran colonial warrior married and had a companion to share his lonely exile in the tropics.

Verster, for a joke, put the advertisement in his paper. Sixteen persons responded to the appeal, and the letters were brought to MacLeod by Verster; he later recalled that the debilitated captain read all of them with some amusement but kept only one—M'greet Zelle's. It had been the last to arrive, which suggests that she had sent it with hesitation. The others had spoken of dowries; M'greet had had the wisdom to send a photograph—a flattering, sun-printed sepia studio portrait that caught the jaded officer's eye. He wrote to her in The Hague.

Given his position as a colonial army officer and the easy sexual mores of Java and Bali, MacLeod had never had to live a very celibate existence. But the notion of a pretty Dutch teenager who was, it appeared, throwing herself at him, struck a chord.

After nearly two decades in the Indies, he had had several tropical diseases, and he suffered from rheumatism. He had been wounded in action and, although a diabetic, he drank heavily. He had lost his hair. They had had to carry him aboard the leave ship on a stretcher. Perhaps "settling down" was the answer. Being a respectable married man might even help with promotion.

He offered to meet her on a stated date in front of Amsterdam's Rijksmuseum. He came in uniform, and she had inherited her father's taste for elegance in male dress. Much later, she would say that she preferred officers, who carefully folded their clothes before going to bed with her, to the dukes who dropped their pants on the floor. She found him waiting—she was rarely on time, all her life—tapping his swagger stick against his thighs.

One can imagine that this hot-tempered, coarse-tongued rake who had spent all his adult life commanding the dregs of the Dutch population—often sent out to the colonies as soldiers as an alternative to imprisonment—was suitably shy and respectful on the first occasion. The man who had spent seventeen years killing rebellious natives or fornicating with their sisters, and hitting the bottle under his mosquito net, must have been at his gentlemanly best. M'greet, for her part, was enthralled, although, judging by photographs of the time, MacLeod was an unprepossessing figure: his bald head and dissipated face seemed to belong to a man ten years older; he was paunchy and had a doleful expression, enhanced by drooping mustachios. But thank God, he was taller than she.

They soon found that they were two of a kind. Because, much later, in search of extra money, MacLeod gave her love letters to Dutch reporters, we know that she was not afraid to court and tempt him physically, archly referring to the exhilarations they had produced in each other at their previous tryst. From one of the letters, however, it appears that she never gave herself to him until the brief period of their engagement. Contraceptives were virtually unknown, abortion was as illegal as murder, and a girl with an illegitimate child was finished. The implications are that there had been some heavy petting in the captain's quarters, itself temerarious behavior in its day.

M'greet's letters also show that MacLeod was decidedly hesitant at first to see the relationship blossom into marriage. He was frequently sending telegrams or letters to cancel meetings, arguing crises of rheumatism and the like. On one occasion, he had his sister Frida write, claiming to be in too much pain to be able to use his hands.

M'greet responded understandingly, signing off with "Farewell, Johnie [sic], with a delicious kiss from your loving little wife, Greta." The little girl M'greet Zelle had already become, in her own mind, the woman Greta MacLeod. However frequently the captain might stand her up, Greta was always on the train for Amsterdam a few days later. Finally John proposed and was quickly accepted. They had been meeting on and off for about two months.

Shortly afterward, Greta was writing: "You ask me if I am ready to do something silly. Ten times, if you like! Do with me as you wish, because in a few weeks I will be your wife. Isn't it marvelous that we both have the same wild temperament?''

In an obvious reference to her menstruations, she added: ''Don't worry about me being indisposed. It happened exactly on time, a few days ago, so you can ask of me exactly what you wish.''

Greta's attraction to MacLeod is not hard to understand. Since her platonic affair with her headmaster, she had been looking for another replacement for the doting father she had lost. Without a dowry, too tall, almost breastless, and with no desire to go into teaching, she needed above all a husband; but a pimply Dutch youth was not what she was after. That she had found an older man who was not a dour Dutch burgher but a battle-scarred warrior who seemed to be rather fun was perfect—she thought.

She had told MacLeod that she was an orphan, and no doubt the fact that there was no boring family to court as well had appealed to him. Now, however, as she was under twenty-one, she would have to produce proof of her parents' death and an authorization to marry from her guardian, Mr. Visser. She confessed to the lie and admitted that her father was still living, with a new wife, in a poor section of Amsterdam.

Adam Zelle made no difficulties about agreeing to her marriage to an army captain, but he insisted that he had a right to meet him first. They should come, he said, not in an ordinary one-horse cab but in a rented carriage, so that Zelle, now a part-time salesman, could impress his neighbors. MacLeod agreed.

In July, a few weeks before her nineteenth birthday, they were married, with Adam Zelle at City Hall in his top hat. Why they were not married in church is not clear; there is no evidence that MacLeod had been married before. It may merely reflect the fact that neither John nor Greta had much time for religious rites, or that John was thinking of the costs.

In an open carriage, the couple and the proud father drove down Adam Zelle's modest lane, and the neighbors cheered. Adam, however, was not invited to the wedding supper at the American Café. MacLeod made it clear, in interviews after Mata Hari's death, that he had formed the same poor opinion of Adam as had the latter's neighbors at Leeuwarden.

At Greta's request, they spent their honeymoon at Wiesbaden, then as now a fashionable German spa. But back in Amsterdam, MacLeod began taking nights off in the local brothels, on one occasion asking Verster, the reporter who had brought them together, to keep company with his wife while he was out.

Because of his marriage, MacLeod was allowed to extend his leave to March 1896. Then it was again put back to September because the army doctors said his health was not yet ready for another long term in the tropics. He was anxious to return; he had gone through his savings and was having difficulty keeping up with his wife's love of pretty clothes.

By September, Greta was pregnant and could not travel. A son was born on January 30, 1897, and baptized Norman John. Norman was the name of the great-uncle, the retired court general, and John was the name of MacLeod's father, John van Brienen MacLeod. The great-uncle had the couple and the newest addition to the MacLeod clan presented at court to Queen Regent Emma, the mother of Queen Wilhelmina. This must have required a whole new wardrobe for Greta, from hat to shoes. The little family finally set sail for the Indies on May 1, aboard the *Prinses Amalia*.

Greta was now twenty, her husband forty-one. It was already clear by then that John was not the perfect husband; but the baby had brought them together, and her letters to relatives and friends indicated that she was looking forward to being a captain's wife in the colonies. She would have at least one servant again, as in the halcyon days of her infancy at Leeuwarden.

3. Griet

CAPTAIN MACLEOD was posted first to Ambarawa, near Semarang, in central Java, and then to Toempoeng, in the east, not far from Bali and close to Malang, where there was a sizable European community. At Toempoeng, Greta had her second child, Juana-Luisa, always known as "Non," an abbreviation of *nonah*—"little girl" in Malayalam, the Indonesian dialect of Malay.

Back on station and in his natural element, MacLeod clearly had even greater difficulties balancing his life as the head of a Dutch family, composed of a vivacious wife and two babies, with his inclinations to spend nights drinking with other officers and sleeping with the local girls. From Greta's letters, it was at the pitch of a particularly rough period of violent quarrels that MacLeod was posted again, this time to Medan on the Sumatran coast across the Straits of Malacca from Malaya. It was now December 1898.

MacLeod saddled up and rode off at dawn, stopping at the bungalow of the local administrator, a Mr. van Rheede, to say that his wife and children would be coming to stay at the Rheede house until he could make arrangements for them to join him in Medan. Greta related in a letter that van Rheede, a hospitable host, had mildly complained that the captain had not even gotten down from his horse to impose his request.

For two months MacLeod sent no money; but he wrote constantly, sometimes letters of twenty or more pages, describing the country, the people, and his experiences at Medan, which is today the principal city of Sumatra—a pleasant resort with beach hotels that draw vacationers from Europe, Japan, and North America. MacLeod was observant, and he clearly had ambitions to be a writer; the letters were, in a sense, a literary diary, because the only reason we know of them is that he painstakingly wrote out copies, which he much later passed on to writers who seemed sympathetic.

Medan was a step up for the officer: he was promoted to major and garrison commander. The town was an improvement on Toempoeng. Some of the little port's streets had electric lighting and, despite the climate and the fact that horses are more vulnerable to malaria than humans, horse-drawn carriages were to be seen. In the letters, Greta had now been abbreviated to "My dear Griet," and he signed them "your husband, John."

As well as interesting descriptions of Medan, the letters also contain lectures to his wife about the need not to leave the children so much in the care of the Javan *ayah* and his objections to her letting other officers call at the house. A few paragraphs after describing the charms of the Sumatran coast, he is referring to "our shocking differences of character." There seems little doubt that Margaretha Zelle was not the perfect mother and that she loved leaving things to servants. But one senses that perhaps her allusions to the kindness and wit of some of her officer visitors were intended to make John jealous and encourage him to send for her sooner.

Those who knew them at the time and who later talked to journalists trying to reconstruct Mata Hari's life seem to have broadly agreed on two things: that Griet MacLeod might have been a good wife if John MacLeod had not been such a dreadful husband, but that she also enjoyed the admiration and attention of single officers and planters who were exiled, without family, so far from home.

As always, she got along better with men than with the few Dutch women, mostly middle-aged wives of senior officials and administrators. She took to wearing Malay clothes and jewelry, which were regarded as beneath the dignity of the other Dutch women; at the officers' club on Saturday nights, she would give her imitation of native dances. Another wheel of Vedantic destiny had begun to turn.

Finally MacLeod sent for his family. By now, however, he had apparently decided that his flattering picture of Medan might give his wife the wrong ideas, and he returned to sermonizing:

"There is much work for you to do here, Griet," he wrote, "for these houses are dangerous to live in unless they are kept completely clean. They have to be swept continually, and the flower pots picked up, otherwise one is invaded by all sorts of vermin. Last night, I saw the largest scorpion of my life."

Scorpions, he noted, were not good for children. Griet must be sure to "monitor all the cleaning *yourself*." She should also not leave the making up of the children's beds and the moving of the flower pots to the servants. None of this seems unwise advice, but it is a reflection of MacLeod's character that he put it into a letter which would take sixteen days to reach Toempoeng, rather than mention it after her arrival.

At Medan, Griet was delighted to fill the role of the garrison commander's wife, which gave her the same status as the wife of the civil administrator—who happened to be away. At twenty-two, she was the first lady of the post. She enjoyed standing apart at receptions so that the other wives, all older than she, should be obliged to come forward and present their compliments.

That was the only pleasure of the assignment. Neighbors would later recount that the noise of the MacLeods' quarreling interfered with their sleep. Griet would complain that her husband would become violent after drinking; on one occasion, she said, he had struck her with his horsewhip. But worse was in store.

About a month after Griet and the children arrived in Medan, Norman and Non fell sick. The hospital diagnosed poisoning, later traced to the sauce poured over their rice. Two days later, Norman died. His sister, who had eaten very little of her supper on the fateful night, survived.

Although the poisoning was assumed to be intentional, no one was ever charged and the case was never solved. The prime suspect was the *ayah*, the children's nurse. There was a story that she had put cat's whiskers into the sauce, but this would be more likely to cause internal bleeding than poisoning. MacLeod had once ordered one of his Javanese soldiers out of the kitchen, where he was courting the girl; he had forbidden all contact between the soldier and his servant.

Griet told her family in letters that she believed the *ayah* had poisoned the children in revenge. The officers' club gossip was that, since the *ayah* was pretty, MacLeod was sleeping with her and had driven the Javanese private off in jealousy. The latter, they thought, obsessed with the thought that his commander was sleeping with his beloved against her will, had either persuaded her to revenge herself in this way, or had done it himself.

The Dutch authorities reacted to the crisis in the MacLeod household by posting the major elsewhere, to Banjoe Biroe, a jungle station in Java. There Griet soon contracted typhoid. By then, the MacLeod disputes had increased still further both in decibels and in violence, with MacLeod accusing his wife of being responsible for Norman's death by not preparing the children's food herself. Whatever his other faults, MacLeod was clearly devoted to his children. He wrote to his sister that, whenever he heard Norman's favorite "Monte Carlo" military march played on ceremonial occasions, he was unable to maintain his demeanor at the head of his troops.

Griet was sent to a cool hill station, Kroework, where she stayed with a coffee planter's family while recovering. MacLeod complained to his sister that his wife's convalescence was costing him more than he could afford, including five bottles of milk a day at thirty cents each.

MacLeod's own health was by then a serious problem, and Banjoe Biroe was no place for his infant daughter. The following year, on October 2, 1900, he retired. With his major's pension, based on twenty-eight years' service, the family could live in the favored hill city of Bandung, where the climate was healthy and the life cheaper than back in Holland.

Griet settled with John and Non in Sindanglava, on the outskirts of Bandung, but her heart was not in it. The retired major was no less choleric than the harassed field commander had been, and his visits to the local bordellos became more frequent. Griet wanted to divorce. She wanted to return to Europe. She was talking more and more of a desire to go to Paris, then the center of the occidental civilized world. She had lost her teenage faith in love—and her attraction to MacLeod seems to have been only a foolish fad, in the first place. She knew that her only sure asset was her physical attractiveness. When a French journalist asked her later why she had chosen Paris to live, she said: "Where else does a divorced woman go?"

In letters to his sister, MacLeod was more and more preoccupied with his distaste for his wife. In one, he expressed the wish that she would marry someone else. Griet, now reconciled with her father, was writing to him to complain of John's meanness with money, his "brutality" and "cruelties," and his numerous "adulteries." She claimed that he had even threatened her with his pistol.

Their family doctor at Bandung later told a writer: "During the year and a half that I knew them, Mrs. MacLeod was always patient and well-behaved, despite the insults which her husband would lavish on her in public." MacLeod, he said, was "unbalanced."

In March 1902, the little family set off back to Amsterdam. After a brief stay at Frida's, with the two sisters-in-law in frequent dispute, they took a small apartment at 188 van Breestraat. One day Griet returned to the building to find that MacLeod had packed his bags and gone to Arnhem, taking Non with him. Griet pursued them, staying with one of John's cousins in the town. She was awarded a separation in August. Non would stay with her mother, and MacLeod was ordered to pay support of one hundred florins a month.

MacLeod came back, and there was a brief attempt at a reconciliation. After he deserted his wife the second time, he never sent money, and he soon found an opportunity to abduct his daughter, whom Griet would see only once again. Major Rudolf MacLeod then published an announcement in the local papers saying he would no longer be responsible for the debts of his spouse. Although a second separation later re-established the terms of the original one, MacLeod resisted both the financial and guardianship requirements, and he was never seriously challenged. His wife set off, instead, for Paris. She was tired of fighting John, and she was never going to succeed in Paris with a baby in her arms.

4. *Marguérite*

WHEN MARGARETHA GEERTRUIDA ZELLE MACLEOD came to Paris in 1903, she was nearly twenty-seven. She had been unhappily married for about eight years and had borne two children; by the standards of the day, she was contemplating middle age. Five years in Indonesia, the frightful life with MacLeod, two children, and the tragedy of her son had all taken their toll. The broad-shouldered, long-limbed, overly tall Frisian Amazon had no evident qualifications for the limited employment opportunities then open to women; she possessed, at the time, little more than her train fare and enough florins to spend a few weeks in a working-class hotel.

Only her attractiveness to men could land her a job somewhere, or a protector. But Paris was for Margaretha a totally strange city, where the people were impatient with accented and less-than-fluent French, and where she knew no one. Looked at objectively, her decision to go to Paris reflected both one of her strongest qualities—her fierce tenacity—and one of her even more obvious faults: her refusal to be realistic or "logical." She was clearly outside the establishment and would have to look for help from people as unconventional as she. From her modest *pension de famille*, she set out to find work as an artist's model.

A letter to Jean Guillaumet, a painter then fashionable with the middle class, led to an invitation to visit his studio. Most of his pictures were of beautiful women. After the amenities, Guillaumet was to recall later, he said to her: "Well, you can lay your clothes over there."

She looked, he remembered, startled, even shocked. In one of what were to become her trademark—her multiple and contradictory bursts of mythomania—she explained that she was Lady MacLeod, married to a British lord from whom she was estranged.

It would be unthinkable for portrayals of her unclothed body to hang on the walls of living rooms. Her husband would be justifiably furious, and she would be "finished." Her idea, she said, had been to model for the head alone. She had been told that her features were "sculptural."

Guillaumet, convinced that her accent was English and that he was dealing with nobility in distress, explained patiently that modeling for the head alone would make finding work considerably more difficult; she would not earn much of a crust. He told her that she was pretty and that she appeared to have a good body. She protested once more that modeling the figure was unthinkable and rose to go.

Then, at the door of the studio, she suddenly changed her mind, put down her purse, and began to disrobe. As she stood before him, Guillaumet observed that she had the sort of generous, well-formed legs and arms and "Greek" shoulders that were then favored by many painters and by sculptors of monuments, with an attractively rounded belly. But the disproportionately tiny breasts, which had fed two children, had become—in Guillaumet's later words to a French journalist—*blettes*. This is a word normally used to describe fruit that has gone bad and squashy. Indeed, she had what is often referred to in French bar-counter slang as tobacco pouches, and small ones at that. *Faute de mieux*, a painter could always invent a different torso; but in a city full of poor girls with excellent qualifications to model, there was no need not to be inspired by the reality. Guillaumet, noting that the rest of her body was good and that she wore clothes well, sent her to a friend who used costumed models for his paintings.

For the rest of her life, she managed to preserve the secret of her ignominious bosom. The woman who was to become the prophet of striptease and one of the most famous and expensive courtesans of the period, sleeping with literally hundreds of men and sometimes with only one for a year or more, never uncovered her breasts except to her mirror and perhaps to her servants. Theater spectators would see her rounded and inviting buttocks, her heaving loins, and her wide mouth open in the expectation of ecstasy as she danced, but they would just have to imagine what existed in between. What she wore—dancing, making love—was a garment of her own design. It was not referred to as a *soutien-*

gorge, which literally means a support that enhances the throat—a French euphemism for the cleavage—and which we in the English-speaking world call by the archaic French word *brassière*, which means something supported by the arms. It was always described as a *cache-seins*, a fetching "breasts-concealer" that she devised herself.

Onstage, it was metallic and bejeweled and meant to suggest a traditional garment from India or the Indies. During the day, like millions of other women, she stuffed the upper portion of her corset, appearing in studio portraits to have a truly egg-timer figure. In her boudoir, the little room beside the bedroom where middle- and upper-class women would undress and bathe themselves in a water basin, she would don her *cache-seins*, filled with the soft belly-down of ducks or geese. No one apparently noticed or cared that the feathers never went hard under the impulse of desire.

How could this pretense endure for so long? Surely, one thinks, a drunken German crown prince must have wrenched it off in the fires of passion? Ever the mythologist, she had an explanation that she gave everyone with the right to ask and that even the most depraved, dissolute, or inflamed lover would not have the effrontery to question. Indeed, it was an explanation that enhanced the lover's pity and protectiveness toward his mistress and thus perhaps even fueled lust. She would admit, with her hands to her face in shame, that her husband, in one of his alcoholic rages, had bitten off both her nipples.

When countless music-hall dancers, encouraged by the "Indian dancer's" success in private salons, emulated her for the broad public and went one further—undressing better bodies of everything except a brief shield for the pubic hair—countless explanations inevitably gained currency as to why the arch-priestess of naked dancing, not noted for her prudery, was so coy about displaying her bosom. While working on this book in France, the writer spoke of Mata Hari to one of a small handful of French friends who knew the subject being researched; the octogenarian country squire, who had been sixteen years old when the lady was shot and had read numerous accounts of her life in his student years, leaned across the dining table in his mansion and asked in a half-whisper: "Was it true that she had only one breast?"

*   *   *

Unable to pay her way with only occasional modeling assignments, Griet returned to Holland and stayed briefly with an uncle of John's at Nijmegen. When MacLeod learned that she was there, he protested to the uncle; his wife, he said, was spreading lies about him; the fault of the separation lay with her. He was apparently successful in creating a cold climate in the house, and Griet left.

After living, briefly and miserably, off other friends and relatives, including her ruined father, and failing to find a job in The Hague or Amsterdam, she decided to try Paris again; this time, she would profit from her first mistakes. By now, she had a friend whom she had met at a Hague reception and who was about to return to Paris, where he might help her. This was the Baron Henry de Marguérie, second secretary at the French legation in the Dutch capital.

She had not told the French dandy, who was described as a "confirmed bachelor" in the days when this did not imply homosexuality—quite the contrary—how poor she was. Arriving in Paris with, as she later claimed, "fifty centimes in my purse," she took a room at the Grand Hôtel, which overlooks the Opéra, and sent the baron a *pneumatique*. The wealthy lover whom she at once acquired was glad to pick up the bill and to buy her some badly needed clothes. If she suddenly found that she had not had enough time to go to the bank and needed a few francs for a taxi, Marguérie was not to know that what he was giving her was all she would have until the next time he came calling. Instead of starting from the bottom, this time she would start from the top: she had nothing to lose.

She had by then decided that she had one other small talent that might be exploited to find work: she was a good rider. She went to an equestrian school, run by a certain Ernest Molier, who agreed to find her part-time work as an instructress. The job was respectable but barely remunerative. If she was in real distress, Molier suggested, she might like to take the plunge into something a little more daring: he had formed a dressage team to appear in circuses. She agreed to participate, but Molier then had difficulty getting bookings for his act. Lion tamers and high-wire artists had begun to put jugglers and pretty riders out of fashion. It was clear that a little jumping in a circus arena would not bring home the bacon either. Molier, noting how graceful she was, asked her if she had ever tried dancing.

The notion of appearing at the Folies-Bergère or at one of its less prestigious imitations terrified her at first. It was true, she knew by then, that many of the girls who danced the can-can, and who occasionally raised their skirts a little higher than the ankles, usually acquired lovers who paid their bills and that a famous few had even married rich or titled men. Marguérite—the name given her by Marguérie—needed a way to achieve this life without the sordidness of nightclub dressing-rooms and the need to sleep with stage managers.

She had begun to talk about, and embellish, her Asian experiences. Since she had never been trained in dancing, and her Amazon form might not lend itself to light ballet, she decided she would have to launch something new: what she was to call Hindu or Indian dancing.

Orientalism was in vogue. Japanese prints and fans and a vast bric-à-brac of the fabled East were beginning to appear in the homes of the affluent. She had learned from her brief contact with circus people how performing artists often invented baroque, mysterious, or exotic backgrounds to enhance popular curiosity. Her Woudker features would lend themselves to a whole new incarnation.

By now, Marguérie, who had moved her from the high-priced Grand Hôtel to a respectable *pension de famille* near the Champs-Elysées, was aware that she was penniless and entirely dependent on him. They were in love, sort of. She called him "Robert." It was in the diplomat's interest to do anything that would help her to earn a living, and the notion of introducing her in French salons as a genuine child of the Orient appealed to his sense of fun. In the initial stages of the subterfuge, the two accomplices seem to have varied the myth. At first, she was the daughter of a Buddhist priest in Java and a nubile Dutch neophyte attracted to the philosophy. Next, she was the offspring of a high Dutch official in the Indies and a local girl. By the time of her first performance, her mother had become Indian, her father a British lord, and she had been raised as a sacred dancer in a Hindu temple on the Ganges.

Her true name was now sanctified as Lady MacLeod. Since the French called India "the Indies" and Indonesia the "Dutch Indies," who would notice any contradiction?

It was as Lady MacLeod that she first danced in Paris for an audience—a private gathering in the home of Mrs. Kireyevsky, a retired singer. The hostess was one of many women who spent their time organizing a salon, a necessary amusement for the affluent in a day when there was no cinema, radio, or television and when, apart from the opera and the classical theater, most public entertainment was essentially for the hoi polloi. Mrs. Kireyevsky frequently put on "charity" affairs in her commodious house, with her guests contributing money to some worthy cause and with part of the funds being paid to the performing artists as a *cachet.*

Because of her previous profession, most of Mrs. Kireyevsky's artists were singers; the idea of a sacred Hindu dancer, fresh from the Orient, who would take off her clothes while dancing solely in the cause of cultural authenticity, was clearly something to break the monotony of endless ballads and arias and would draw wealthy men in profusion. A violinist was found who had actually heard Indian music. He would play a suitable background that the audience, incapable of judging how genuine it was, would accept.

By then, Marguérie had left for a new diplomatic assignment in St. Petersburg, and he did not see his protégée's triumph. However, according to a description passed on to the press by one of the guests, Lady MacLeod explained to her spectators that she was going to dance a tribute to the Hindu god Siva. She told the audience, with their evening-dress jackets and monocles, their lorgnettes and ballroom dresses, that she had been trained from puberty to serve Siva, much as a nun was the bride of Christ; the dance would simulate her reactions to his demands on her. In her presentation, since she knew no Hindi, she threw in a few words of Malayalam.

As the bow stirred the violin strings, she began to move sensuously across the floor, her features fixed. This was an easy expression for Margaretha Zelle to hold, since she rarely smiled. She was swathed in diaphanous veils purchased in the rue St.-Honoré, because she had somehow forgotten to bring her real temple garments from Benares. From the veils, her long sculptural arms emerged; her hands, delicately pointed in the Javanese fashion, supplicated the invisible god. As the contortions became more sexual and she was drawn irresistibly into the celestial embrace, the veils were cast away one by one, and her tan figure, now clad only in the stuffed metallic breast-cups and a bejeweled adornment at the groin, began heaving voluptuously; she finally submitted to the invisible one, then collapsed in adoration or satiety.

Unrehearsed and probably grotesque as the performance almost certainly was, this was cultural education of a sort that a generation of jaded boulevardiers in evening clothes could appreciate: a woman taking her clothes off in the name of art. The fact that she was also apparently the daughter of a British peer, with the title of "lady" in her own right, also made this "authentic" Ganges temple dancer one of them. She could, and did, reappear after her exotic act, dressed once again like their own wives and mistresses, and could quaff champagne and exchange small talk like everyone else. Moreover, for a half-British half-Indian, her French was becoming pretty good.

By all accounts, "Lady MacLeod" was a thunderous success that night. Numerous invitations to appear at other salons followed. But the true success of her outrageous subterfuge came when one of Mrs. Kireyevsky's guests, a wealthy businessman named Emile Guimet, invited her to dance at his museum of oriental art.

5. *Mata Hari: The Dancer*

DESPITE HER IRRESPONSIBLE FANTASIES and her superficiality, there was an introspective, ego-conscious side to Margaretha Zelle, which fell in with her spurious "temple dancing." Having spent her most formative years in Indonesia with MacLeod, she had returned to Europe sensitized to what she thought of as Hinduism and with what appears to have been a deeper, instinctive attraction to its Vedantic roots. The Vedas and Upanishads, of which she never seems to have had more than a glancing knowledge, are essentially a body of intuition rather than a religious philosophy. Always an audacious maverick in her younger years, and audacious in some ways to the end, she had defied colonial mores by wearing Indonesian clothes, thus seeking to identify herself with a culture despised as folkloric and immoral by the Christian Dutch officers, administrators, and their wives—a society that eight years with MacLeod had helped her to reject. Islam did not then dominate the archipelago as it does today. For all their problems, the sin-free Indonesians seemed more in harmony with the universe than the colonials, and she had developed at least a dilettantish interest in finding out why.

Since the Dutch called the Indonesians, the descendants of a Malay empire, "Indians" (after all, the West, because of Columbus' mistake, calls the Caribbean peoples "West Indians" and the native peoples of the Americas "Amerindians"), she always seems to have confused Hinduism, the principal religion of Indians, with Buddhism. Hinduism is a mix of the Vedanta and the pantheon of gods brought in by the Aryan peoples across the Himalayas when they conquered most of the subcontinent. Buddhism was a return to the Vedantic source, rejecting the pantheon and the superstitions that flavored Hinduism, much as Christianity and Islam were attempts to return to a purer Judaism. With a little reading and a dose of intuition, she appears to have found, in her limited knowledge of the Vedantic tradition, something that gave meaning to her troubled life. In her case, it produced not a compassionate aesthete but a self-centered hedonist who did many un-Buddhist things, such as collecting furs and claiming, untruthfully, to have hunted tigers.

She seems to have accepted that life was an illusion. Doting fathers became deserters; dashing officers became monsters; an innocent child could die suddenly in the most improbable manner. The impact this had on oneself was the impact one chose. Escape from a continuous cycle of rebirth was difficult because that too depended on oneself. What appears to have made her describe herself continually as a Hindu rather than as a Buddhist was the centrality of sex in much of Hindu art and illusion and the roles ascribed to women and to men in the comedy of love.

What she clearly accepted all her life was that sex was more important to men than to women, in that it was always pleasurable and even ecstatic to men but only occasionally so to women—and more important for women than for men because of the power that it gave to women. As Shaw made Julius Caesar say of Mark Antony's dalliance with Cleopatra, "a grain of sand in a man's flesh and kingdoms fall." This factor, then virtually true everywhere and still true in most cultures, would have been impressed on Griet in Java; there, women's submission to men as a source of man's subjection to women was more exuberant and obvious than in a less liberated society such as the Netherlands, where sex could only be discussed by professors of medicine and never intellectually confronted except by pornographic poets.

The dark side of her personal illusion was that her childhood universe had turned to ashes. Her father's bankruptcy had not only shattered her childhood cocoon; it had also impressed her with the problem of being poor and the greater problem of being poor and female. The positive aspect of her illusion was her power of seduction, despite her big and rather ungainly frame and its malassorted bust. Men would always provide material support in return for sex; a poor man, in contrast, could not pay the rent by offering himself to the ladies. As the women in the Hindu temple carvings seemed to imply, she would say to a potential lover, as she had said to MacLeod, years before, in Amsterdam: "You may do with me as you wish." However, she would say afterward of a Crown Prince of Germany or a French minister of war, "I conquered him" or "I can do with him whatever I want." Sex was her inexhaustible pot of gold, always on tap. Men inherited a patrimony—the family farm or savings. Women inherited a matrimony—with benefit of clergy or not.

The keys to her ability to direct the illusion of her life were seduction and apparent submission, while suppressing real physical participation or—until once, much later—emotional involvement. The dance she launched on Paris was the one in which she seduced and submitted to a Hindu god—her conquest of him in competition for submission with her rivals.

The Musée Guimet is today a respected institution in Paris; scholars use its collections and library for research; the Sorbonne sends its orientalist students there. In the late 1900s, however, Emile Guimet was simply a dilettante who had inherited a collection of oriental art from his father, Jean-Baptiste, a wealthy chemical engineer. Emile reportedly made one trip to Japan, stopping off in Egypt on the way home, adding to his father's iconoclastic collection of objects from Japan, China, India, the Indies, the Near East, and elsewhere. Neither of the Guimets invented the French attraction to what collectors call Orientalism; but France was then colonizing much of southeast Asia, and ships' captains often brought back cheaply purchased pieces that could be sold at impressive profits to Paris dealers. Emile Guimet, like his father, was an ardent customer; the family collection had finally overflowed the mansion and Emile had offered it for public view by building a splendid museum on the place d'Iéna.

If Guimet was captivated by Lady MacLeod, so too was his museum director, a Mr. de Milloué, and it was decided to use the museum as a setting for her performance. Both men insisted that she needed a stage name. Few artistes of the period mounted the boards with the names they had inherited: as with the stars of the *belle époque* in Hollywood a generation later, the men and especially the women of the Paris theater invented names to enhance their attraction, much like the names of modern brand products.

Griet had danced for the officers in the Indies and had written to relatives as far back as 1897 to say that, on the first of these occasions, she had taken the name of Mata Hari. The phrase means "the light of day" in Malayalam and is synonymous with "dawn." Word for word, it means "the eye of the day." Why a dancer from an Indian temple on the Ganges should have a Malayalam name does not seem to have puzzled anyone in Paris, including Guimet and his "expert" curator, when she revived the appellation at the Guimet Museum.

Her appearance there on March 13, 1905, conceivably the watershed event of her stage career, transformed her from a *succès de salon* into a triumphant artist. The two dilettantes, Guimet and Milloué, made this first truly public spectacle of Mata Hari a feast for the eye, transforming the round upstairs library of the museum into a Hindu temple, complete with authentic carvings of female figures mounted at the head of the columns that support the ceiling, and even "tropical" creepers growing on the columns.

No longer was the god invisible: a half life-size carving of Siva, with four arms, was placed on the improvised stage with a bowl of burning oil at his feet. Mata Hari was dressed from the museum collection, as were four supporting dancers who, in the course of the rite, would vie for Siva's attentions but retire in humility as the god directed his invitation to Margaretha Zelle alone. Bracelets from the collection embellished her wrists, biceps, and calves. A belt from India, encrusted with precious stones, held a translucent Indian sarong in place. Her similarly bejeweled metal breastcups were stuffed for the occasion with cotton wool.

The diaphanous shawls she wore as the dance began were cast away to tempt the god until finally, as the candelabras were capped and only the flickering oil light gleamed on Siva's features, the sarong was abandoned and her silhouette, with her back to the audience, writhed with desire toward her supernatural lover. The four dancing girls chanted their jealousy as Mata Hari groaned and worked her loins deliriously. All passion spent, she touched her brow to Siva's feet; one of the attendant dancers tiptoed delicately forward and threw a gold lamé cloth across the kneeling figure, enabling her to rise and take the applause.

A few moments later, dressed in the latest Paris fashion but playing with a *majong*, an articulated Javanese marionette from the museum collection, she joined the audience to be complimented again. Among those who went away ostensibly impressed were the ambassadors of Japan and Germany.

Two nights later, she danced for Mrs. Kireyevsky again, to raise money for the Russian Red Cross, to help treat the wounded of the Russo-Japanese war. This event was attended by, among others, a sprinkling of self-exiled Russian princes and grand dukes, along with their friends in the French nobility. Thereafter, there was no segment of French society so haughty and restricted that the brash hatter's daughter could not penetrate. She danced three times that year for the Baron de Rothschild and once at the famous Cercle Royal, a club limited to men of the highest ranks of the aristocracy and whose premises are today the Paris office of *Time* magazine. On another occasion, she appeared at the larger and almost equally prestigious Grand Cercle.

By now, she was insisting on the sort of impressive backdrop that had been provided at the Guimet. When the famous actress Cécile Sorel—a classicist of the Théâtre Français notorious for having also performed, for the right price, at the Folies-Bergère—invited Mata Hari to perform, she transformed her greenhouse for the occasion. There was a profusion of every type of trailing plant, to suggest a Hindu temple in the heart of the Tamil forest.

At this performance, Mata Hari had the occasion to meet Gaston Ménier, the great name of French chocolate, who invited her to dance in his mansion also. Ménier, an enthusiastic amateur photographer, later took the first pictures of her in, and largely out of, her oriental costume.

At this point, Mata Hari (always written, accented, as Mată Hări) was her accepted stage name, but invitations were addressed to "Lady MacLeod." To her friends, she had become Marguérite.

There were, of course, a few who discerned a certain amateurishness in her performances. Fellow performers like Cécile Sorel were supportive: if the public liked it, good luck! The press was largely supportive also: she was what would later be called hot copy. But the novelist Colette, herself a concupiscent mistress of famous men, wrote in 1923: "She hardly danced at all, but she knew how to undress herself slowly and move her long, proud, bister body." Despite Mata Hari's later fame for style in dress, Colette also implies that she did not become a parisienne overnight. The writer called the dancer "someone with no taste in clothes. . . . She dressed like a German."

A few other learned writers inconveniently noted that the dancers portrayed in the Hindu temple carvings had revealed only the one part of the body that Mata Hari hid—the breasts—and added that in any event the figures were mythological, like angels, and that there was actually no such thing as a temple dancer. This is not strictly true, but it can be said that there are no "sacred" dancers of the sort hastily invented by Margaretha Zelle.

For blasé groups, she would shorten the dance, starting with fewer veils. She would vary it in other ways for an occasion: Molier, who had by now started his own small circus, complete of course with equestrian acts, invited her to perform, and she managed to do a half-naked "temple dance" while riding a horse.

"Lady MacLeod, Mata Hari" also danced for the Society of Amateur Photographers, and this led to her dancing before the lens of Gaumont, who was, with Pathé, one of the pioneers of silent motion pictures before the fad reached America.

Shortly after her appearance at the Guimet, she had written to John, asking to see her daughter. Her estranged husband agreed to a meeting—at the railroad station at Arnhem. Mata Hari arrived in great style, helped down from her first-class car by a liveried footman brought along to carry the luggage.

There was a short, awkward conversation with the retired major and the bewildered Non. Mata Hari asked John if he would allow her to have Non in Paris for a while. John refused, but said he could use some help with the bills. Mother and daughter never saw each other again.

It was later that year that she met the wealthy sixty-three-year-old lawyer Edouard Clunet, later to be one of a very small, hardy group of spurned lovers who were to remain loyal to the end. Some authors have placed this meeting in Monte Carlo, but this appears to be incorrect. Clunet fell in love with her and found her a manager whom he knew personally, Gabriel Astruc. Astruc was one of the great impresarios of his day; he had brought Sergei Diaghilev and the Russian Ballet—soon to become the Ballets Russes de Monte-Carlo—to France. Astruc booked her into the Olympia, the leading Paris music hall. For the ten thousand gold francs offered—comparable to the purse offered today to a major attraction in Las Vegas—she was prepared to drop her carefully nurtured aristocratic image and enthuse the vulgar Paris crowd.

Appearing on the bill with her that week was Fred Karno, the American mime who later discovered Charlie Chaplin, as well as a troupe of Arab dancers, a film projection, and someone called "Leo and his infernal violin." There was massive promotion, the public saw what it was told that it would see, and Mata Hari moved from the review columns to page one. She had become, in the words of *Le Matin*, "the greatest and most sensual temple dancer of India." She was, of course, the only one.

Like most overnight successes in the entertainment world, then as now, she was hugely overspending. Her father's naïve belief that one was rated by the sumptuousness of one's clothes was exaggerated in his female offspring: a fortune went on dresses, hats, shoes, and jewelry, despite lavish gifts from admirers and lovers. She was Adam Zelle's daughter in orbit. Soon, we learn, a jeweler was suing her for nonpayment of a twelve-thousand-franc bill, and a court ordered her to pay two thousand francs a month.

The attraction of Mata Hari was, of course, her brazen novelty. She had made stripping artistic, exotic—and acceptable. But there are just so many times that one can repeat the same act, and as 1905 wore on she was having to work hard to keep up the momentum of her fame. As other exponents of naked dancing appeared, as she herself put it, from "out of the ground," to cash in on the fall of the taboo, she would harp constantly and righteously on the artistic and even religious nature of her dancing. She told a Dutch reporter that her altruistic aim was to educate Europeans into the culture of the Orient and that, when that was done, she would retire to a monastery and spend her life in contemplation. She carefully did not, however, specify how long it might take to sensitize the Occident to the Orient enough to permit her to abandon her apostolate.

What had brought her to Paris in the first place was the degradation of her marriage and the destitution created by her separation. Although she enjoyed her fame, and enjoyed it immensely, the best revenge is living well. She had not come to Paris originally to conquer the stage but to move up from poverty to luxury, and the obvious route to that was marriage to an affluent and attentive husband. Playing Salome in a sarong, and even on horseback, was only a means to an end. Or was it? As her artistic career began to falter only months after it had started, the Frisian obstinacy began to obtrude. As market forces challenged the momentum of her faddish shooting-star career, she wanted more and more to maintain it and to move on to even greater heights in the entertainment profession.

This dichotomy, between wanting to marry a duke and wanting to be a world stage celebrity (which, of course, would always enable her to marry a duke if the right one came along), was to track this strange woman—self-indulgent but often loyal, brashly arrogant and reckless but never quite stupid—all her life and finally lead to her perdition in a comedy of human frailty in which she at last achieved the dignity that had eluded her before.

She was then living, above her means, in a magnificent apartment at 3 rue de Balzac that contained a beautiful grand piano. It was the building in which Marguérie lived. She now had a servant from Holland, Anna Lintjens, who was to remain with her virtually all through the rest of her life. Anna was a natural choice—a fallen woman: she had borne a child out of wedlock in 1886, when she must have been about twenty-five. Unmarriageable, she had drifted into domestic service.

For a while, Mata Hari let it be known that she was "engaged" to a Russian prince whose name she would not reveal but who does seem to have existed. At the time, something happened that would have made such a marriage possible: MacLeod sued for divorce, sending a lawyer to Paris with a photograph, procured somewhere, of Mata Hari in her most naked pose. The lawyer argued convincingly that such a photograph would persuade any Dutch judge that she was depraved. She reluctantly agreed to be divorced for adultery, knowing that this would deprive her of any claim to her daughter. The decree was signed in Amsterdam on April 26, 1906.

John, now fifty-two, remarried the following year. His bride, Elisabeth-Martina-Christina van der Mast, twenty-four at the time, soon bore him a new daughter, Norma. Non disliked her stepmother and was sent off to live with a local family. The couple separated in 1912, and Non came back to live with her father. By then, MacLeod had brought suit, successfully, to prevent Griet from using his name; the double appellation, often used before, disappeared from billboards. Now the invitations came in the name of Mata Hari or Marguérite; but she would still revive the distinguished name of the lords of Dunvegan when it suited her.

Well before her divorce was declared final, and in search of new worlds to conquer, Mata Hari danced for two weeks in Madrid at the end of 1905. A local newspaper article described her performance as "discreetly voluptuous."

For her ardently Roman Catholic audience, she wore a "skin," which enabled her to appear to drop everything else on stage. Although deprived of a real look at her heaving loins and resplendent buttocks, the Spaniards could at least catch a hitherto censored glimpse—through the *collant*—of her cantilevered, supposedly amputated nipples.

In Madrid, she developed a relationship with the French ambassador, Jules Cambon, later the leading diplomat of his day. He was probably her greatest intellectual conquest. As ambassador to Washington in 1898, he had mediated the Spanish-American War at the personal requests of President McKinley and the Queen-Regent of Spain, leaving the United States with Cuba and the Philippines. The Spanish must have been satisfied not to have lost even more because, four years later, in 1902, he got a rousing royal welcome when he arrived in Madrid as the French envoy there. In 1907, he would go on to Berlin, where he was to be preoccupied with competing French and German claims to Morocco; he would stay there until 1914, credited by historians with having come within an ace of singlehandedly staving off World War I—and once again renewing his relationship with Mata Hari.

In his Madrid mansion, the French envoy who had been, for a time, in Washington, the appointed representative of both Spain and the United States in a delicate negotiation, had no compunction about giving a "brilliant" reception for the Dutch apostle of Indian culture and presenting her as "a true ambassadress of France." What more could one of the greatest diplomats of all time do for his mistress?

Mata Hari returned to Paris to learn that Astruc had booked her into the Monte Carlo Ballet. A role had been created for her in Massenet's new work, *The King of Lahore*. She was ecstatic. The première at the Monte Carlo Opera House took place on February

17, 1906, with Massenet present in the box of Prince Albert I of Monaco. When Mata Hari was once more lured into the four arms of Siva, the deity now had a voice—curiously, that of the American contralto Geraldine Ferrar. Although she was reluctant at first, and petulant and difficult during the exercise, Mata Hari had agreed to be taught some of the rudiments of dance, and she got flattering reviews from the improved result. But she was onstage with La Zambelli, one of the great ballerinas of the day, and the comparison was not flattering.

Zambelli is reported to have told the stage manager: "She is as much an Indian dancer as I am a Chinese waiter! I have only lost my temper about two hundred times in my career, a royal tribute to my overweening forbearance, but this time I was sorely tempted."

No matter; Mata Hari was a celebrity, and a celebrity who took off her clothes! She was led through the streets of Monte Carlo in a carnival procession in which she depicted Venus. Massenet sent her a measured note of congratulations, and Puccini, also in the audience for the première, sent her flowers. But, apart from a brief première for a Paris show, she was never invited back to Monte Carlo again, despite strenuous efforts on her part to persuade Diaghilev.

The apparent triumph in Monte Carlo was perhaps the ideal moment to withdraw, while she was ahead, from the undignified hustle for theater jobs. The occasion to do so presented itself when, during a short appearance in Berlin that followed, she fell into the arms of a Hussar lieutenant, Alfred Kiepert of Westphalia—coincidentally, the province from which the Zelles originated. The couple had originally made acquaintance in Monte Carlo.

Kiepert was a very rich Junker and landowner. He set her up in style at 39 Nachodstrasse in Berlin, well away from the castle where he lived with his beautiful Austro-Hungarian wife and their children. He introduced Mata Hari into the highest ranks of the aristocracy, got her invited to the annual maneuvers of the Imperial Army in Silesia later that year, and gracefully looked aside when she occasionally satisfied the amorous demands of the higher nobility, including his royal liege, the Crown Prince. (Waagenaar doubts that she actually made this princely conquest, but it seems to be too well attested by others, and by Mata Hari herself, to be untrue.) This period in Mata Hari's life was to be looked at with a bilious eye by the French, and especially the British, a few years later.

German is a fairly easy tongue for the Dutch to learn, and from pillow talk and parties she was soon as fluent in German as she was in French. She was never a great reader and therefore had a good aural understanding of languages. Mata Hari apparently saw this interlude in a different city as a way of putting some space between herself and the feverish search for appearances, through Astruc or others, in Paris, and as a preamble to a new chapter in her career as a dancer—a career that ideally would be limited thenceforth to prestigious opera and ballet occasions.

From her luxurious Berlin niche as a royal courtesan, she wrote to Massenet, urging him to write a ballet around her. He wrote back, discreetly, that he was flattered by her proposal but was unfortunately tied up with work for months to come. However, if he was dubious about her dancing, the great composer, then in his sixties, was not indifferent to her charms. He took advantage of his hold on the dancer to visit her in Berlin. A note from him left in her album indicates that they had had a brief, passionate relationship; with Massenet, however, Mata Hari never again got beyond the casting couch, and the composer completely omitted to mention the Berlin idyll in his memoirs.

Writing to Astruc later that year, she mentioned Massenet's visit. She said that the composer had given her an introductory letter to the Vienna Opera and that she had been invited to play in a Christmas pantomime for children in London—a bizarre role for a striptease dancer but one that she was prepared to undertake. After all, she had never been to London, and Edward VII had been one of the most notorious libertines in Paris in his days as the Prince of Wales; surely there would be an invitation to Buckingham Palace.

Astruc seems to have been unable to follow up on either possibility, but the lure of the prestigious Vienna Opera was irresistible. She left Kiepert to his wife for a while, at the end of the year, and set off for the Austro-Hungarian capital, where she performed her traditional Siva dance at the Dissident Art Theatre and, in a *collant*, at the Apollo. There the orchestra, presumably lectured by Mata Hari that her dancing was religious, played as an introduction a musical adaptation of Martin Luther's poem-prayer "A Mighty Fortress Is Our God!"

The Opera itself, alas, was to prove to be beyond her reach. No doubt word had arrived from Monte Carlo that the girl didn't really know how to dance and that she was a royal pain at rehearsals.

Indeed, Vienna largely resisted her charms. Isadora Duncan, a true dancer, had already cavorted naked there and had been followed by another talented transatlantic terpsichorean, Maud Allen. It was only as her own best press agent that Mata Hari could prove superior to such as these.

In interviews with Austrian journalists, and probably not thinking of the shameless stare of history, she reinvented her biography once again. She told them she was a Dutchwoman whose grandmother was the daughter of a Javanese priest, adding that "this means that pure Indian blood flows in my veins." Her father had now become a Dutch officer. She had been born in Java and educated in . . . Wiesbaden! (After all, she had been there on honeymoon, and so could describe the city.) Her ex-husband was no longer a coarse redneck who had never seen the Indonesians as anything but savages; he was now a scholarly Dutch aristocrat who had read the Vedas and had been naturalized Indian. By this, she apparently meant a citizen of the Dutch East Indies; needless to say, since Indonesia was a colony, there was at the time no such thing as "Indian" citizenship. Her former spouse, she said, was still living the life of a native in Malang, a town near where the MacLeods had once resided.

The real MacLeod had used the seeming indecency of her performances to get a divorce. Adam Zelle, still living in dejection at 65 da Costakade in Amsterdam, saw his chance to benefit differently from his daughter's fame, and in a way that seems as ahead of his time as his interest in oil had been: He would write a book about her! Since her own accounts of her life for the journalists of Paris, Madrid, Berlin and Vienna had been a tissue of lies from beginning to end, she could hardly blame him for emulating this meticulous scorn for facts.

An Amsterdam editor showed interest in the work that Zelle produced but took the precaution of checking with MacLeod, who indignantly pointed out that the book was fiction. However, Adam Zelle, like his daughter, was not someone put off easily by a first rebuff, and a book of 266 pages appeared in December 1906 with another Amsterdam publisher. The title was *The Life of Mata Hari: The Biography of My Daughter, and My Grievances Against Her Former Husband*. The title attests to the contents and to the old hatter's confidence that if the litigious scoundrel sued, surely his grateful and wealthy daughter would come to his aid.

According to Zelle, Margaretha now descended from a long line of kings and dukes in Germany. His name, he insisted, proved that his family had been the landowners of Celle. But little M'greet had always had the supernatural gift of being able to move from one time capsule to another, so that she benefited from numerous cultures and manifestations in history. If this fraudulent work shows nothing else, it demonstrates how much the genes of the father had shown up in the daughter. Most of the book, he unflinchingly claimed, had actually been written by Mata Hari herself "in the United States of America"—a country she never saw.

At the request of MacLeod, who in his penury always seems to have had florins enough to pay for lawyers, a Dutch attorney published a pamphlet denouncing Zelle's work, saucily entitled "The Naked Truth About Mata Hari." Zelle profited from the polemics to issue a second edition of his book. Waagenaar, who read Zelle's effort (the present writer cannot read Dutch), noted with some wit that Zelle's reasoning that his name implied descent from the princelings of Celle was the equivalent of Jack London claiming that his family had once owned the British capital.

A less audacious and more legitimate initiative was taken by a Dutch cigarmaker who mixed Javanese and Turkish tobaccos to produce a good imitation of the Russian cigarettes then favored by the wealthy of western Europe; he gave his cigarettes the brand name of Mata Hari. The lady was flattered, and insisted in his publicity that she never smoked anything else.

If Adam Zelle had been slow to get out of oil, or perhaps too brilliantly fast in getting into it, he had been right in not delaying his book. From then on, with a few brief moments of revived glory, M'greet-Greta-Griet-Marguérite-Mata Hari was to spend her time trying to resaddle the comet. The battle between the lure of stage fame and the attractions of a simplified, luxurious life as a lady continued and was never finally resolved. She at least had Kiepert's money to tide her over for a while. After a brief visit to Russia, of which no records appear to have survived (another shot at the prince?), she set sail for Egypt.

6. Mata Hari: The Courtesan Who Sometimes Dances

MATA HARI WAS DISAPPOINTED by the cruise to Egypt aboard the German steamer *Schleswig*. She found no exotic dances to bring back. But as soon as she returned to Paris, she began lobbying for the lead role in a new opera with a decidedly Near Eastern theme: Richard Strauss' *Salome*, which was adapted from a play by Oscar Wilde and which Astruc was putting on at the Châtelet Theatre. She wrote to Astruc literally begging him for the part and enclosed a letter for Strauss himself—written, curiously, in French, despite her fluent German. She offered to meet the composer in Berlin and told him: "I am the only person who can dance the mind of Salome." Astruc never forwarded the letter: he had another dancer in mind for the role.

When all her efforts to get the part failed, she returned to Berlin and Kiepert for the rest of the year, at the end of which the liaison finally came to a close. The German aristocrat paid her off handsomely—100,000 marks at once and two drafts for 100,000 marks each, postdated for the end of 1908 and 1909.

She was now without a home in Paris, so she stayed at the Hôtel Meurice, where she told a reporter for *The New York Herald*'s Paris edition that she had just spent two years in Egypt and India gathering material for new dances and going tiger-hunting with a maharajah. She did not dance again until September 20, 1908—an unpaid charity performance at the home for retired actors at Pont-aux-Dames, near Paris. She still managed to get her name from time to time into the gossip columns, always announcing major theatrical plans; but her career as a dancer was clearly winding down fast, and her main fame was more and more as a courtesan. Articles of the time compared her with Cléo de Mérolde, the mistress of Leopold II of the Belgians, with Lola Montez, the Irish pseudo-Spanish dancer who had much earlier conquered the heart of Ludwig I of Bavaria, and with "la belle Otéro" who, like Mata Hari, had made limitless bedroom conquests. But whatever she earned in that profession was soon spent, and when she checked out of the Meurice she left unpaid bills.

The following year, she gave two more charity performances— at Houlgate, for the local poor, and at the Femina Theater to raise funds for a Bulgarian hospital. She had added a new dance, the *Ketjoeboeng*, which she explained, perhaps significantly, was an Indonesian flower that bloomed and died in a single night. It was not until January 1910 that André Antoine decided to put her into a ballet, *Antar*, derived from a play by the Algerian writer Chekri-Ganem. The setting is a sort of "fabled Araby," with a generous mix of historic periods. Antoine gave Mata Hari the role of Cleopatra, to be danced to an Arab air composed by Rimsky-Korsakov. But Mata Hari was now decidedly overweight for ballet and proved to be more petulant than ever during rehearsals for the première in Monte Carlo, where she got mixed reviews. When Antoine took the show to Paris, he fired her.

She sued for three thousand gold francs—the fifteen days' pay that she would have earned if she had appeared during *Antar*'s short Paris run—and five thousand francs damages for the injury to her reputation. The court awarded her only the three thousand francs.

By then, she had encountered an investment banker, Félix "Xavier" Rousseau, and had told him that she was tired of the social round of life in the capital. They had met at a private concert at which Rousseau's teenage son was playing. He seemed to be a promising catch: his office, at 41 rue Vivienne, was literally a stone's throw from the Paris Stock Exchange.

Suddenly she dropped from sight: Rousseau had set her up in a country mansion, the Château de la Dorée, at Esvres in Touraine. From the spring of 1910 until the end of 1911, she spent all her time at Esvres except for an occasional trip to the Auteuil races with Rousseau and a visit to the Vittel spa to "take the waters." For nearly two years, her principal activity was riding horses, especially her favorite, Radjah.

Rousseau had rented the château from the Countess of La Taille-Trétinville, having been recommended as a tenant by a fellow businessman who knew the dowager. The friend had explained that the house would be occupied full time by "Madame Rousseau," who was described as a lady of Dutch origin and the widow of a former governor of India, Lord MacDonald. (Rousseau later corrected this to "Lord MacLeod.") The banker became a weekend husband: he would take the train to Tours every Friday night and reach Esvres by taxi, setting off back to Paris early on the Monday.

The mansion had no gas, electricity, or running water. The woman who loved to lounge in milk baths in Paris did her ablutions in a basin filled by bucket from a well, having the water heated in winter on a woodstove. Fireplaces were the only source of warmth. Rousseau, however, installed a raised bed, reached by steps, for his beloved, gave her four horses, and draped the stables in the crimson velvet she had coveted since her high school days.

Waagenaar, who spoke to Pauline Piedbout née Bessy—who as a twenty-two-year-old maid had shared the housekeeping duties in the château with the Dutch servant, Anna Lintjens—recounted a charming anecdote of Pauline's about "Madame Rousseau's" riding abilities. One day, a sixteen-year-old boy belonging to the La Taille-Trétinville family brought her a letter, boasting that he had ridden all the way from Tours. Mata Hari mounted his horse, sidesaddle in the style of the women of the day, and, to the youth's amazement, rode it into the house and up and down the wide central staircase. "When you can do that," Pauline remembered her saying, "you will be able to say that you know how to ride." Mata Hari was never noted for her modesty.

One day, Rousseau's mother arrived. Her intention was to try to persuade Mata Hari to give up her son so that he could return to his wife in Paris. But Mata Hari and the older Madame Rousseau got along so well from the first meeting that the old lady was invited to stay. She became Mata Hari's companion, on and off, for six months.

At Esvres, the now apparently settled chatelaine tried again to strike up a correspondence with her daughter; but the letters, and a gold watch that she sent for a birthday, were returned by John.

The frustrated mother was eventually to become the frustrated country wife: during 1911, Rousseau's bank began to collapse. At the end of the year, he was forced to give up the lease on the château and move Marguérite back to Paris, renting a small but attractive Norman-style house with a garden at 11 rue Windsor in Neuilly, the most exclusive of the Paris suburbs. Under strain and soon to be bankrupt, he became quarrelsome about her bills, and the couple parted.

The rent was paid for a while, and Mata Hari stayed on in the house. She kept the many gifts that Rousseau had given her, including the four thoroughbreds. Later that year, she is reported as unsuccessfully trying to borrow 30,000 francs and offering the horses as collateral.

Astruc managed to get her a brief but prestigious engagement: two performances at La Scala Opera House in Milan, one as the princess in Gluck's *Armide*, and one as Venus in a modern ballet called *Bacchus e Gambrinus*. She told the Italian press that she felt at home in both roles, explaining her attraction to the first by the fact that her grandmother had been a real princess in Java, where she had been born. Her biography now had a new and sophisticated twist: orphaned at twelve, she had been educated in Britain, France, and Germany.

Once again, the reviews were mixed. As a dancer, Mata Hari was hardly of the class expected in what was then Europe's most famous opera theater. One critic suggested that, since she had no talent for ballet, La Scala should fatten her up even more and let her do some belly dancing. To a critic who suggested that her dancing was erotic, she said: "When a dance is well performed, it extinguishes in those who watch it exactly those desires which they would like to be stimulated." To which the reporter added the comment: "In India, perhaps."

She returned to Italy briefly a few weeks later for one more appearance, dancing Salome in the private palace of the Prince di San Faustino—the Palazzo Barberini on Rome's via delle Quattro Fontane, now a museum. The prince kept her on in his quarters long enough to have her painted as Salome by an unknown artist. In the picture, she is reclining almost naked on a couch and fingering the severed head of John the Baptist.

But the appearance at La Scala had revived old hopes of glory, and she was back on the rollercoaster again, searching for parts, in need of money. She asked Astruc to forward a letter to Saint-Saëns, urging the composer to write a ballet for her. She still dreamed of appearing with the Ballets Russes and even went to Monte Carlo to see Diaghilev and Nijinsky. Diaghilev did agree to try to find her a cameo role, perhaps as Scheherazade or Cleopatra, but he wanted her to audition first. Mata Hari flounced out of the meeting, saying she had never been so insulted. Astruc was instructed to get her engagements in Vienna, London, or the United States. When he failed, she fired him—then changed her mind.

The maidservant Anna, who had become an indispensable companion, was still with her, and this continually brought back memories of Holland. Mata Hari had still not given up hope of recovering her daughter, who was now thirteen. One day that year, she actually sent Anna off to Velp, where John and the young girl were living, with orders to kidnap Non as she came out of school. Anna's instructions were to take a taxi to Antwerp with the girl at once, then the train to Paris.

At Velp, the scared servant found someone who knew Non by sight and who agreed to stand at the school door and point the child out. But as the bell rang for the end of class, the accomplice came running to Anna to explain that MacLeod himself had turned up to take his daughter home. Anna accosted the father and daughter, explaining that she had a gift for the girl from Paris. MacLeod gruffly sent her packing.

In the summer of 1912, Mata Hari wrote to Jules Cambon to ask him to help her get engaged by the Berlin Opera. The ambassador wrote back on July 26 to say he would do what he could. Nothing came of this. Cambon was preoccupied with Morocco, which France was then conquering to the chagrin of the Germans, who also had designs on the country.

In the fall, she gave a party at Neuilly, hiring an Indian orchestra led by a certain Inayat Khan, described as the "master of music of the Maharajah of Hyderabad." She danced the *Ketjoeboeng* in the moonlight, her long hair braided in what she claimed was the Tamil style. A few weeks later, she danced for a group of ethnographers. The biographical significance of these two minor performances lies in the fact that they took place at a time when numerous writers have placed her at a school for women spies at Lorrach in Germany. (Interestingly, in view of Mata Hari's own fate, Inayat Khan's daughter, Nur, became an officer in Britain's Women's Auxiliary Air Force during World War II, was parachuted into France as a radio operator with the Resistance, and was caught by the Germans. Since she was captured in civilian clothes, she was refused prisoner-of-war status and was shot at Dachau.)

The following year, 1913, Mata Hari appeared for a month in a cameo role in *Le Minaret* at the Théâtre de la Renaissance, then briefly at the Folies-Bergère in the role of a Spanish dancer, fully clothed and squeezed into an hourglass corset. Her dance was billed as a "living painting by Goya." Her only other engagement in 1913 showed how far down the line she had come: two shows a day for two weeks at the Trianon Palace in Palermo, Sicily. She shared the bill with nine other acts, including a troupe of performing dogs. She was now begging Astruc to get her engagements at private parties and writing to him that "if you believe that one thousand francs is too much, ask for six hundred."

The need for a rich protector was greater than ever. Rousseau, now a salesman for Heidsieck champagne, could be of no help. She wrote to Kiepert in Berlin. He wrote back guardedly that, if she returned to the city, he would of course enjoy seeing her again. This was enough for her to take the train, leaving Anna in charge of the house. On May 23, 1914, she appeared for two weeks as part of a music hall bill at the Metropol. She was offered a return engagement in September, but the war was to put paid to that.

At the Metropol, the sight of the fleshy thirty-eight-year-old woman doing her "Hindu" dance struck some spectators as indecent, and a complaint was lodged. A police officer called Griebel or Griebl decided to judge for himself. He watched the show, concluded that it was all pure art, and took her off to dinner. (Waagenaar discounts this anecdotic explanation of their subsequent relationship but does not say why. She herself later, under interrogation, did not deny it.)

Nearly every account of Mata Hari's life confuses Griebl with his superior, Traugott von Jagow, the head of the Berlin police. Von Jagow is then promoted to head of German espionage, and the story goes that he and his exotic mistress lunched together on the day following the outbreak of war—which took place on the night of August 4—and drove together afterward through the streets to the cheers of a crowd. This was to be cited by writers after her trial as additional proof that she was a German spy.

The notion that the head of German espionage would have exhibited himself in public with a spy whom he was about to send back to enemy territory can only raise a smile, and the true head of German espionage, Major Friedrich Gempp, was presumably too busy on that fateful day for a leisurely lunch and a drive through the streets with a foreign courtesan.

In fact, there was no such lunch, but she did dine one evening in late July with Griebl to thank him once again for quashing the indecency charges and to bid farewell: Austria had invaded Serbia on July 28, Germany was expected to be at war at any moment, and she was about to return to Paris. This final meal with Griebl, whom she later agreed had been her lover, was not in public but in a private room at a restaurant. While they were eating, the sound of shouts came from nearby streets, and the city policeman reflexively rushed outside to see what was happening. Mata Hari followed, and the two drove in Griebl's car to the Emperor's palace, where they watched a patriotic crowd march by singing *"Deutschland über Alles."*

Otherwise, her situation as a Francophile neutral in Berlin was unpleasant. "The police treated all foreigners like animals," she would recall later, under interrogation. She was arrested "several times" in the street and was "accused of being Russian."

She tried to get out of her theater contract for reasons of *force majeure* in order to return home to Paris. Partly because of this, her theatrical costumier, in a desperate rush to be paid for his work before she disappeared, had much of her jewelry and one of her fur coats seized. Her Berlin agent, she later said, held on to some of her money. When she went to the bank to draw funds, she was told that since she was a long-term resident of France, she was considered to be French; her account had been blocked.

The lady had a facile temper and a commanding tongue: at this point, we can be sure, she was beside herself. However, the important thing for the moment was to get home, especially after Germany actually entered the war on the night of August 4.

On August 6, her exit papers finally in order, she boarded a train for Switzerland. Like everyone else aboard, she was ordered off the train by the frontier police for questioning. The main purpose was to prevent Germans leaving for their neutral neighbor with valuables. She soon found that she had problems. Few people carried passports in those days, but they had suddenly become necessary. She needed official papers certifying that she was Dutch and a Swiss passport to cross the border. The word "passport" then had two meanings: one type of passport was a proof of nationality, the other a permit from the country to which the traveler was traveling, authorizing him or her to pass through the port or other frontier post—a document now replaced by a rubber-stamp visa. Mata Hari had neither.

While she was still trying to argue her way into Switzerland, the train left without her, but with her baggage, including her last fur coats, aboard. Because she had naïvely announced that she was returning to France—enemy territory—instead of Holland, she found little more sympathy for her plight from the German border guards than she had found from her Berlin bank manager or her dressmaker. She was later to claim that *"les sales Boches"* had cost her about eighty thousand francs' worth of lost clothes and valuables.

She returned to Berlin the following day, without even a change of clothing, and stayed at a hotel. She called Griebl but, because of her French residence and sympathies, he was afraid of further contact with her. At the hotel, she poured out her troubles to a Dutch businessman who was about to return to Holland. She told him that, after paying her hotel bill, she would not have enough money for fare. She too now wanted to go home to Holland. The friendly businessman bought her a ticket for Amsterdam.

By the fourteenth, she was in Frankfurt, where the consul-general of Holland, H.H.F. van Panhuys, issued her with a Dutch passport—then a broad sheet of high-quality paper folded into six sections. The next day she was in Amsterdam, as penniless as she had been when she had left that city for France for the first time eleven years before. Her father had died in 1910. In desperation, she went to the house of the Dutch businessman, who had left Berlin a few days ahead, and asked for shelter. Despite the penury in which she arrived and her problems in leaving Germany, it was later to be alleged that she was already a German spy when she returned to Holland.

Nearly fifty years later, Waagenaar found the businessman's wife, by then a widow. To conceal her identity, he calls her simply Mrs. K. She told him that, when she got to know her temporary guest better and realized that they had the real Mata Hari in their home, the courtesan assured her that her husband's generosity had not been in return for any bedroom favors. Mrs. K. recalled having said that, since Mata Hari was penniless, she was surprised that the famous siren had not seduced her spouse. Mata Hari had explained that she would never have done this without a change of clothes or a bath, and she had had access to neither at the time.

The visitor moved out a few days later, still penniless. With her habitual gall, she took a room at the expensive Victoria Hotel. The next step would be to find a man to pay the bills. In the event, a man found her.

In the street the next day, she noticed that she was being followed. It later transpired that her Parisian dress and French style had convinced a passerby that she must be an elegant prostitute. Mata Hari hurried into a church to be safe from her pursuer, then peeped out for a look at him. He was expensively dressed, middle-aged, and ostensibly affluent, so she reemerged and looked him in the eye. He addressed her in French.

Responding in the same language, she told him that she was a Russian tourist. He offered to show her the house in which the Czar Peter the Great had once lived in Zaandam, near The Hague. For several weeks the man, a banker called van der Schalk, was a frequent and generous visitor at the Victoria. Waagenaar believes that he discovered one day that his mistress was as Dutch as he and that his ardor for exotica was deflated, bringing the relationship to an end. Actually, she must have told him of her Dutch identity without mishap, because van der Schalk sent a lawyer to Berlin who succeeded in unblocking her bank account and recovering some of her seized jewelry.

From Amsterdam, Mata Hari wrote once more to her daughter, who was now sixteen. Anna Lintjens had recounted, after the Velp escapade, that the girl closely resembled Mata Hari—tall, with the same sepia features, black hair, and brown eyes—and that Non, despite her father's jaundiced views about her mother, carried her lunch to school in a biscuit box that bore a picture of Mata Hari as a dancer in her Guimet Museum period.

No reply came from Non. Instead, MacLeod wrote to say that all correspondence should be addressed to him. She sent him a polite letter—pretentiously, in French—asking to see her daughter. He wrote back, setting a date for a meeting in Rotterdam; he also asked for five thousand florins so that Non could have piano lessons. Then came another letter from MacLeod, who was then supplementing his army pension with a job as courthouse reporter for an Arnhem paper, saying he could not afford the train fare to Rotterdam. He apparently did not want to be seen with his notorious ex-spouse in Amsterdam and had chosen Rotterdam because nobody there knew either of them.

Her only known legitimate earnings that year came from two brief appearances: one was at the Koninglijke Schouwburg, the Royal Theater in The Hague—a cameo dance performance called *Les folies françaises* that was bizarrely served as a dessert to Donizetti's *Lucia di Lammermoor*. The other was a one-nighter at the Municipal Theater of Arnhem, near where MacLeod lived, in which her dance followed Rossini's *The Barber of Seville*. In both the December 14 role in The Hague, where she lost her footing and tripped onstage, and the Arnhem appearance four nights later, she was fully clothed.

But security was in sight. Two months before the Royal Theater engagement, she had renewed acquaintance with a lover from the distant past: the Baron Eduard Willem van der Capellen, a career colonel of fifty-one; it was he who pushed van der Schalk out of her life. On October 31, the baron signed a lease for her on a charming little house in The Hague at 16 Nieuwe Vitleg, facing onto a canal. The lease, for three years, renewable, was to start on November 15, at a rent of 750 florins a month. By this time, Non was attending a teacher-training school in the city, but the paths of mother and daughter never crossed—although MacLeod's last wife recounted later that Non was aware that her mother was in The Hague and had discovered the address; she had walked past the house, noting the "pretty curtains," but had not knocked at the door. She later returned to Velp as a trainee teacher, still carrying her lunch in the biscuit box bearing her mother's picture.

With the German army swirling through Belgium, Holland was

and remained on invasion alert and had mobilized its forces. The colonel, whose home was in Amsterdam, was serving on the frontier. Putting his mistress in The Hague enabled him to visit her regularly, leaving his wife to believe that he was either at "headquarters" in the capital or on the frontier with his troops.

While the house in the Nieuwe Uitleg was being totally redecorated and furnished at the baron's expense—including, notably, putting in a bathroom—Mata Hari lived at the Paulez Hotel, in constant and angry dispute with her slow Dutch decorator. (The hotel was destroyed in the final stages of World War II, and the American embassy was built on the site.) Finally, the place was ready, and the faithful Anna came back from Roermond, her home village, to rejoin her employer. Despite the pleasure of frequent visits from her illegitimate son, now a private in the Dutch army, Anna was to find that life with Mata Hari was no longer the round of excitement that she remembered from the Paris days. The fallen star had become an increasingly bored and bad-tempered woman.

The Hague was not Paris. The generous but dour Capellen was not Marguérie or Kiepert. Like Rousseau, he only needed Mata Hari's companionship when he could get away from his work; but for her, being a chatelaine in Touraine had possessed a charm that being a baron's concealed mistress in Holland did not. If only the war would end soon! But a year later, it showed no signs of reaching a conclusion.

On December 15, 1915, she went briefly to Paris to collect her silverware and other belongings; the four horses, including her beloved Radjah, had long since been sold. Because of the occupation of much of Belgium, she had to take a circuitous route. The Dutch ship put her off at Harwich, on the British coast, and she spent a few days in London before getting another ferry to Dieppe and the train for Paris.

In Paris, she stayed at the Grand Hôtel, spending several days with Marguérie, who had now been her on-and-off lover for eleven years in between diplomatic assignments. After helping create her career as a dancer, he had gone off to St. Petersburg in 1904, then to Vienna two years later, in time for her visit there and her efforts to dance at the Opera House. He had been back in Paris in time to help her forget Alfred Kiepert, before going off to Tokyo in 1909, and then Lisbon two years later. Having reached ambassadorial rank, but without a posting, he had been placed on the "availability" list in 1912. With the war, the wealthy nobleman had returned to the Quai d'Orsay, refusing pay, to help with the organization of codes and ciphers.

It was also at the Grand that she met the Marquis de Beaufort, a Belgian major who came in frequently from the Front. He took the room adjacent to hers and became her lover. Marguérie and Marguérite were two of a kind, and the libidinous diplomat had never minded sharing her favors.

On Christmas Eve, she wrote from her hotel to Gabriel Astruc, explaining that she was returning to The Hague "in a few days' time" and beseeching him to get her an engagement the following year with Diaghilev. She would now deign to be auditioned. Astruc did not reply. Perhaps he did not have her confidence that the madness of the war could not possibly go on much longer. Her one-night performance in Arnhem was to prove to have been her last stage performance. The last clipping in her album was the back cover of the March 13 issue of a Dutch magazine: a full-length photo of her. Across it, she wrote "March 13, 1905–March 13, 1915." It had been exactly ten years since her appearance at the Guimet Museum.

Returning to Holland, she was forced by British troop movements across the Channel to take a ship from Vigo, Spain, that called briefly at Falmouth. She took advantage of going to Vigo, which is near the Portuguese border, to visit Lisbon briefly, sending "Robert" de Marguérie a postcard from there—his own last posting abroad.

III

LOVE AND BETRAYAL

1916—1917

1. *Wartime Vacation*

THIS IS PERHAPS THE MOMENT to look at the situation in Europe in the first two years of the war.

A week after the Austrian invasion of Serbia—officially to avenge the assassination of the Archduke Franz-Ferdinand in Sarajevo a month before—the Germans had launched their own attack on Belgium on the night of August 4, 1914, following the long-established "Schlieffen Plan." Other armies were poised to march on Paris; the French pre-emptively invaded Alsace-Lorraine, but were soon repulsed.

German preparations had been afoot for some time and, as we shall see later, Kiepert and another of her lovers had talked openly about them to Mata Hari. It was no secret that the Germans had amassed 1,500,000 troops, grouped in seven armies under the overall command of General Helmuth von Moltke. Their purpose was to realize the worldwide territorial ambitions of the Kaiser Wilhelm II, a pompous but none-too-intelligent man whose grandmother, Queen Victoria, had called him "Silly Willie," but who saw himself as a modern Napoleon. The commander of the 5th Army—based in Luxemburg, next to the Dutch frontier—was a former lover of Mata Hari's, the Crown Prince Wilhelm, of whom we shall hear more again later.

Despite the long German preparations for war, France and Belgium had failed to mobilize sufficient forces. Their armies were soon thrown back. General von Kluck entered Brussels on August 20. Soon all of Belgium was occupied except for the Ypres salient in the west and some coastal ports, which soon fell. Only Ypres was to remain in Allied hands throughout the conflict, and only in the final weeks of the war were substantial parts of Belgium liberated; Brussels was to be in German hands virtually until the end.

One result of the successful German drive into Belgium was that that country and neighboring Holland soon became nests of spies for both sides.

France, which hastily mustered five armies, was able to offer stronger resistance than Belgium, but only relatively. A 6th Army was to be formed late in 1914 specifically to try to take on the German 5th, under the *Kronprinz*. But by September 8, the Germans had reached Meaux, twenty-three miles, as the crow flies, east of Paris. Virtually all available public motor vehicles, especially buses and trucks, were requisitioned to get forces to the Front. It was the time of the famous "taxis of the Marne," when Paris hackies helped to drive the troops to a front line which was then in the rural exurbs of the city. Most of northeast France was occupied, with only the Verdun salient holding out.

The French government had fled to Bordeaux on September 3, and the prospects looked bleak. But the French armies rallied bravely and drove the Germans, with their extended supply lines, back. The government was able to return to Paris in December. The Germans were pushed to as far as what became known as the Hindenburg Line, still well inside France, and were to hold it, more or less, for the rest of the war.

Besides Belgium and Britain, France had one very important ally: Czarist Russia, which had thrown 800,000 men into battle on the Eastern Front against Germany's ally Austro-Hungary. But Russia's was an undertrained, underpaid, underfed citizens' army; it had been defeated by Japan in 1904 and was to prove a poor match for the forces of the Vienna empire.

The British, equally unprepared, had initially mustered only 90,000 men, all volunteers. They were to build up the force only slowly. A threat to draft unmarried men, which spawned thousands of hasty marriages, was rejected as too unpopular. It was not until David Lloyd George took over the leadership of the Liberal Party and the premiership of the coalition government in London in December 1916 that "bachelor conscription" was passed, and the British Expeditionary Force finally surpassed a million men, or about half the number of the French.

It was to be a long and murderous war, fought in terrible conditions, mostly from trenches that overflowed in heavy rains or were frozen solid in winter. Vermin and disease were rampant, and medical conditions appalling. The death tolls were enormous—sometimes amounting to nearly half a million men, on both sides, from a single battle lasting only a matter of weeks, despite the fact that a bolt-action rifle could fire only one bullet at a time. As late as March 1918, the Germans were to muster forces for a major offensive, which in July of that year was to bring them once more close to Paris—to Thierry, fifty miles away—before they were thrown back again.

The war was fought not only in western and central Europe, but in distant places like Tanganyika and Mesopotamia (modern Iraq) because Germany and Turkey had colonies in Africa and the Middle East; but mostly it engulfed nearly all of Europe. Italy was neutral at first. Then, in the hope—later partially realized—of capturing territory from Austro-Hungary, it joined the Allies on May 23, 1915. An early pro-Allied politician of the time was Benito Mussolini, who broke with the Italian Socialist Party over his demand that Italy join in the war against the Central Powers. The Italians were to fight a largely unsuccessful war, however, and French and British troops finally had to go to their assistance.

To Mata Hari, the nuisance of a war was going on too long. Rusticated in The Hague, she was soon bored again—with Holland, perhaps with her colonel. War or not, Paris still beckoned. During her brief December visit, she had seen that it was now a city of uniforms, and she had always had a penchant for the military. Would she have married a man with all of MacLeod's blemishes if he had been a planter? She loved dress and, with the passing of the costumery of previous ages, the military was almost alone in offering men a chance to dress up in colorful absurdities of brass and braid, to cut what was called a dashing figure. Moreover, for a woman who supported herself by seduction, Paris would always be a more natural home than the sedate and straitlaced seat of the Dutch government. Mata Hari had never pretended to be French, but she rightfully claimed to be parisienne. Although the years were taking their toll, she still had her magic name and the courtesan's image of being both naughty and patrician. Her career as a paramour for the upper class could not be sidetracked in The Hague.

She applied for a new Dutch passport, which was issued on May

15, 1916; it is now in the military justice files in Paris. It was still a huge single-page affair folded into six, but it bore an innovation that had been introduced to make passports more difficult to sell to such wartime novelties as refugees and spies: a photograph. It is the cropped head-and-shoulders version of the pretty studio portrait that had appeared on the back page of a Dutch magazine the year before—the last clipping in her album. The slim handsome face has now become rounded, hinting at her increasing weight. A new waved-and-bobbed hairstyle emphasizes the ovularity of the features. The generous lips seem to bear the hint of a smile, as though she had just made a remark to the Dutch photographer. She is wearing a hat with pale, probably osprey feathers, and a garland of pearls is at her throat.

She had already obtained a new passport, in the other sense of the word, from the French. This booklet, similar to modern passports, is also in her file in the military justice archives. The photo it bears is more of a "mug shot" and follows the requirements of identity photographs today: there is no hat, and the hair is combed back to reveal the ears. The passport states that it is not valid for the *Zone des armées*—the war zone.

Despite the long list of battles lost by the Allies on the Western Front, Britannia once again ruled the waves, or at least those that lapped the shores of England and France. However, to take a ferry to England, and then a British ferry to France, required a British "passport" also, but the British consul in Rotterdam—presumably the port from which she intended to sail—had already refused her request. It was to be the first indication that she was under suspicion, but she saw it only as one of the absurdities of bureaucracy that proliferate in wartime even more than in time of peace.

One possible reason for British concern that the dancer who had been in Berlin at the outbreak of war, with a German policeman for a lover, might have sympathies for *les Boches* comes from a message sent by Italian intelligence to Paris in June 1915 and copied to London. This said that a Japanese ship that had docked at Naples on its way from Marseille to Egypt had had Mata Hari aboard as a passenger, with her home address listed as Berlin. She was reported as speaking German on board "with a slight Oriental accent."

The Italian message has apparently been lost, but its existence is attested to by Edmond Locard—a key figure, of whom more later—and it is first mentioned in print in a fairly serious British book, *The Story of the Secret Service* by Richard Wilmer Rowan, which appeared in 1938.

When the indefatigable Waagenaar read it in Rowan, it reminded him of something he had read somewhere else, and he dug up a report in *Le Temps* dated March 21, 1907. René Puaux, a writer for the paper, happened to be on the *Schleswig* when it took Mata Hari from Marseille to Egypt. He quotes her from a shipboard interview as saying that she is "a Berliner now," and he tells his readers that when she speaks German, it is with an accent "as un-Oriental as she can manage." Puaux clearly believed her legend that she had been born in India or Java.

Thus Graham Greene's character, in *Our Man in Havana*, who persuades his controller that the diagram from a vacuum cleaner manual is actually the blueprint of a secret weapon, had his real-life counterpart in Italy in 1915, using a 1907 press report to fabricate a piece of "intelligence" eight years later. No one seems to have questioned why a Berliner who was headed for Egypt during the war would take ship from France rather than from a port controlled by the Central Powers such as Trieste, or how the *Schleswig* became Japanese. The Rome message convinced the British that she was still established in Berlin about a year after the war began, at a time when she was actually savaging her inefficient decorator in The Hague and soothing the brow of her colonel when he came back from guarding the Dutch frontier.

As early as April 27, 1916, the Dutch ministry of foreign affairs, at her request, had gone over the head of the British consul and instructed the head of the Dutch legation in London, Marees van Swinderen, to appeal to the Foreign Office to issue her with a document enabling her to go ashore in Britain on her way to France:

> Message 74. Wellknown artist Mata Hari, citizen of the Netherlands, whose legal name is MacLeod Zelle, wishes for personal reasons to go to Paris, where she lived before the war. British consul Rotterdam refusing visa despite acceptance French consul. Please request British government to instruct consul Rotterdam issue visa. Respond by cable.

This message, now in Scotland Yard files, bears the scribbled mention "H.O." The Home Office, Britain's equivalent of what other European countries call a ministry of the interior, controlled the police.

Marees van Swinderen replied to The Hague on May 4:

> British have reason consider entry into Britain of lady described in your 74 undesirable.

This meant she would have to take the Iberian route. She booked passage aboard the *Zeelandia* for Vigo, Spain. The ship sailed from Amsterdam on May 24, steamed slowly through the Channel, stopping in Falmouth for a British inspection, and reaching Vigo about a week after its departure. The neutral Spanish did not then require a visa issued in advance. Her Dutch passport shows that she reported her arrival to the Spanish authorities in Madrid on June 12 and left for Paris on June 14.

On board the *Zeelandia*, she was to encounter more evidence of "espionitis," as she recounted later in one of her interrogations by Bouchardon, the military examining magistrate. She recalls that among the passengers was "a Jew of Dutch nationality called Hoedemaker" who described himself as a businessman. Other passengers, she said, told her that Hoedemaker was constantly on ships plying between Holland and Spain and that he was "in the service of the British." His task, she was told, was to report on neutral Dutch, Danes, and Norwegians going to Spain to take ship for Latin America, there to manage German firms whose executives had been interned. When the ship stopped at Falmouth for inspection, she recalled, Hoedemaker stood by the British officer who stamped passports and occasionally whispered in his ear. Some of the passengers would then be led ashore for questioning.

Mata Hari, whose destination was Paris and who had a French "passport," was not detained, but she told Bouchardon of a conversation she had had on deck with a Mr. Cleyndert, a rice merchant from the Dutch city of Zaandam.

"Cleyndert said to me: Keep your eye on that obnoxious Jew. He is telling everyone that he has searched your cabin."

With Cleyndert's help, Mata Hari soon found other passengers who agreed that Hoedemaker had boasted to them about the search; then she brought about a confrontation between Hoedemaker and the witnesses. He denied everything; but when the passengers gathered in the summer sun to take tea on the deck with the captain that day, "I insisted, in front of everyone, that Hoedemaker apologize to me," she told Bouchardon. "I asked him again if he had been in my cabin. He said he had not. I then asked the witnesses if he had made such a revelation to them. They said he had."

Mata Hari then slapped Hoedemaker "so violently that blood flowed from his mouth," she claimed, while the passengers, she recalled, shouted "Hurrah!" and "Bravo!" A Uruguayan consul on his way home from Holland later warned her that Hoedemaker was threatening to make trouble for her in Spain.

At Vigo, she recalled, Hoedemaker placed himself immediately behind her on the gangway, and he was beside her as she entered the lobby of the Continental Hotel. She had asked two other passengers, an American and a Dutchman called Buber (most books mistakenly say Rubens), to stay with her until she was safely in her room. Later, she claimed, when she was staying at the Palace Hotel in Madrid, she spotted Hoedemaker and a companion watching her.

The British were clearly seeking evidence of her possible links to Germany, and a typically hamfisted "agent" of the period was doing his limited best to check on her. But the trial records agree that she made no suspicious contacts in Spain.

When the train from Madrid reached Hendaye, the French frontier post, she was searched and interrogated by "three gentlemen." Then, despite her French "passport," she was refused entry and sent back to San Sebastian on the Spanish side.

She decided to write to Jules Cambon, her old friend from his days as ambassador to Madrid and later to Berlin, who was now the secretary-general of the Quai d'Orsay, the highest post in the French foreign service. But sending the letter to Paris and waiting for Cambon to telegraph back to Hendaye would take some time, and the great man presumably had other things to do besides facilitating a vacation for a courtesan in the middle of a disastrous war; so instead of mailing the letter she returned to Hendaye the following day and showed it to the French officers. Her threat to send it to Paris apparently impressed them, and they let her through.

Had Mata Hari been on a German espionage mission, the refusal of the British visa, her problems with the British agent Hoedemaker, and her rejection by the French officers at Hendaye would have made it clear to her that she was under suspicion and would therefore be followed everywhere, as was to prove to be the case. Safely back in San Sebastian in neutral Spain, one would have expected her to seek fresh instructions. There was a German consulate in the city, one of whose tasks must surely have been collecting information from across the border.

To Mata Hari, however, all these contretemps seemed to be simply the problems of war, interfering with her vacation. But at last she was in Paris again, taking a room once more at the Grand Hôtel, at 2 rue Scribe, on June 16. The French, alerted by the British, got around to a surveillance two days later.

Two police inspectors, Tarlet and Monier, were assigned to the task. Although she spotted them early, they were never replaced, not even when she later left Paris for Vittel. In their raincoats and derbies, they soon became familiar to the hotel staff, who reported all her telephone calls and visitors and showed them her mail. With her constant round of shopping, eating meals in the Bois and elsewhere with a great variety of escorts, and calling on friends, the two men were occupied for six months, seven days a week, hunting for horse-drawn or automobile taxis, frequently unable to find one in time, and often losing their elegant prey in traffic jams.

The reports of the two inseparable inspectors—curiously, almost the only documents in the voluminous French military justice dossier on Mata Hari to be typewritten—sometimes seem to be the stuff of a Mack Sennett comedy or of the early silent films of Fred Karno, who had appeared with her at the Olympia. They are also, filled out by Mata Hari's own account of the time, during her interrogations, a striking portrayal of the life she led—what the French call *fainéantise*, do-nothingness—in a city that was once more, as in 1871, living in danger of capture by the Germans.

Says Monier, who seems to have been the senior of the two policemen: "This tracking [*filature*], begun on June 18, 1916, continued, in a not uninterrupted fashion, until January 17, 1917." (Actually, it appears to have ended two days sooner.)

On June 18, the two inspectors followed her as she visited various fashionable shops and waited when she returned to the hotel for a manicure. The next two days were equally boring for the police, with rain keeping her in the hotel for most of the time and the *flics* sheltering as best they could in a local café or in the doorway of a nearby apartment building.

It was on June 21 that she first complained to the hotel doorman that she was being followed by two men. Learning of this, "we believed it inadvisable to continue the tracking," they reported. But apparently headquarters did not agree with their implication that two new faces be supplied, because the following day Monier and Tarlet were back on the trail.

They reported that she was alone most of the time, even at dinner in the hotel. She was, as it happened, waiting for the Marquis de Beaufort, the Belgian major of the previous year, to get leave from the Front. Occasionally, she chatted with officers staying at the hotel, but her bedroom, the inspectors learned from the hotel servants, remained inviolate. There were visits to take tea with old theatrical friends, notably a Mrs. Dangeville, who lived at 30 rue Tronchet.

She was leading a fairly typical life for a single woman staying in a luxury French hotel of the day, and since she was to spend half a year doing this, a brief description of such an existence is perhaps in order.

The daily routine was determined by the timing of the two meals, *déjeuner* (literally "breaking fast") and *dîner*. The first meal was at 10:00 A.M., and a hotel servant would walk along the corridors at nine-thirty swinging a bell to warn guests in time for them to don the right attire for meals in public or to rise if they were still in bed. *Dîner* was usually at 5:00 P.M., similarly preceded by a warning bell, a practice that would be continued for a few generations more on ships and trains.

In Paris, the demands of the sophisticated had pushed back the hour of dinner to five-thirty or six or even later, thus necessitating a new way for hotels to earn money—introducing the British habit of "high tea" in the afternoon. Guests who arrived after the early closing of the dining room in the evening could get a dish of cold *charcuterie*—known, after the British demand for it, as an *assiette anglaise*—in their rooms.

Restaurants, except for the working-class establishments, were more flexible; you could still get a dinner until about 8:00 P.M. However, quality restaurants, and many others, would not serve an unescorted woman, and those that did could draw the same conclusions as their customers about the reason for her presence. For more modest visitors to Paris, *pensions de famille* were more popular than *garnis*—small hotels that supplied no meals. That a woman traveling alone like Mata Hari could only go to a restaurant if someone invited her helps explain her (otherwise apparently promiscuous) willingness to indulge in a broad spectrum of escorts.

Eating à la carte—ordering from a menu with a choice of dishes—was gradually becoming popular in luxury hotels and was probably an available facility at the Grand; but most people were served a fixed meal, known as *table d'hôte* ("guest's table") from the long table at which all guests still ate together in most hostelries in Paris and in virtually all of them in the provinces. In a hotel like the Grand, however, the guest's table would certainly have been replaced by the new fashion of smaller, separate tables. This luxury was demanded by the heavy spenders of the day, the British travelers, who objected to sitting down with a whole host of strangers babbling in French and waving their forks about to make a point.

Table d'hôte meals, which were probably what Mata Hari ordered when eating in the hotel, were not as dreary as they sound: they ran to as many as twelve courses: soup, hors d'oeuvres, a fish dish, a vegetable dish (eaten separately), a poultry dish, another vegetable dish, a *plat de résistance* made with serious meat, another vegetable dish, cheese, dessert and fruit, for instance, plus a carafe of wine and coffee. What choice a traveler had was confined to refusing some of the dishes, but this still enabled anyone to eat an adequate repast.

It was the numerous British visitors to France who had brought about nearly all the modernizations in the French hotel system. The British, like the Japanese, were used to eating a meal before getting dressed in the morning, and the French had to find a way—for an additional charge, of course—of satisfying this barbaric habit. While they could not be expected to supply bacon, eggs and mushrooms, porridge and grapefruit, they could at least cook up some eggs and coffee. The French themselves began to drink coffee in the mornings and chew on some of yesterday's bread, grilled to relieve its staleness, thus inventing toast. This became the *petit déjeuner*, or "minor breaking of the fast."

Life in hotels was a good deal less complete for the guest than it is today. A seasoned modern traveler is distinguished by the ability to carry his or her needs in a folding garment bag and either a briefcase or a flight case, and by looking with scorn at the once-a-year vacationer who trundles through airports with a cumbersome set of matching luggage. In Mata Hari's day, it was the exact opposite: a practiced traveler brought *everything*. He could not expect to find towels or soap or writing paper or shampoo samples in his room, and he would be wise not to count on clean sheets if the previous guest had stayed only for a night or two. Guidebooks advised men to bring at least six suits and eight pairs of shoes to satisfy the dress codes for varying times of the day; women needed more changes of clothing, and their wardrobe required more voluminous space for the long dresses with ample skirts, the stiff corsets, the ankle-length shoes, and so on. A wise traveler took pens, spare nibs, bottles of ink, a library of books, perhaps a "rug" for protection in the dirty and unheated trains, whose "carriages" were filled with locomotive smoke if a window closed badly. Huge trunks were needed to carry everything, and those who could afford it brought a servant along to handle all the personal cargo. When automobile travel became more popular, a big rack at the back of the car supported the trunks and thick leather cases.

Those hotels that had installed running water on the upper floors had begun fitting individual basins with faucets in rooms, to replace the traditional pitcher and bowl, filled each morning by a servant who trundled a pail of warm water down the corridors. Running water in the rooms (usually cold) was essentially a feature of the luxury districts of Paris and of the more fashionable spas, and baths were slower in coming—once again, because the French saw no more need for them than for *petit déjeuner*. To get a private bath usually required renting a whole suite, appropriately called an apartment; but newly built hotels were beginning to provide the private baths required by wealthy foreigners, and older luxury hotels were converting some of their bedrooms into bathrooms, at obvious cost in loss of rooms and extensive plumbing. Mata Hari, we know, always insisted on a private bathroom: she may have been parisienne, but she was still a clinically clean Dutch girl at heart. She was known to have taken baths of milk to improve her skin, leading to one of the latter-day myths that she always bathed that way and had supposedly asked for a milk bath in prison— when milk, then in short supply, was reserved for children under wartime regulations.

The Paris she had first discovered in 1903 was, however, modernizing fast. The last horse-drawn buses and streetcars had been withdrawn in 1913, about fifteen years ahead of London, and only the wartime needs of the armies had taken many of the taxis away from the streets, along with trucks and motor-driven buses. This had given a last breath of life to the fiacres, whose horses, as short-tempered as the taxi drivers of today, fought for position in the traffic jams, snapping at each other's necks and frequently causing injuries that would lead to fights between the *cochers* who drove them. But the war had brought surprisingly little inflation—hence the number of relatively junior officers staying in first-class hotels like the Grand when on leave.

Electricity was universal in good hotels—it was the beginning of the age of the Tiffany lamp—and even the economical and more effective central heating was starting to replace the inefficient, labor-intensive, but beloved fireplaces in the rooms. There was even the telephone—usually only one per hotel, available at the front desk, with the concierge turning the handle and getting the number for the guest. Some of the newer first-class hotels contained elevators, operated by young pages, and others had carved elevator shafts out of part of the staircase wells.

Only the streets themselves had changed little. The place de la Concorde had been endowed with electric lighting in 1848, as was the Opéra district a generation later, but most of Paris was to be lit by "gas beaks" until the 1920s and 1930s. The great nineteenth-century buildings in *pierre de taille* had weathered well, while the more modest buildings, their plastered facades seemingly held in place by generations of grime, had also resisted the challenge of the years. Outside of the great hotels, Paris looked and even behaved much as it had for decades.

Inside a hotel, the affluent or relatively so lived in a world apart, surrounded by large, underpaid, tip-conscious staff, within reach of live music at almost all times, spending hours in the salon on the ground floor. There, the age-old tradition of the *table d'hôte*, which had brought travelers together in permissible intimacy for many centuries, survived in the convention of speaking to all and sundry, much as travelers in modern cruise ships do. A solitary lady such as Mata Hari, dressed in the latest fashion, would have had no difficulty striking up chance relationships without appearing to be flirtatious, even if she was.

But there were some chance relationships that she did not welcome. On June 30, she again complained to the hotel staff—who passed on the complaint to the inspectors—that she was being followed; but Monier and Tarlet remained on the job, following her as she rode down the boulevard in a fiacre and went shopping in the rue Royale. They sipped a *marc* in a café and studied the window as she ate in an elegant restaurant across the way with someone who had invited her. On another day, they clasped their derbies and scampered for a taxi as she set off with a different escort for the Bois, and they lingered in the shade of the trees while the lady, who always had a healthy appetite when in company, slurped oysters and tapped into the gourmet excellence of the Pavillon d'Armenonville.

Finally, the war in the Yser valley let up enough for the warrior services of the Belgian marquis to be spared. On July 11, she reserved the room next to hers for Beaufort, whose name was misspelled by the two inspectors—who perhaps had problems deciphering her handwriting—as "Belfort." She told the hotel manager that the marquis would be arriving on the thirteenth or the fourteenth. He finally taxied in from the Gare du Nord at 10:30 P.M. on July 14.

The French required, then as now, that foreigners staying in a hotel fill in a special card, which is sent to the *Service des garnis* at the Prefecture of Police and which asks a number of fundamental questions. Foreign spies and gangsters presumably stay in private homes. Despite the prevailing "espionitis," this formality required the marquis to say with what unit he was serving. As the fashionable couple mounted the staircase to their adjoining rooms, the two policemen eased out of the shadows to read the card and noted that "Fernand de Beauffort" (their new misspelling) was forty-two, a major in the 4th Lancers of the 1st Division of Cavalry, serving in the Army of the Yser.

Mata Hari had not lost sight of the inspectors. They reported that she had again complained to the hotel about the surveillance on July 12. A real spy, one would think, would not have revealed that she had identified them in the first place, for fear that the police would send out new people who would be more discreet and perhaps escape her notice.

Beaufort tipped the porter who carried his luggage to the major's room; then he joined Mata Hari in hers for a quiet dinner—presumably, given the hour, a cold *assiette*. In a distinguished hotel like the Grand, it would have been unacceptable for her to receive a number of different men in her room, since this might lead to complaints from neighbors. In the past, whenever she had had what might today be called one-night or one-afternoon stands, she had always insisted on her escort renting a room in one of the elegant brothels to be found in the luxurious districts of the city, especially the very famous one in the rue de Galilée. Dr. Léon Bizard, who was to be her visiting prison doctor, claimed to have spotted her on one occasion in the rue de Galilée establishment while he was performing another of his state duties—giving a weekly venereal inspection to those ladies of the *maison close* who had a governmental license, known as a yellow card, to ply the profession on a full-time basis. But a relationship like that of Mata Hari and the marquis, using the subterfuge of adjoining rooms, was conventionally tolerated.

On the first night, the tired inspectors left Fernand and Marguérite to their midnight supper and took a fiacre to the Prefecture on the Ile de la Cité to file their report. They were back in the morning to see the lovers take a taxi and to follow them as they drove around the city and returned to lunch in her room. Nothing further was seen of them until the evening, when they ventured out to dine at the famous Restaurant Larue in the rue Royale, a pleasant summer stroll away.

The liaison between Beaufort and Mata Hari, and the fact that she had clearly come to Paris to meet him, was of course passed on to the Belgians. Here was a major who was spending his leave with someone suspected by the British allies of being a German spy. A Belgian police inspector was dispatched to Paris to read Monier and Tarlet's reports and give back-up support. But the French were turf-conscious: he could spy on Beaufort, says the report, "but he should not preoccupy himself with the mistress of the latter." How or if he managed to separate the surveillances, we do not know.

On July 16, the two *flics*, now joined by their Belgian counter-part, waited outside while Fernand and Marguérite dined at the Café de Paris on the Champs-Elysées. On the eighteenth, it was lunch at the Pavillon d'Armenonville in the Bois—a long ride over cobbled streets. Beaufort hailed an automobile taxi, which with the war had become something of a luxury, and the inspectors had to dodge among the neighing horses of the fiacres to find a car taxi to follow. Starting off with a distance handicap, they lost the lovers' car but made a clever guess at the destination and arrived as the couple were sipping their apéritifs on the restaurant terrace.

The hotel staff reported the next day that the major and his lady had been overheard discussing renting an apartment where they could enjoy more privacy on the major's furloughs in Paris. However, when the inspectors followed the couple, it was only to a jewelry shop and then to Rumpelmayer's, where they indulged in ice cream. Mata Hari was finally having her vacation in Paris, and three policemen yearned to know if the problems of the Army of the Yser were part of the pillow talk.

Fortunately for the inspectors, the two lovers were usually in bed by ten o'clock, by which time the wartime city had virtually closed down, so the policemen could hurry back to the Prefecture and dictate their reports from scribbled notes to a typist, read and sign them, then go home to sleep and be back on duty in the morning. Fortunately also, Fernand and Marguérite always rose late.

But however much Mata Hari seemed to enjoy the wealthy officer's company, Beaufort was not destined to be one of her *grands amants*, like Rousseau, Kiepert, or even van der Capellen. She had slept with no one else until he arrived; but after he departed for the Front on the nineteenth, and the Belgian inspector went home (to Ypres?—we are not told), Monier and Tarlet tracked Mata Hari to Larue's again with someone else. This was a certain Antoine Bernard *fils*, a distiller of fine liquors from Martres de Veyre in the

Puy de Dôme region. Since they had this information, the businessman was presumably staying at the Grand. Mata Hari and Bernard were to dine together again on the twenty-first, but if anything came of this flirtation, the hotel staff and the two inspectors did not discover it.

By then, Beaufort had more serious competition.

2. Marina

PRESUMABLY UNBEKNOWNST to the dashing marquis, and unnoticed initially by the inspectors, Mata Hari had met the love of her life a few days before the Belgian major arrived from the Front. Had the object of her new affections not been out of town when the major called, the Belgian's long-awaited dalliance with the courtesan might have faced both emotional and theatrical complications.

The inspectors had in fact noticed that on one of her frequent visits to Mrs. Dangeville, the retired actress, their quarry had been accompanied by a "French sublieutenant" who was spending his leave at the Grand and by an unidentified Russian captain. The "French" officer was Nicolas Gasfield. He is described as thirty-four years old and as serving with the 8th Regiment of cavalry riflemen (*chasseurs à cheval*). He had been born in St. Petersburg and was apparently on his way to serve on the Turkish front in Salonika. Later, pretrial investigation would show that he was actually a Russian, perhaps seconded to the French cavalry in a liaison post. (As the largest of the Allies by far, Czarist Russia had contingents in many places. Russian troops from France started arriving in Salonika on July 30, 1916. Greece, a politically divided country, had been invaded by Bulgarian, Austrian, and German forces, and only its mountains had saved it from occupation.)

The other Russian officer whom Gasfield had brought along was Vladimir de Masloff (whose name is invariably misspelled in many different ways in books on Mata Hari, even by Waagenaar). Before their trysts at Mrs. Dangeville's, they had apparently met for the first time in the salon of the Grand.

The Russians had naturally concentrated the bulk of their forces on the Austro-Hungarian empire, occupying East Prussia (with its capital at Danzig, now Gdansk) and parts of Hungary. They were

83

aided by the Serbs, whose nationalism had ignited the war. Russia's principal role was to tie up large concentrations of Central Powers forces on the Eastern Front. Masloff, however, belonged to the 1st Special Imperial Regiment, an elite unit dispatched by the Czar to fight on the French front. At some point shortly after Beaufort left, Masloff, who was then stationed at Mailly, near Reims in the province of Champagne, returned to Paris, and he and Mata Hari became lovers. More than that, she was acting out of character: she had actually fallen in love.

"Vadim" de Masloff was then twenty-one, but in snapshots taken by his mistress and others that were found in her purse at the time of her arrest and that are now in the military justice file, he looks about eighteen—a slight, thin-featured figure vaguely resembling how the actor Dustin Hoffman might have looked in his student years. His background remains unclear. At one point in an interrogation, Mata Hari said he was the son of an admiral, then later of a brigadier-general. There is no explanation as to why he always signed his name, even on army postcards read by censors who knew his identity, as "de" Masloff. The Russian gentry did not have particles before their names, so at best Masloff was indicating that his family were country squires who, had they been French, would have been entitled to the distinction. Alternatively, like Mata Hari, whom he always called Marina, he may have mythologized about his social rank.

Very shortly after they became lovers, he returned to the Front. There he was gassed by the Germans and lost the sight of his left eye, over which he wore a huge patch when she saw him again. The poison also affected his throat, a condition later relieved by operations.

This battle-hardened but probably still battle-scared youth, with his halting French, awakened something in the aging courtesan that seems to have had no equivalent elsewhere in the story of her life, not even in her unfortunate infatuation with marriage that had led to eight years of holy deadlock with MacLeod. For her, it involved a complete switch in roles.

For thirteen years—indeed, if one includes MacLeod, for all her adult life—Mata Hari had relied for her existence on men more affluent and usually older than she. Now she set out to become the protector of a much younger man, giving him money from her allowance from the Dutch baron to pay his gambling debts, buying him meals in great restaurants he could not afford. It is perhaps not unfair to say that the seasoned trollop had found a gallant war-hero gigolo.

The mutual attraction is not hard to understand. She was becoming flabby and had just reached forty; she was finished as a dancer, and her chances of a great marriage with a wealthy lord were diminishing. Perhaps she had finally and wisely decided that any union based only on her own selfish interest would not last and that happiness lies even more in loving than in being loved. Although well past her prime, she remained a *name*, and one that summoned up an image for the rich young officers whom she met at the Grand and who lavished attentions on her.

In her midlife crisis, moreover, the famous siren rigorously rejected the thought that advancing age would diminish her charms. A year before, she had still been trying to be engaged by Diaghilev's demanding Ballets Russes. She had never been the sort of woman who looks in her mirror and sees the truth—only the possibilities. Now, as proof that she was still irresistible, she had won the passion of this handsome and dashing youth who, at the age of twenty-one, was an officer responsible for the fate of perhaps a hundred men, fighting in the twenty-four-hour nightmare of trench warfare, severely wounded but still heroically anxious to return to battle. Curiously, no one seems to have observed (although it can scarcely have escaped Mata Hari's notice) that Vadim was, within a few months, the same age as her son Norman would have been—the son who had tragically died, perhaps because of her own carelessness, and about whom she may still have felt pangs of guilt.

Nor is it hard to analyze the relationship from Vadim's side. The attraction felt by very young men for older, more sexually experienced women is common to all cultures. "Marina" had the added attraction of being famous, fawned over by bowing *maîtres d'hôtel* and others, in possession of a seductive name that no one could forget, an exciting celebrity who had made the orgiastic spectacle of naked dancing both artistic and respectable.

What young soldier with a less-than-fifty-percent chance of survival on the Western Front (where the average "longevity" of officers was then five months) would hesitate when this Venus beckoned? And then this frightened, wounded young man, far from home in a country whose language he spoke inadequately, found that he had not just acquired a famous mistress but also a mothering figure—someone in whose ample embrace, despite the inevitable stuffed bodice that she still wore in bed, he could rediscover security.

With security, one can also see Masloff acquiring an illusion of maturity. Half blinded and in pain from his throat, how could he not feel manly and protective himself toward this woman whose nipples had supposedly been torn away by the fangs of a drunken husband? And surely he must have thought that he was the only one to whom she had confided her tragic (and of course mythological) secret. Her *cache-seins* and his eyepatch hid the scarifications that made them members of the same tribe of misfortune. What more could one ask of a wartime romance?

This passion was to transform Mata Hari's life and to cause her death, through a whole chain of circumstances.

On July 28, she went twice to the nearby ministry of foreign affairs. There is no record of what she accomplished there, but we know that by then she had made up her mind to travel to Vittel, near where Vadim was a patient in a military hospital. She had learned the news of his being wounded but did not know the full story yet. Vittel was in the *Zone des armées*, and at the Quai d'Orsay she presumably went to see one of two men. Either she asked for Cambon, who was perhaps absent or unavailable, and then returned at a fixed time for a meeting, or her quest may have been limited to the less powerful but more intimately friendly Henry de Marguérie—using one lover to help her rejoin another, much as she was using van der Capellen's money to feed and entertain his most threatening rival, Vadim. What she needed powerful help in acquiring was a *carnet d'étranger*—rather like a small internal passport—that would enable her to enter the war zone.

She still, however, needed escorts if she wanted to eat meals away from her hotel. On the thirtieth, thanks to Monier and Tarlet, we find her talking to a Montenegrin major staying at the Grand and going for a ride in a fiacre with him in the Bois. He was, we learn, Nicholas Yuilchevich (the inspectors' spelling), aged thirty-four. (Montenegro was, like Serbia, a separate Balkan kingdom carved out of—or restored from—the Ottoman empire, and which had been invaded by the Austrians; it is now a part of Yugoslavia.

One can only assume that a Montenegrin unit was fighting on the Western Front or, more probably, that Yuilchevich—whose name was more probably Jovilchevich—had a liaison post in Paris. His attraction for Mata Hari was perhaps that he was, like her Vadim, a Slav.)

The next day, she called at a police commissariat at 43 rue Taitbout, seeking permission to go to Vittel and also asking for a safe-conduct for Calais. The latter would seem to have been a precaution, in case the German army should one day send her scuttling back to Holland, or perhaps it was simply in the hope of finding a shorter route home whenever she needed it. Both permits were refused.

She went back to her hotel and wrote three letters to suppliers, including a dressmaker and a jeweler. The telephone was still a luxury that few shops possessed. If an order was slow in being delivered, the only solution was a letter or a *pneumatique*. Her letters were steamed open, then sent on.

The next day, she called at the Prefecture of Police, trying to get someone to overrule the commissariat in the rue Taitbout. Presumably they referred her back to the commissariat, where she made another stab at getting a *carnet* on August 3. The season at Vittel, a fashionable spa that she had visited in 1911, ends sometime in September, when the weather cools and the main hotels close. She was running out of time.

The permission she was requesting was for twenty-one days, and the reason was "to take the waters." Later, Bouchardon was to question why she was so desperately in need of a Vittel cure when she was writing to van der Capellen at the same time that she was in excellent health. By then, however, he knew the answer: the only cure she really sought was the youthful loins of her wounded Russian warrior.

The same day, August 3, Masloff managed to get leave and come to Paris. It was the first time she was to see him with his eyepatch and to learn about his poisoned throat. They dined together and went back to Mrs. Dangeville's to spend the night, the inspectors noted. The following day, she saw him off at the Gare de l'Est.

That afternoon, she eased her cares over Vadim's departure by going for a drive in the Bois and to dinner at the Pavillon d'Armenonville with an Italian captain of military police who was staying at the hotel. A professor in civilian life, his name was Mariani and he was born in Genoa, the inspectors learned from the hotel card. Back at the hotel, Mata Hari wrote a note to Gasfield, one of the two men (the other, we learn later, was a French Hussar) responsible for introducing her to Vadim and mailed it to him at his future address on the Turkish front.

Mariani apparently had hopes of becoming Mata Hari's lover, because the French police noted that he took a room in another hotel the following day, giving his name as "Martini," born in "Rome." But thanks to Monier and Tarlet, we know that Marina did not deceive Vadim by following the Italian captain.

On August 8, she was to meet the man who would prove to be her nemesis. This was Georges Ladoux, a regular army captain who had come out of St.-Cyr, the West Point or Sandhurst of France. A protégé of General Joseph-Jacques-Césaire Joffre, the overall commander of French forces, Ladoux had been given the interesting and physically safe job of organizing counterespionage. That this was entrusted to a captain gives some idea of the embryonic nature of the service; and that a *St.-Cyrien* was still a captain at forty-two, in the middle of a war that offered rapid and easy promotions to fill dead men's shoes, indicates that he had had a troubled military career—which was to end under an even more disastrous cloud.

He had been given the intelligence job in June 1915, after being denied a requested posting to the Zouaves, in which his father had served in the Franco-Prussian war. Ladoux reported to Colonel Antoine Goubet, the head of all French intelligence, whom Mata Hari never met. The captain's job was to take on the better-funded and -organized German service, which was headquartered in the Thiergarten in Berlin, and to collaborate with the Special Branch of Scotland Yard, which had been made part of Britain's Foreign Office. Initially, Ladoux and his colleagues had spent most of their time censoring soldiers' letters.

It was on the well-meaning but ill-fated advice of Jean Hallaure, whom she had known as a teenage horse-trainer with Ernest Molier and who was now a cavalry lieutenant, that Mata Hari had gone to Ladoux's office at 282 boulevard Saint-Germain. Hallaure, who also arranged the appointment, had counseled her that Ladoux was the person best able to overcome any suspicions about her request to enter the war zone and to get the trip to Vittel authorized. Hallaure, severely wounded, now had a headquarters job in Paris that brought him into contact with Ladoux.

The latter was a trim, black-bearded figure, much smaller than Mata Hari, with waxed moustaches and brilliantined hair. He habitually wore uniform and a leather belt and puffed on an English pipe. In his memoirs, published in 1932, he recalls his first meeting with the stately courtesan. He was in civilian clothes that day and must have looked even less impressive than usual. After she had swept into his office and the two had exchanged amenities, she sat in a stiff-backed chair, and he told her that Hallaure had recommended her to him.

"It was in August 1916 that I met Mata Hari for the first time and I can see her still, as if it were yesterday, dressed, in spite of the summer weather, in a dark two-piece and wearing a large-brimmed straw hat with a gray feather," Ladoux wrote. He noticed that she swung her hips "like a dancer" as she walked in.

He recounts that he told her he had learned that she wanted to go to Vittel and that he had the authority to have a *laissez-passer* issued. Why did she want to go to Vittel? She insisted that she wanted to take the waters. If she could not go to Vittel, she would go to Fiuggi, near Rome, where the waters were similar. He says he told her that he knew about her affair with Vadim de Masloff and that Masloff was at a hospital near Vittel.

By then, the British, whose "secret service" the Frenchman believed to be vastly superior to his own *Section de Centralisation des Renseignements* (Centralized Intelligence Section), had told Ladoux they believed she was a German spy with the code number AF 44. The letters were said to mean that she was under the control of a German spy headquarters in Antwerp, Belgium, run by a German woman, Dr. Schragmüller, who was known to the Allies, because of pronunciation difficulties with her name, as "Fraulein Doktor." This center was said to run French-speaking spies, and the British thought that Mata Hari's two trips to France meant that that was where she was deployed.

Ladoux consequently asked her if she had retained her prewar links to Germany; he claims he frankly told her she was under suspicion. She said she had assumed that something like this might be the case because she was under surveillance by two policemen. She complained of this constant shadowing and of the searching of her luggage while she was out of the hotel. Ladoux says he told her bluntly that it was the British who believed she was a German spy, but he added reassuringly that he didn't believe it himself. She recounted the story of her violent altercation with the supposed British agent, Hoedemaker. She then learned what may have been a bizarre reason for her problems at Hendaye in June.

"Who was the black man who traveled with you in the train from Madrid to Hendaye?" Ladoux asked.

"He was the husband of the Russian dancer Lupochova, who had the next berth to mine," she said. "In the morning, he asked me if he could bring his wife's breakfast into our women's compartment."

In his memoirs, Ladoux does not explain the significance, if any, of his question. He listened while she prattled on about her misadventures at the frontier post at Hendaye. He asked about her Dutch colonel. What were his views about France? She said he was a Francophile. She pointed out that he always corresponded with her in French. Ladoux had read the letters and he recognized a phrase that she quoted from one of them: "Marguérite, you who love France so much . . . "

Since she was so fond of France, he said, was she prepared to use her status as an "international woman" to help the French war effort with "great services"? She appeared surprised. She was to say later that she recognized that, since the suggestion came from Ladoux, he could only be referring to intelligence work.

According to the interrogation, which Ladoux confirms in his book, the conversation then went as follows:

"Would you do it?"

"I've never thought about it."

"You must be very expensive!"

"That's for sure!" (Ca, oui!)

"What do you think such work is worth?"

"A lot, or nothing."

She explained that if she spied for France, she would expect to be paid well if she were successful, but not paid at all if she were not.

Ladoux recalls that he said: "Think about it. See if you can't do something for us. I will give you your card for Vittel. Only promise me that you won't seduce any French officers." He was, he tells us in his book, particularly anxious that the military aviators from nearby Contrexéville not discuss their work with the likes of Mata Hari.

According to her own account, she replied: "No danger of that. I'm too much in love with a Russian." In his memoirs, Ladoux says he had read her letters to Masloff, which had even been tested—negatively—for invisible ink.

Ladoux told her he had seen her dining with Vadim at the Ambassadeurs restaurant. He says he concluded the conversation with "Whatever it is, when you have made a decision on what I have said to you, come back and see me."

She said she would. He gave her a blue *laissez-passer* to enable her to enter the building freely.

Her first priority was to get to Vittel before the season ended and the more suitable hotels closed. Ladoux sent her to a police officer called Maunoury at the commissariat in the rue Taitbout, saying Maunoury would issue her with the *carnet* she sought. She had given Ladoux a photo for his files and now she gave another to Maunoury. Then she went to the Quai d'Orsay to see Marguérie.

The following day, Hallaure called at the hotel, presumably to ensure that his introduction had been useful. Although Ladoux tells us that he believed that Hallaure and Mata Hari were lovers, the inspectors found no evidence of this, and her letters to him, now in the military justice file, use the second person plural and end with such unromantic sign-offs as *Bien à vous*. (Waagenaar, however, records that when Hallaure was performing his military service in Britanny in 1910—when he was twenty and she was thirty-four—she visited him there; a photograph of them together exists, and she is wearing his Hussar uniform.)

An army postcard from Vadim arrived that day, assuring "Marina" of his love and his impatience at waiting for her. He gave his address as "1st Special Regiment, Sector 189." It had been passed by the army censor.

Ladoux's apparent approval did not get her the *carnet* right away. Possibly Ladoux and Maunoury were playing a cat-and-mouse game with their enigmatic prey. On August 11, she was back at the office on the boulevard Saint-Germain.

By now, despite her regular and affectionate exchange of letters with the baron in Amsterdam, discreetly sent through her Hague servant, Anna Lintjens, she had become so much in love with Vadim that she had apparently decided to resettle in France, in spite of the war. On the fourteenth, Monier and Tarlet followed her as she went apartment-hunting in the fashionable Passy district. She also apparently deceived Vadim for once, since the inspectors noted that she dined with a "French lieutenant of about thirty" and later took him back to her room. This was presumably not Hallaure, because the lieutenant wore the uniform of the infantry, not the cavalry.

The next day, she returned to the commissariat but was told that her *carnet* was not ready. Although Ladoux knew that she wanted to go to Vittel to see Vadim, it may have been the congenital liar in Mata Hari that led her to give the "taking the waters" pretext to Maunoury; she also went to the Italian embassy the same day and asked for a visa to go to Fiuggi. She then went to the Prefecture of Police for an exit visa for Italy. Was she seriously thinking of Fiuggi? Was she naïvely trying to establish that her main concern was to visit a spa for a cure? Was she perhaps even questioning her infatuation with Vadim? We do not know.

On the eighteenth, she went again to see her old flame, Baron "Robert" de Marguérie, at the Quai d'Orsay. (She almost always referred to him as a marquis, and sometimes as a count, but he is listed in French foreign service records as having joined in 1869 as a *stagiaire*, or probationer, under the name Baron Henry Jean-Baptiste Joseph de Marguérie. Perhaps at some point his father had died and he actually had inherited a marquisate.) Whether Mata Hari went to see him to enlist his help in getting to Vittel or even in making a hasty exit to Italy, we do not know, but all the indications are that she was exploiting her hold on Marguérie to get to Masloff.

She had not heard from Vadim for nine days, but two cards from the captain were waiting at the hotel when she returned. They had presumably been delayed at Ladoux's office. In both cards, he complained that he had not heard from her, although we know from the inspectors' reports that she had written to him more than once.

On the twentieth, the mysterious infantry lieutenant was once again in her company. He was described by the inspectors as "Lieutenant X." This odd discretion about his identity would seem to indicate that the only man who had persuaded her to deceive her lover was an intelligence plant. Was he one of Ladoux's men, and had he won her favors by promising to expedite her *carnet*? She had apparently told the lieutenant about her desire to find a home in Paris, and he accompanied her to an apartment at 33 avenue Henri-Martin. On her return to the hotel, the inspectors noted, she told the manager that she had found an apartment but would not be living in it until after she had been to Vittel. Perhaps she finally had confidence that, with others supporting her request, she was going to get there after all.

Now the prospect of a vacation in Vittel with a nearly penniless Russian officer seems to have prompted her to refurbish her finances. It seems likely that van der Capellen's drafts were not keeping pace with her orders to dressmakers, her purchases in the city's shops, and her entertaining of Vadim. Ladoux, in his memoirs, is uncharacteristically generous, saying: "Mata Hari lived simply and almost in poverty." He says the money she received from lovers was only enough for her to exist parsimoniously in her luxury hotel. She flirted and slept with officers, he says, but he concedes that he never found any evidence that she had asked them serious questions "dealing with the military."

All her life, whenever she was short of money, there had always been one sure way for Mata Hari to refloat the bank account; and with the prospect of moving soon from the Grand Hôtel, she ceased to be so circumspect about the unwritten hotel rules regarding one-night stands. On the twenty-first, the inspectors went off for the night after noting that she had retired to her room with a Belgian officer, and they were back in the morning in time to learn that she had just emerged from her chamber with a British captain. Her principal preoccupation, however, had not changed: earlier on the twenty-first, the inspectors reported, she had been to Ladoux's office for permission to send a telegram "to a Russian officer at the Front," and later she had gone to a post office in the rue de Bourgogne "where she probably sent the said telegram."

She was, in short, not so much being unfaithful as working hard to make money to spend on Vadim in Vittel. Her principal conquests that week were two British army officers, both from Ireland

and both twenty-three years old. The inspectors noted their names as being James Plankett (Plunkett?), from Dublin, and Edwin Cecil O'Brien, from Tipperary.

She was also seen sipping tea with a French lieutenant-general, Maurice-François Baumgarten, aged sixty-three, who was similarly about to leave Paris to take the waters at Vittel, and she was showing further concern about how she would finance life with Vadim after breaking with van der Capellen: since the apartment in the avenue Henri-Martin was not furnished, she talked to the hotel manager about exchanging it for a furnished one.

On the twenty-eighth, she was summoned to the Prefecture, then went from there to the commissariat in the rue Taitbout, where she received her *carnet*. This black booklet is now also in the military justice file, boldly stamped VALID FOR THE WAR ZONE.

The next three days were spent collecting the new toilettes she had ordered from dressmakers to take Vadim by storm in Vittel— many subsequently never paid for—and being manicured and coiffed for the trip. She also found time to discuss Ladoux's request that she spy for France with Marguérie. The latter, she later recounted, told her that such work was extremely dangerous, but that "if anyone could serve my country well in such work, Marguérite, it is you." It was to prove to be ill-fated advice.

On the thirty-first, she returned to what seems to have been her favorite restaurant, the Pavillon d'Armenonville, with a Scottish officer of twenty, James Stewart Fernie. She was clearly developing a taste for juveniles. The next day, she took the express train for Vittel.

If Ladoux's memoirs are to be believed on this, Vittel was to be the first testing ground of her loyalties. If she spent her time in the war zone making love to Vadim and not collecting information about troop movements and the like, he was prepared to try her out as a spy, if she were willing, and as one who would use her German contacts and knowledge of the German language to pretend to the Germans that she would work for them. The British, of course, believed that the Germans had already recruited her— and Ladoux could not lose sight of that fact.

Vadim had written in one of his cards that the Grand Hôtel in Vittel was still in good order despite the war and that he was sure she would be satisfied with it. The lonely boy in his hospital cot was clearly in awe of his famous paramour and her need for the greater creature comforts; his tiny army postcards—the only mail permitted from the actual frontline trenches by the censors—make it clear that he was waiting feverishly for "Marina" to come.

She arrived in the spa on September 1. The larger hotels in the watering stations of those days sent buses to the station to pick up their guests and their heaps of luggage. We may assume that Vittel's motorized buses had all become troop-carriers at the Front and that the reduced wartime clientèle were collected by the familiar old horse-drawn vehicles, with their *impériales* on top for baggage. She checked in at the Grand and was given room 363. She had already noticed that the familiar faces of Monier and Tarlet were aboard the train; they were busy the next day reporting that she had taken the waters. On the third, Masloff arrived from his hospital; room 362 was waiting for him. He was wearing the long silk patch over his left eye, tied by a ribbon around his head. At five-thirty P.M., Monier and Tarlet, from the hotel grounds, could see them kissing by the window of room 363, with Masloff clearly recognizable by his patch. By her own account in the interrogations, her youthful lover was now seriously worried that he would lose the sight of his right eye as well. In each other's arms that night, she promised him that she would look after him if that should happen. He proposed marriage, she said, and she accepted at once. Nothing like this had happened since 1894, twenty-two years before.

Masloff had four days' leave, and was to depart on the seventh. We know little or nothing of how they spent their time. Vittel was relatively new, more modern and more expensive than established watering stations such as Vichy, Aix, or Evian. Mata Hari and Vadim probably found life there almost as comfortable as in Paris and in many ways more romantic. Hotels still had stables dating from the not-distant days when people had arrived by carriage, before regular express trains were available, and this enabled them to offer one of Mata Hari's favorite distractions—horses. We know from the photos in the Mata Hari dossier that the couple went riding. There would have been regular music in the square and dancing in the hotel itself. The one-time professional dancer could presumably be led by her young companion into a sensuous waltz.

After Vadim left to rejoin his unit, Mata Hari stayed on, chatting and drinking tea with various officers on leave but apparently having no affairs. General Baumgarten was one of those who talked with her. She told him that the Russian officer he had seen her with was her nephew. By then, however, Masloff had introduced himself to another elderly officer, Brigadier General Jules de Rolland, as her fiancé.

With the hotel about to close, she returned to Paris on the thirteenth, once more staying at the Grand Hôtel. She told the manager she was planning to return to Holland, probably via Switzerland and Germany.

This spontaneous admission of plans to visit enemy territory apparently reflected the fact that she had decided to agree to Ladoux's request. Despite her gifts for dissimulation, the potential French spy never did acquire the discretion needed for such an occupation. Now, with bills all over town, and urgently needing money to finance life with Vadim, the sooner she left the city the better.

On the morning of her return to the Grand, she had found that the manager of the Hôtel Meurice had obtained a court order to seize part of her luggage because of an unpaid bill for thirteen hundred francs. Waagenaar says this debt dated from 1913, but it seems equally probable that it dated from as far back as 1907, when she had stayed at the Meurice on arriving from Berlin. She paid two hundred francs, and on the seventeenth a further three hundred francs, after which she got her luggage back. Thus more or less free of taint, she went that day to Ladoux's office and agreed to spy for France. Too ungainly to dance Salome or Cleopatra anymore, but still a proven seductress, she had found a role. Since it would involve risking her life among the Germans, the *cachet* should, she obviously thought, be much better than at the Opéra or the Folies-Bergère.

According to her own account under interrogation, she and Ladoux had discussed her espionage assignment: it would be Brussels. Because of the fighting, Belgium could be entered only from the east, through Holland. Ladoux had asked her by what route she would prefer to return to her native country. Because the British suspected her and might give her problems, she had considered going through Germany, but she feared this might be dangerous. If Ladoux could arrange things with London, she told him, she would prefer to travel via Spain and the Channel. Ladoux agreed. She may well have suggested getting help in convincing London from Jules Cambon's brother, then the French ambassador to Britain.

The counterintelligence chief confirms in his book that he had told her frankly what she later told Bouchardon: that the police reports had stated that she had done nothing suspicious in Vittel. She told him equally frankly that she was undertaking the work he had suggested to her solely to earn money. She wanted to be able to spend the rest of her life with Vadim. This would only be possible if she had a substantial sum, since Vadim would be dependent on her, especially if the worst happened and he became completely blind.

"I want to be rich enough not to have to deceive Vadim with others," Ladoux quotes her as saying at one point. The sentence certainly sounds like vintage Mata Hari, a woman who did not mince her words. She even, Ladoux claims, gushed on about her plans. When the war ended, she would bring the furniture (that van der Capellen had bought for her) from The Hague to Paris and live in the avenue Henri-Martin apartment with the fortune that Ladoux would certainly pay for her services.

"I see things big," she said.

Even in the employ of a major government involved in a world war and a life-or-death struggle, the irrepressible courtesan was determined to set her own agenda and not get sidetracked into chicken-feed assignments that would not earn enough to establish her love nest for Vadim. The amateur spy had already mapped out what she could do for the French in Belgium.

During her brief affair in 1914 with van der Schalk—the Dutch banker who had originally thought she was a Russian tourist—she had met one of his friends, Wurfbein, a Brussels businessman who was then operating partly out of Holland to provide food supplies to the German army of occupation in his own country. Wurfbein had invited her to visit him in Brussels and had promised to introduce her to General Moritz Ferdinand von Bissing, the German officer who commanded the occupation in Belgium.

Once she was in The Hague, Ladoux recalls Mata Hari saying, she would write to Wurfbein to announce her arrival and take him up on his promise to introduce her to the officers of the German general staff in Belgium. It would not take long, she thought, to get the general to bed and find out secrets about German troop movements, new offensives, and the like. Then she would work her way back to the Crown Prince, and soon France would be learning, via her pillow, everything that was going on at the highest levels of German planning.

"I have a very spontaneous character," she said she told Ladoux. "I've no intention of hanging around for months getting tidbits of information. I'll bring off one big coup, and then go."

This was an age of amateur spying, but even Ladoux, the little captain who was learning the art on the job, seems to have had understandable doubts about her ambitions. Although she had in effect answered it already, he asked her the stock question: "What are your reasons for agreeing to work for France?" he says he demanded.

Modern spymasters have learned to be hesitant about those who volunteer for romantic or ideological reasons. By their standards, her response might have been reassuring: "To be financially independent so that I can marry my lover."

"Have you thought about a price?" he says he asked her.

"A million."

It is hard to set the modern value of a million gold francs at that time, but the dividends or interest from such a sum would indeed have been enough to support the couple in the style to which Mata Hari aspired for the rest of their lives.

Her amateurishness shows up not only in the fact that her first thought was not about communications—she did not ask at once how she would send her information back to Paris—but also in her courtesan's approach to business: she did not demand an advance of funds, not even to cover travel expenses. Presumably Eduard van der Capellen could take care of that aspect of the French national defense budget—and if she did not bed von Bissing, well, there had been other disappointments, such as the trip to Monte Carlo to join the Ballets Russes.

In one of her interrogations, Mata Hari said Ladoux responded that the sum of a million francs was high, but that if she produced even one piece of information that would turn the tide of war, "we will pay it." She claimed that he boasted that France had once paid two and a half million francs for information which he did not describe.

Ladoux says in his memoirs that her price was so high, he suggested jokingly that she work for the Germans and try to penetrate the French general staff instead. As he describes the conversation, she answered: "But if I become the mistress of the Crown Prince, would you give me a million?"

"Not yet," he says he replied. "It ought to be he who gives it to you, he's rich enough, and—well, you'd be worth it."

She ignored his flippancy, and said: "I have already been the mistress of the Crown Prince, and it would be up to me if I wanted to see him again. . . . Here, I am just a lady of the night; there, I was treated as a queen."

Ladoux says she got up and, being a "marvelous artist," depicted how she had the Germans "at her feet." Having agreed to Ladoux's suggestion that she spy for France, she now had to convince him of the plausibility of her plan to become what we might now call a one-woman fifth column. Wasn't it worth trying? she asked. She said she could make contact with the Crown Prince through Kroemer, the honorary German consul in Amsterdam, who was involved in furnishing supplies to the German army in Belgium.

Ladoux says he recognized the name and asked: "Do you really want to serve us? Be careful, the job is dangerous."

"I don't doubt it," he says she answered. He notes that it was at this point that he finally asked her how she proposed to transmit her information. She asked if there was someone to whom she could report in Amsterdam. He claims he said no, that that was why they needed her, and that she naïvely accepted this answer. He says he then asked her if she knew how to use invisible ink. He insists that she said that she would learn.

Using a ruler and a wall map, he says, he showed her the line of the Front, telling her at the same time that he was now "sure" she had worked for the Germans and would be risking her life to work for France. (Clearly, he could not have been "sure," and we do not know if this is a true relation of what he said. He mentions no riposte on her part.) He says he gave her "a night" to consider. He claims that the next morning she changed her mind about her route and asked to go to Holland via Switzerland and Germany—although he testified otherwise to Bouchardon; in his book, he claims that the choice of the Spanish route was his, while to Bouchardon he confirmed her own story that it was hers. This is one of many disquieting instances in which Ladoux appears to have little concern for truth where either or both of two imperatives are involved—to load the case against Mata Hari, or to cover his rear. Obviously, if Ladoux wanted to keep an eye on her, he could do this more efficiently in Spain than in Germany—although she could have been useful to the French, and no use at all to the Germans, going through Germany.

Ladoux says, without explaining this bizarre confidence, that he told her that all her movements would be reported and that her instructions would finally come from someone who would approach her in Holland. He recalls that he gave her permission to contact her lover in Amsterdam through the Dutch legation in Paris.

The next day, Mata Hari moved to a less expensive hotel. She was still being pursued by the Hôtel Meurice for the remainder of her old debt, so she took six trunks of her luggage to the safety of the apartment in the avenue Henri-Martin, which was still unfurnished. Later, Monier and Tarlet saw her dining and "walking arm in arm" with a man she had met in the new hotel. For the next few days, she passed her time with others in this way while waiting for Masloff to come again to Paris on leave. Most of the acquaintances she acquired in the hotel this time were civilians, including an American.

He is described in the military justice files as "R. A. Moore, aged forty-one, a businessman, born at West Plains, USA." That was presumably what he wrote on the hotel registration card for foreigners. Mata Hari later described him as an engineer who had told her that he had patented his invention of a new type of rifle. He had claimed that he had sold a quarter-million of them to the Rumanian army and that he was trying to sell them to the French. (Rumania, which had been neutral but leaning toward the Central Powers when war began, had become more genuinely neutral after the death of King Carol late in 1914, then more and more pro-Allied. On August 27, 1916, it had joined in the conflict on the Allied side—hence Moore's sales journey. Rumania, however, did little more in the war than help to tie up some of the forces of

Austro-Hungary and its neighbor, the kingdom of Bulgaria, which had joined the Central Powers on October 29, 1915.)

There are indications that she was beginning to understand the problems of the extraordinary assignment that she had agreed to undertake, although her first priorities can only raise a smile. She sent Ladoux a *pneumatique*, asking for an advance to buy dresses with which to seduce von Bissing and to buy furniture for the future love nest in the avenue Henri-Martin. The chief of counterespionage, needless to say, did not see this as the sort of thing one discussed in the public mails and did not respond. When she followed up her missive with a telephone call, he was "not in." It seems fair to suppose that his confidence in her as a spy, which had never been strong, was by then diminished.

On the twentieth, we find her returning to the Centralized Intelligence Section. Both parties agree that Ladoux told her that she was on probation. He had given her to understand that she was being tested for her aptitude and her loyalty—although he would later inexplicably insist to Bouchardon that he was sending her out of his reach solely to test her true allegiance.

He told her, they both agree, that she would be paid on results only, but paid handsomely if she came up with something significant, as she had asked at the start. Ladoux, defending his judgment in taking her on, was to emphasize in his book that she had never been more than a freelance spy: she had not been given a precise mission or an identifying code number; she had not been offered a cipher to use, names of agents to contact, or invisible ink. She had received no money.

If Bouchardon, the future interrogator, is to be believed, Ladoux is telling less than the truth, here as elsewhere. Bouchardon claims in his own memoirs, published posthumously in 1953, that Ladoux gave her names to contact in Belgium. Major Emile Massard, in his book on women spies, makes the same assertion. Bouchardon also says that when Ladoux asked her if she would agree to use invisible ink, she had categorically objected because—as she agreed in her own testimony—"that doesn't go along with my character." After all, ambassadors don't put their reports into cipher: some minion does that. And, as she told Ladoux, "I don't plan to spend long out there." All she wanted was one major coup as the Great

French Spy—not unlike, perhaps, her cameo appearance at Europe's number-one opera theater in Milan.

On the twenty-third, Masloff arrived in Paris with a forty-eight-hour pass. He appears to have overstayed by a day, because the inspectors watched her put him on the train at the Gare de l'Est on the twenty-sixth. The young man's ardor seems now to have conveyed itself fully to his middle-aged paramour. On the twenty-eighth, she wrote him no less than three letters in the course of the day. By this point, there was less time for shopping, especially as she owed money in most of her favorite boutiques. On the thirty-first, she was back in Ladoux's office, once again vainly pleading for an advance. By now, she was offering an extra coup: while in Germany, she would renew relations with the Duke of Cumberland—by then a British traitor—and turn him around. Later that day, she went to the Dutch consulate-general, where a letter from van der Capellen, sent through the Dutch diplomatic pouch, informed her of a fresh draft of funds to a Paris bank.

She went at once to the main office of the Comptoir National d'Escompte de Paris (now the Banque Nationale de Paris) on the place de l'Opéra to collect the funds, but they were not there. She finally received them on November 4, then swept past the Opéra to the post office on the rue Gluck, where she bought a money order for five hundred francs and mailed it to Vadim.

She was ready. The last great performance awaited: the seduction of Moritz von Bissing, perhaps the reseduction of the Crown Prince and of Cumberland, a million francs, and paradise with her handsome boy, chained to her for life by his encroaching blindness and her money. On the fifth, she went to the Gare d'Orsay to leave her substantial baggage for the Madrid train that would depart that evening. She had dinner with the faithful Marguérie, who took her to the station to catch the express, which set off, the inspectors said, at nine-fifty P.M. She took sleeping car 2492A, berth number eight; this was carefully noted by Monier and Tarlet before, one assumes, they finally went home for a well-earned rest.

Their last report ended with the words: "The usual telegrams have been sent." All down the line, French defense attachés and other spies would be on the lookout for Ladoux's latest probationer.

* * *

The little captain remained cautious about this extravagant foreign woman who defied definition. At his last meeting with Mata Hari, Ladoux had asked her if she had been to Brussels before: she had replied that she had been there with van der Capellen for the Miniatures Exhibition—in 1903. Had she ever been to Antwerp? She said she had not. He told her she had been photographed there. She laughed and repeated that she had never been there in her life. There was, Ladoux recounted later, no photograph; but of course the British thought she was "AF 44" of the Antwerp network, run by Dr. Schragmüller, "Fraulein Doktor"—and, as Ladoux was to tell Bouchardon later, there was also a vague report that she had been spotted once in an Antwerp hotel.

Ladoux's final instructions to the courtesan had been, he and she both say, to return to The Hague and rest up from her travels in the Nieuwe Uitleg house. About two weeks after she arrived, he had told her, "someone" would contact her and give her precise instructions. She had asked how she could be sure that it was the right person. Ladoux said the agent would give her a password. He wrote something on a paper, folded it, and passed it to her. She opened the paper and read "AF 44." He noticed that there was no reaction to the sight of the German intelligence code-number that the British thought was hers.

"Don't you recognize the number?" he asked. She said she didn't understand. "I thought AF 44 was you," he said.

Ladoux had thus prepared the ground for saying later that he had remained suspicious of her even when sending her out on a freelance assignment. If, against all the evidence that he had then from his own surveillance, she turned out to be a German agent after all, he could say that he was trying to fool her into thinking that she had fooled him when she accepted his request to work for French intelligence.

Ladoux records that when he explained what AF 44 meant, Mata Hari was apparently indignant that suspicions remained. Ladoux assured her that he had great hopes for her and that, if she succeeded, the money would be generous. He said they had regularly paid twenty-five thousand francs for every spy for the Germans identified by a French agent. Arithmetically, she noted, she would have to deliver forty names to make a million; but she was, she said, after the *grand coup*, not just identifying "a few spies here and there." She would prefer to furnish "military or diplomatic intelligence." How she genuinely expected to make a fortune out of this seems to have been as unclear to Ladoux as it must remain to us. Vadim's Marina, however self-confident, had never been a very pragmatic woman.

3. Clara

At this point it seems worthwhile to draw back for a moment and consider how confused were British and French intelligence—and also how Ladoux and those elements of British intelligence who furnished the information for such extravaganzas as Thomas Coulson's *Mata Hari*, and the whole fictional legend about the woman, later embroidered the story to their own advantage and for the greater entertainment of a gullible public.

For instance, even well after the war, when Coulson was writing, the British—who thought she had been in Berlin, Naples, and Cairo in 1915, when she was in The Hague—thought, or said they thought, that she had been in the war zone at Vittel just before "the battle of Chemin des Dames" and had contributed information to the Germans that had cost the lives of hundreds of thousands of Allied troops. The Germans won the first battle of Chemin des Dames in late 1914, while she was in The Hague, penniless and shopping for a lover. The French launched an offensive that retook the area in October 1917, the time of her execution, and the Germans took most of it back the following year, when she was dead. These were the only battles of Chemin des Dames.

This is only one particularly ludicrous but not otherwise exceptional example among many of how glaringly self-deceiving at best and plainly deceitful at worst was this band of amateur spies and spy-hunters—with and among whom the sophisticated innocent or proud nincompoop who was Mata Hari had decided to play the improbable role of the woman whose middle-aged charms would win the Great War from a four-poster bed.

Before leaving Paris, Mata Hari—blissfully unaware of how all her movements from now on could be misinterpreted at will—went to the consul-general's office at the Dutch legation to collect the information about money from van der Capellen and to inform the consul-general that she was leaving. Coulson insists that she gave the consul-general a letter for her daughter—which makes little sense, since she was leaving for Holland herself—and that the letter was opened by the French, who found it to be in code and to contain "information of major importance on an espionage technique which enabled the French to repair the enormous damage done to them by the enemy." Tantalizingly, he does not elaborate. Had this startling fact—that Ladoux's long surveillance had at last borne fruit—been the case, it would of course have figured in her trial, which it did not. Moreover, of course, she would never have been allowed to leave the country.

Ladoux says in his memoirs that he found her call at the consulate-general to be suspicious, although in contradiction he agrees that she had asked him if it would be in order for her to tell the functionary that she was returning to Holland, and he says that he had told her there were no objections.

Mata Hari arrived at the frontier post of Hendaye-Irun on November 6, went through customs, and joined the narrow-gauge Spanish train on the other track. Ladoux says in his book that he was having her shadowed, and we must suppose that this was true. She spent the night at the Grand Hôtel in Madrid. A French agent, Ladoux says, reported that she had noticed that he was observing her there. He is said to have reported that she came down to the hotel lobby the following day at 7:05 P.M., apparently to take the 8:13 train to Vigo, but had walked up to him and said that she had decided to spend another night in Madrid.

Although it is not hard to imagine that she talked to someone who was obviously following her, the story itself is unbelievable since she had to be in Vigo to board the *Hollandia* for Holland at a fixed time. According to Ladoux, the agent claimed she asked him not to follow her around the following afternoon because she had an appointment with "a compatriot" between two and four. Ladoux recounts that, the following day, a different agent followed her on a bicycle (he says he was a young man wearing a false gray beard) to a café called El Palmario, where she made two telephone calls, one to a German bank in Madrid and the other to the German consul in Vigo. Frustratingly, he does not tell us how the agent knew this or what was said. Research shows that there was never a café called El Palmario in Madrid, and no mention of this episode was made in the interrogations or at her trial. The tale was presumably invented to embroider the book. By the afternoon in question, she was actually in the Atlantic off northwest Spain. Mata Hari, herself an exuberant liar, had met her match.

Ladoux also says that a French agent at Hendaye had informed "the British admiralty" of the lady's journey, and that a British naval vessel, *Marvellous*, intercepted the *Hollandia* and took her off to Liverpool for questioning. In reality, the *Hollandia* was never intercepted, and she was never questioned in Liverpool. She traveled on the *Hollandia* to Falmouth, where the British came aboard for the usual search of the cargo and the passengers.

Mata Hari told the story herself in one of the later interrogations: "At Falmouth, the boat was invaded by police, soldiers and suffragettes, who had the job of searching the women passengers. Two of them searched my cabin, looking under the bunk and even unscrewing the mirror from the wall, to look behind.

"An officer checked my identity, looked at me closely, and produced from his pocket a snapshot of a woman in Spanish dress with a white mantilla, carrying a fan in her right hand, and with her left hand on her hip. The woman resembled me slightly, but she was shorter and plumper than I."

The officer was apparently on the lookout for the person in the picture and thought "Madame Zelle MacLeod" was the woman in the mantilla. Mata Hari says she laughed at the idea but that the officer insisted that the photograph "had been taken at Malaga, where I insisted I had never been. I was made to disembark."

The officer who arrested her was George Reid Grant, a career policeman who had gone to France as a soldier in 1914 and then returned to Scotland Yard the following year to help in the organization of counterespionage. He and his wife, Janet—who was also enrolled as a counterespionage policewoman—had been posted to Falmouth, where Mrs. Grant's job was to interrogate female suspects.

Interviewed in 1964 at the age of seventy-eight, George Grant remembered clearly everything about the episode. He said he had first met Mata Hari in January 1916, when he was the officer who had stamped her passport at Falmouth as she returned to The Hague from her first wartime trip to France. He recalled her as "one of the most charming specimens of female humanity I had ever set eyes on."

Grant and his wife and their fellow police officers had been told to look out for Clara Benedix, a much-sought-after German spy who was living in Spain, pretending to be Spanish, and ostensibly earning her living as a flamenco dancer. Because the photo of Clara Benedix resembled Mata Hari, the two Grants concluded that they were the same person. "Clara Benedix," they decided, was an alias (like Mata Hari) for Margaretha Zelle MacLeod.

Because of the war, merchant ships did not sail up the Channel between sunset and sunrise, and the *Hollandia* spent that night tied up at Falmouth. Early in the morning, George and Janet went on board to remove the Dutchwoman. Forty-eight years later, George recalled that Janet had "stripped Mata Hari and searched her thoroughly," while he ordered the ship's carpenter to unscrew the mirrors in her cabin, and the suffragettes—campaigners for the right of women to vote, and who had volunteered for war work—went through her belongings. Nothing incriminating was found.

Mata Hari, whose responses to questions were interpreted by a Mr. Adams—whose father had been the prewar director of a mission for English-speaking seamen in Rotterdam—protested volubly, as did the ship's captain. The skipper noted that his ship was neutral property and that his passenger was a neutral also. Grant recalled the Dutch merchant marine officer as saying: "You are making a terrific mistake this time. This woman is the most popular passenger aboard." He was apparently emphasizing the point that the complaint that he intended to make to the Dutch government would be widely supported by the other Dutch passengers.

The Grants took Mata Hari to their Falmouth home, where she was allowed to take a bath. She refused food, "cried a lot," and "drank an awful lot of coffee," Grant recalled. In the evening, Grant took her aboard the night train for London. Since the British police would not allow a male officer to travel alone with a female prisoner, his wife went along as "chaperone."

The police had reserved a compartment, and Mata Hari had insisted that it be first class. The prisoner took off her skirt and hung it over the light so that she could sleep. The train had no running water, only washbowls that were filled at stations, so on their arrival in London the Grants agreed to Mata Hari's request that they all go to a hotel to enable her to take another bath and change her clothes. Only then was she taken to Scotland Yard, where Grant handed her over to Chief Inspector Edward Parker, who gave her a room that served as an overnight cell. Her jewelry and money were removed. It was now November 13.

By the time they handed the prisoner over, the Grants had begun to have doubts about their arrest, and the improbable trio—the humble English bobby, his amateur policewoman wife, and the sophisticated Parisian courtesan—had become friends. Janet Grant asked Mata Hari for a photograph, and the lady fished out several from her bag, autographing one of them. She also gave Mrs. Grant a small glass toy dog as a souvenir, which Grant himself, a widower when interviewed, had on his mantelpiece. Mata Hari invited the Grants to visit her in Holland one day and gave them her calling card. Grant—a well-schooled British plebeian used to looking out for such things—noticed that it was embossed with a small crown, implying that *Vrouwe* Zelle MacLeod belonged to the aristocracy.

At Scotland Yard, Mata Hari was interrogated for three days by "three gentlemen in uniform," she later said. During this time, she also met Sir Basil Thomson, an assistant commissioner of police and the head of Scotland Yard's Special Branch—counterespionage.

(Sir Basil, who also wrote his memoirs later, was a former colonial civil servant who had returned to London from Fiji to take the bar exams and had then had a career as a prison governor. An Old Etonian and an alumnus of Oxford, he had been given the job equivalent to Ladoux's in 1914. By the time he met Mata Hari, he was fifty-five. Thomson reported to the Foreign Office and to General G.M.W. MacDonagh, the director of military intelligence, who was the British equivalent of Colonel Goubet.)

Thomson expressed astonishment that his men had unknowingly arrested Mata Hari, the famous "naked dancer." He confirmed what his officers had told her already—that they had believed that she was Clara Benedix. (In the trial records, the French, notoriously poor about foreign names, refer to this well-known figure as "Clara Bénédict.")

Because Thomson's men, although arresting the wrong woman, had nevertheless actually brought in someone of whom the British were suspicious, he and they questioned her carefully. Then Thomson sent a letter by hand to the minister of the Dutch legation in London saying that Margaretha Zelle MacLeod had arrived carrying a "French passport" and had been arrested on suspicion of being "a spy of German nationality bearing the name Clara Benedix, of Hamburg." He said Mrs. MacLeod "refuses this identification, but investigations continue to substantiate the charge." We must recall that the Grants had hypothesized that Benedix and Mata Hari might be the same person. Thomson told the Dutch minister that his prisoner had asked for paper to write to "your Excellency" and that she had been supplied with the "necessary material."

In the afternoon, Thomson wrote another letter—also now in Scotland Yard files—and sent it through the mails. It arrived at the legation the following morning. Curiously without reference to the previous letter, the officer wrote:

> I have the honour to inform you that a lady bearing a Dutch passport and named Mrs. Zelle MacLeod was asked to disembark from the Dutch ship *Hollandia* on its arrival at Falmouth, being under suspicion of activities in breach of neutrality law. She has asked me to send you the enclosed letter.
>
> An investigation is in progress, as rapidly as is possible, by telegraph, and she will not be detained any longer than is necessary. However, if it appears that she is guilty of activities in breach of neutrality law, it may become necessary to arrest her.

In fact, Mata Hari's letter was written on November 13, at her arrival, and Thomson must have taken a few liberties with diplomatic procedures by holding on to it. Perhaps he wanted it translated from the Dutch. It said:

> Excellency,
> May I with deference request of Your Excellency to come to my assistance as quickly as possible.
> I have been implicated in a terrible affair. I am Mevrou MacLeod, daughter of Zelle, divorced. I am going to Holland via Spain, traveling on *my own completely authentic passport* [underlined in the original].

The English police insist that it is a forgery and that I am not Mevrou Zelle.

I am at my wit's end, imprisoned here since this morning, at Scotland Yard; I beg you, come to my help.

I live in The Hague, 16 Nieuwe Uitleg, and I am as well-known there as in Paris, where I resided for many years. I am all alone here, and I swear that absolutely everything is proper in my situation.

There has been a misunderstanding but, I beg of you, help me.

Sincerely,

M. G. Zelle MacLeod

In articles and in a later book, despite his written admission to the Dutch minister, Sir Basil never mentioned that Mata Hari had been suspected of also being Clara Benedix. He claims that he knew all along that she was Mata Hari and no one else. He recounts that she told his officers that she was simply going home to Holland. When he persisted in having her questioned for days, she decided that it would be safe to tell a very senior British Secret Service officer that she was working for French intelligence. Thomson naturally sent a message to Ladoux for confirmation.

Ladoux, to judge by his reaction, seems to have had no clear idea of why the British had arrested his probationer-spy. Sir Basil had carefully made no mention of the Clara Benedix mistake. Ladoux drew the conclusion that the British were even more sure that Mata Hari was a German agent. He would now look very silly if he admitted that he had sent her to spy, on however freelance a basis, on the German general staff in Belgium. He was later to claim to Bouchardon that he had connived with Thomson at her detention at Scotland Yard; but he confirms in his memoirs that he telegraphed back the words that Thomson recalls: *"Comprends rien.* [Understand nothing of your message.] Send Mata Hari back to Spain."

Now, unless we accept the connivance claim, with both men unnecessarily lying to—instead of congratulating—each other in secret telegraphic traffic, it must have been the turn of Sir Basil to be perplexed. If she was not Clara Benedix, and she was not Ladoux's agent, why not send her home? However, under the circumstances, having asked his French counterpart for instructions, there was nothing Thomson could do but return her to Spain, as Ladoux had requested. Mata Hari assumed at the time that the decision to send her back to Vigo was Thomson's own, because she later quoted him as saying: "We now realize that you are not Clara Benedix; but we cannot let you go to Holland." She also quotes his interrogators as saying something that it is hard to believe is accurate: "We don't allow any Dutch people to go to Holland."

The minister in charge of the Dutch legation in London, Marees van Swinderen, who had been ineffective in getting Mata Hari a British visa six months before, had by then begun checking, through the Hague, with the Dutch legation in Paris. Ladoux, the wily dissimulator, had assured the Dutch legate there that he had not given Mata Hari a mission and that if she said she was going to Holland for intelligence work, it must be for the Germans.

While this was going on, the complaint of the *Hollandia*'s captain was working its way up through different channels of the Dutch foreign ministry. On November 25, a functionary there sent van Swinderen a message *informing* him of Mata Hari's arrest in Britain. The message referred, not to the legate's recent dispatches, but to his telegram of May 4 about the British visa!

Van Swinderen read this message on the morning of November 26. He had by then apparently had at least two meetings with his compatriot, and he now reported to The Hague that she was "returning to Spain of her own free will." It was, of course, the only way she could get out of Scotland Yard.

On November 28, Thomson told Mata Hari that she was free to return to Madrid. The elegant and exasperated lady with the numerous trunks could at last move out of the gas-lit overnight cell and into the Savoy Hotel. Although the British still regarded her with some suspicion (why would anyone have been the mistress of a German police officer in Berlin in August 1914?) they clearly had no evidence that she was a spy, so they released her. (The following year, they arrested Dr. Bierens de Haan, the director of the Dutch Red Cross hospital in Paris, as he was sailing home to Holland, because he had a photograph of Mata Hari and himself in his luggage. It had been taken when she had visited the French wounded at his hospital. After six weeks in prison, he was allowed to travel on to Holland.)

Ladoux's ambiguous message to Thomson is not hard to fathom. He was still disturbed by the British suspicions—which he later claims he shared all along, although this is at least only partially true, since he had authorized her to leave France. Obviously, at this point he didn't want her in Holland, where she might well complain to her government and to the press, thus embarrassing his much-higher-ranking British counterpart Thomson, whose suspicions he would now be flagrantly challenging by continuing her on the Bissing mission. The little captain had been cautious all along about contesting the conjectures of British intelligence, which he admired. Let her spend the rest of the war in Spain!

Thomson claims in his memoirs that her passport was "altered"—his pretext for having initially presumed it to be false. Waagenaar assumes that she changed a digit and made herself ten years younger than she was. Knowing what we know of Mata Hari, this was not an unreasonable assumption, but a close look at her Dutch and French passports and her *carnet d'étranger* shows no sign of 1876 having been changed to 1886. The documents, especially her Dutch passport, are written in exquisite script that would be hard to alter, and nothing anywhere shows signs of tampering. In any event, logically there would be no need to alter the date of a false passport, only a genuine one. But Thomson implies that her pretense at being thirty instead of forty explains his advice to her: "If you would please take the advice of a man almost twice your age, give up your undertaking."

By then, with both the British and Dutch making their inquiries in Paris, Thomson knew there must be more behind Ladoux's original "*Comprends rien.*" If she was not under orders from Ladoux, how could he order her to Spain instead of allowing this neutral citizen to continue home to Holland? If Ladoux thought she was working for the Germans, as he had told the Dutch legation in Paris, why had he let her leave France in the first place, and why did he not encourage the British to keep her under lock and key? If the Dutch thought she was not working for Ladoux, why had they consented to their citizen being sent to Madrid instead of being allowed to pursue her journey home? Writing well after her execution, Thomson never admits that she was probably not a German spy, but he appears to have recognized that she was in a situation in which, if she got into trouble, the French would disown her. She had in fact gotten into trouble at Falmouth because a policeman and a policewoman had thought she was Clara Benedix, which had created a discreetly unannounced international incident. This is partly conjecture, but it would seem to explain why he released her and paternally advised her to give up spying for anyone. How wise he was—especially as she had not then even started to try her skills at that occupation.

She left Liverpool on December 1 on the *Araguya*. (The irrepressible Major Coulson has her in Amsterdam by then, working with a German spy called Max Neuder, who he says managed to send her back to Paris through the German and Allied lines.)

At the Hotel Continental in Vigo, where she arrived on the sixth, she met Martial Cazeaux, a Frenchman working as a clerk at the honorary Dutch consulate in the town. She told him of her problems with the British and she asked who Clara Benedix was. She later recounted in an interrogation that he had told her that Benedix was a famous German spy who was often in Spain and who was then, he said, living at the Hotel Roma in Madrid. The woman had been to France three times since war began, he said. In return for this briefing on the whereabouts of spies in Spain, Mata Hari later said, she confided in him that there had been a Belgian couple on the *Araguya* called Allard and that passengers had told her that the husband was a spy for Britain while the wife was an agent of Germany. Bouchardon, who must have been a great man for a straight face, was to ask her why she was giving the name of a British—Allied—spy to an employee of the Dutch consul! This is only a partial picture of what appears to have been the musical comedy of much of World War I espionage. There is more: she later told Bouchardon that on her second day in Vigo she was taking a stroll along the sea wall when she ran into Cazeaux again. She said he asked her: "By the way, would you like to go to Austria for the Russians? I hear they're looking for someone."

She says she answered "Why not!"

At least, after her shattering experience at Scotland Yard, her limited good humor seems to have returned. She says Cazeaux's next remark was: "How much would you ask?"

"One million, with one hundred thousand in advance." ("I was joking, of course," she told Bouchardon.)

"That's very expensive," said the consulate clerk.

"If I save one hundred thousand lives, aren't they worth ten francs a head?"

Mata Hari recounted that Cazeaux warned her that the Russians were "talking to the Americans, who would do it for less."

This ludicrous conversation, which seems to have come out of a Graham Greene entertainment, ends with Cazeaux asking where "a Russian" could find her in Madrid. Reading the transcript of the interrogation that recounts the exchange, one would be tempted to believe that Cazeaux was a French agent who principally wanted to know her address in the Spanish capital and who was testing to see how strong were her first loyalties among the Allies; after all, she was known to be committed by then, as only a human being can be, not to a Frenchman but to a Russian; but neither Ladoux nor Bouchardon, in their books, claim that France had Cazeaux on its payroll. She apparently told Cazeaux that she would be staying at the Ritz, this time. How would she recognize the Russian? Cazeaux tore one of his calling cards in half, gave a portion to her, and said the Russian would bring the other half with him.

The next day, the eleventh, she left for Madrid. She had telegraphed Anna Lintjens from Vigo, saying that she was returning to Paris and telling the servant to ask "the Baron" to send her five thousand francs there. In Madrid, she indiscreetly telegraphed van der Capellen himself, saying she was unable because of wartime conditions to reach Holland now and repeating her request for him to send her funds in Paris. In Madrid, she also wrote a letter to Ladoux, explaining what had happened in Falmouth and London and asking for fresh instructions.

She told Bouchardon later that she had been expecting a response by telegram—which would have had to be in clear, so that she (and everyone else) could read it. Ladoux, of course, did not respond. (Five days later, she was to send a telegram to Cazeaux in Vigo, asking when the Russian was coming. He responded by letter, asking her to be patient; the Russian, he said, was in Switzerland.)

She was without instructions, needing money, and unable to

get to Holland and Belgium and von Bissing. She was roughly in the situation of a freelance reporter who has promised to get to Beijing during the Cultural Revolution but has ended up without a Chinese visa in Rangoon, Burma. She would have to recoup and once again set her own agenda. Perhaps she could do something to impress Ladoux in Madrid?

4. Mata Hari: The Spy Who Almost Never Was

WE ARE NOW IN THE second week of December 1916. The fortnight that would be the basis for her trial and for her enduring legend as a world-class spy of the first magnitude was about to begin. Since von Bissing was several hundred miles away and the Imperial Crown Prince even further out of reach, the next best thing would be—as she later recounted to Bouchardon—the German envoy in Madrid. To get to him, she would need an introduction. Since the Belgian scenario laid down with Ladoux involved her pretending to be on the Germans' side, she needed to contact German intelligence, which would probably be in the hands of a military attaché.

The Germans had several of this species in Madrid, working under the ambassador, Prince Ratibov. The most important was naval Commander Herbert "Hans" von Krohn. Then there was Major Arnold Kalle. A few days before she arrived on the scene, a junior member of the whole group had arrived—naval senior Lieutenant Wilhelm Canaris, an orphan who had joined the German navy at the age of eighteen and who would eventually become an admiral.

Canaris, whom several authors have described as her contact at the German legation in Madrid, and some as her controller and lover, in fact never met Mata Hari and never knew of her existence until it dramatically ceased. He had been a twenty-seven-year-old naval attaché in Santiago at the outbreak of war and had ended up in internment in Chile. Friendly Chileans had helped the fluently Spanish-speaking lieutenant escape with a false Chilean passport

Il n'a pas su, m'employer
C'est sa faute à lui.
Et pas la mienne —
Moi. j'ai été sincère;
mon amour et mon interêt
en sont la garanti.
aujourd'hui. autour de
moi. Tout tombe — tout
me renie, même, celui
pour qui j'aurais passé
à travers d'un feu —
Jamais. j'aurais cru
a tant de lâcheté humaine
Et très soit. Je suis seule.
Je me défendrai. et Si
je dois tomber; ça sera
avec un sourire de profond
mépris —

Respectueusement

M. g. Zelle
McLeod

"... and if I must fall it will be with a smile of profound contempt. Respectfully, M.G. Zelle McLeod" [Mata Hari]

(*above*) Margaretha and John,
1895: The wedding portrait

(*left*) Presumably the picture
that seduced John

Debut as a dancer, 1905

Debut as a lady, 1905

Mata Hari made stripping exotic—and acceptable.

(above) The house at 11 rue Windsor

(left) The house at 16 Nieuwe Uitleg

Mata Hari, probably
in 1912, when she
danced in "Tamil
braids" in the garden
of 11 rue Windsor

Vadim de Masloff, 1916

Studio portrait of
"Marina" and Vadim,
Paris or Vittel, 1916

"A ma chère petite Marina—ton
Vadime"

Captain Pierre Bouchardon (*left*) and Lieutenant André Mornet, at or shortly after Mata Hari's execution

Captain Georges Ladoux as a retired major, and Inspector of Resorts and Spas. During the war, he wore a beard and waxed the ends of his moustaches.

Mata Hari at her trial, 1917

A letter to Mornet from prison in which she signed herself "Mata Hari"

Mata Hari in her prime

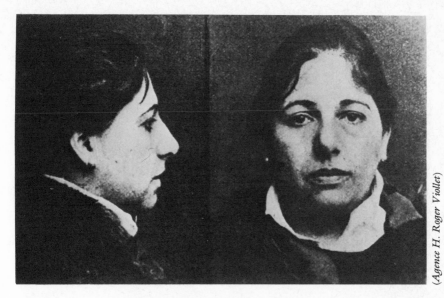

The last pictures taken in prison

Execution scene reenacted with great authenticity for a French silent film in 1922

in the name of Reed Rosas; this had passed the British inspection as he sailed up the Channel to Holland whence, as a neutral Chilean, he had been allowed to continue "on business" to Berlin. The spurious passport later got him back, via Falmouth, to Spain.

Within a few hours of her arrival in Madrid, Mata Hari had asked the desk at the Ritz Hotel for the diplomatic list, saying she wanted the address of a Dutch diplomat in Madrid. Looking through the German list instead, she found, she says, the name of *Hauptmann* (Captain) von Kalle, an army attaché. By then, he had in fact been promoted major, but the list was out of date. German army records show that he was not a "von." Since it seems unlikely that the German ambassador would have given him, in the information sent to the Spanish foreign ministry, a title of gentry he did not possess, it appears probable that Mata Hari, whose memory was not good and who had a "thing" about titles, had simply promoted him in recollection to the sort of aristocratic rank that she thought a relatively senior diplomat deserved. Interestingly, French intelligence knew so little about this key figure that they accepted Mata Hari's mistake and made it their own.

She noted Kalle's address and wrote to him that day, December 12, saying she wanted to meet him and asking for an appointment. The following day, a messenger arrived from the embassy with a letter from Kalle, saying he did not have the pleasure of knowing her but that he would receive her at three o'clock that afternoon. Under interrogation, she remembered this as a Saturday, but actually December 13, 1916, was a Wednesday.

She had written to his residential address, which was where she met him. She told Bouchardon that a servant (she says "the butler") showed her into Kalle's study, where the major, after inviting her to sit down, said: "I am not in the habit of receiving ladies who could have been sent to me by our enemies, but I am sure with you that this is not the case."

She says she laughed and asked him why he was so sure. He said it was because he had been promoted major ten months before and he was certain that an Allied intelligence agent would not have written to him as "Captain." Knowing Mata Hari, and for that matter the Second Bureau, this was probably misplaced confidence.

To impose herself, Mata Hari had entered speaking in French, a language required of every diplomat of the day but which not all diplomats necessarily spoke as well as she. He said that he had noticed from her calling card, which she had sent him with her letter (also in French) that she was Dutch. (It referred to her as *Vrouwe* Zelle MacLeod.) Did she speak German? She said she spoke it as fluently as French and that her heart was with the German cause.

She says she told Kalle about her arrest in Britain on suspicion of being a German. She asked who Clara Benedix was. He skirted that question and congratulated her on her German.

With the usual Mata Hari exaggeration, she told him: "I lived in Berlin for three years."

He asked her, she later said, if she knew any German officers. She told him she had been the mistress of Alfred Kiepert. She claimed that he then recalled having seen them together at the Carlton Hotel in Berlin and said he knew that she had watched the Silesian maneuvers. Of Clara Benedix, he said he could not discuss intelligence matters, since he had promised the King of Spain that he would not get involved with intelligence. It had been decided, she said he told her, that German intelligence in Spain would be confined to the consulate-general in Barcelona, which was near the French border. But he promised to ask the Baron von Rolland, the German consul-general in Barcelona, if any German (presumably a reference to Clara Benedix) could have been issued with a false Dutch passport. He said the idea seemed odd (*singulier*, in Mata Hari's statement).

She recounted that Kalle loosened up and offered her a cigarette. She did not say so, but at the time—as in many Oriental countries today—this was often a test as to whether a strange woman was "loose" or respectable. She accepted the cigarette and squeezed it into her holder.

"I made myself pleasant [*très aimable*]," she said. "I twisted my feet around." (In those days of floor-length skirts, for a woman to draw attention to what was covered by her skirts was considered seductive.)

She went on: "I did what a woman does in such circumstances when she wants to make a conquest of a gentleman, and I soon realized that von Kalle was mine."

She recounted that at one point, relaxed in his chair, he had told her he was very busy.

"I'm tired," she recalled him saying. "At the moment, I am busy trying to arrange for a submarine to drop off some German and Turkish officers in the French zone of Morocco. It is taking up all my time."

Since there seems to be no reason to distrust Mata Hari's account of the conversation, Kalle was presumably passing off what she was later told was stale information—the putting ashore in Morocco of German and (Arabic-speaking) Turkish officers to foment a rising against the French—perhaps to see what she would do with it.

She says she left Kalle's home "after having made a conquest of him." This was presumably a euphemism for having joined him in his bed and for having convinced him, she thought, of her sympathies for Germany. She had laced her conversation with tales of French resentment of British direction of the war, of mounting opposition to the Briand government, of how a Greek princess was using this for her purposes, and the story circulating in Paris that the Allies would launch an offensive in the spring.

That night, still using the public mails, she wrote to Ladoux to say that she had "renewed acquaintance" with a German "highly placed in the [Madrid] embassy" and to recount what she had learned from him—the submarine story. Because Kalle had said that all German intelligence work was supposed to be concentrated in Barcelona (obviously, his remarks about his labors on the submarine project would suggest that the agreement with Spain had not been honored) and had promised to raise the passport question with the consul-general there, she reported that von Rolland appeared to be the head of German espionage in Spain.

She concluded her letter to Ladoux with the words: "I await your instructions; I can do what I wish with my informer." The letter is not in the files; for its contents, the author has relied on her own recollection of it under interrogation.

Kalle, meanwhile—as was soon to become apparent—had begun checking with German intelligence in Holland, through Berlin, even before she arrived in his study, to see what, if anything, was known about this Dutchwoman who had asked for an appointment with a German intelligence officer. The afternoon must have convinced him that he was dealing with a bumbling *agente provocatrice* sent to him by the French; he immediately, as we learn later, hatched a plan to deal with her.

It was fortunate—or perhaps unfortunate in the light of what happened later—that she had selected Kalle from the diplomatic list instead of von Krohn. The latter was then the lover of Marthe Richard, a French spy also living in the Ritz. Marthe Richard was later the subject of a book by herself and of part of Ladoux's book, after the war, and a French film was made about her. This brave young widow was the true courtesan-spy and double agent that Mata Hari was supposed by legend to have been. Ladoux had not told Marthe Richard about Mata Hari, and the "French farce" of espionage in those days could have been even more in the style of the playwright Courtelines if von Krohn had deceived one French spy with another. After Mata Hari's execution, Marthe Richard would learn, in a leak from the trial published in the French press, that Mata Hari had been the mistress and subordinate of a German attaché in Madrid described as "von K . . . " She recalled later that, believing her turf had been invaded (since Kalle was not a "von"), she had naturally thrown a scene of jealousy with von Krohn, who had justly protested his innocence and fidelity.

Marthe Richard, the true seductress, double agent, and war heroine, was elected to the French National Assembly much later, after World War II, and then became famous for the "Marthe Richard law," which abolished legalized prostitution in France. (In a broad sense, this is ironic, since she was being paid by the Second Bureau, in World War I, to sleep with von Krohn. In her very old age she told the French press she regretted putting through the bill, which had put prostitution back on the streets and into the hands of pimps and gangsters.) When *Ma vie d'espionne* (*My Life as a Spy*), her memoirs, appeared in the 1930s, she told reporters that her situation in Madrid had been similar to Mata Hari's brief role there and that, in the context of the times, she could easily, as a double agent, have gotten into trouble also. "But I got the Legion of Honor and Mata Hari got the firing squad," she said.

In her book, Marthe Richard says that her chambermaid at the Ritz had reported one day that there was an "English artist" called Lady MacLeod who was now staying in the hotel also. The gossip about an "English" arrival was relevant, because the Spanish chambermaid was a German agent, as Marthe Richard was supposed to be. The anecdote is also significant in that it indicates that neither Marthe Richard nor the maid had heard any suggestion from their German controllers that "Lady MacLeod" was one of "theirs."

The next day, Mata Hari met two Dutch consuls in the hotel for dinner; their names, she said, were de With (some sources say de Witt) and van Aerssen. They introduced her in the dining room to Colonel Joseph Denvignes, a French military attaché who was, as it happened, in charge of French espionage in the Spanish capital. The elderly-looking colonel, who limped from a wound, was much taken by the Dutch visitor, especially when she mentioned her theatrical name. As Bouchardon disapprovingly related it in his book, "He behaved like a smitten young sublieutenant."

The following morning, Denvignes was back at the hotel to ask her if she were free for dinner. As was common at hotels in those days, the Ritz had arranged a "gala ball" in the evening to entertain its guests, and she had promised to attend with the Dutch consuls. The colonel asked if he might join her after the dinner, when the dancing would start.

At the "gala," Denvignes took Mata Hari aside and began to flirt with her. She complained in her account to Bouchardon that this public display of affection in Catholic Spain was embarrassing. She said she decided to recall him to his duties by telling him "I'm one of yours. If I had met you a day sooner, I would not have sent my information to Paris, I would have given the letter to you."

She then brought the flirtatious colonel further back to business by telling him of her meeting with "von Kalle." The notion that this attractive woman could be a spy on his payroll seems to have inflamed Denvignes further. He was back at the hotel in the morning to ask her to go back to Kalle and try to get more precise information about dates and times for submarine landings in Morocco. She suggested that pressing Kalle further might look suspicious, but she agreed to try.

The next day, she returned to Kalle's home during the siesta and sought to pry him out. She said he told her that "pretty women shouldn't ask so many questions." From that opening, it seems reasonable to presume that he allowed her to "seduce" him again.

Both the Mata Hari investigation papers and Ladoux's memoirs suggest that, if the submarine story was not new in Paris, it had not been learned through Denvignes nor passed on by him earlier, since he took Mata Hari's "intelligence" on to Paris that month for evaluation. Mata Hari was later to claim that he had tried to pass it off as something he had acquired on his own.

Denvignes' instructions to Mata Hari to question Kalle further on the submarine story must by now have left no doubt in the German major's mind about her role. He asked her about her plans, and she told him of her intention to return to Paris, and then to travel on to Holland via Switzerland.

This would have been the Saturday meeting (December 16) that she confused with the earlier Wednesday encounter. She reported back to Denvignes that she had discovered nothing further about the submarine operation. The French colonel, although busy with a visit by the then French Minister of War, General Lyautey, was courting her as assiduously as he could. On the twentieth, he told her that he was about to return to Paris with the minister—who was in Madrid on his way back from a mission to Morocco—and that if she discovered any further intelligence she should write to him at the ministry of war.

The following day, the amorous colonel appeared once more at the hotel at lunchtime and again at dinner—the easiest times, because of the *table d'hôte* convention, to find her there. He was back the following morning and evening, when they met in the otherwise empty reading room of the hotel; he plucked a violet from a posy she was wearing at her bosom, saying that he would carry it to Paris to remind him of her. He also unwound a ribbon from her bodice to enhance the floral souvenir. He wanted to know if, on his return from France, she would live with him and "brighten my home" (*égayer mon foyer*). She said she would soon be in Paris.

He then asked her if there was anything he could do for her there, before her arrival. She told the colonel to speak to the enigmatic Ladoux and to impress the junior officer with her usefulness. He promised to do so and said that all messages to him should not be sent by mail, as he had instructed her earlier, but rather should be given to his replacement at the embassy in Madrid, the Marquis d'Aurelles de Paladines. When she came to Paris, she should look him up at the Grand Hôtel d'Orsay, where he would be staying.

The day after Denvignes left for Paris with Lyautey, a messenger brought her an invitation from Kalle to come to tea at three o'clock. (The diplomatic working day in Spain ended at two P.M.) Given the public flirtation with Denvignes at the Ritz, Kalle obviously knew that she had been talking to the French. He now had, she would say later, an "authoritarian" manner.

She says he began their conversation stiffly: "Come over to the light. You have certainly passed on what I told you, because the French are sending out messages all over the place to find out where those officers landed."

This was presumably not true but was meant to impress her with the fact that his "indiscretions" had been just that, not artfully planted flummery. She said she told Kalle: "They could have learned about that through others. And how do you know what they are telegraphing?"

"We have the key to their radio cipher."

Needless to say, this most certainly could not have been true. Had it been, it would have been the last thing Kalle would have told anyone without a need to know, even if a questioner had relentlessly pulled out his fingernails or held a revolver to his head.

The conversation, according to Mata Hari, continued as follows:

She said: "Well, that's quite something! How intelligent you are!"

Kalle said: "One must forgive a pretty woman anything, but if it was known that I had told you about the submarine, I would be in trouble in Berlin."

This modest reprimand makes it clear that the submarine story was false, outdated, or already known to the French; and since he had just pretended that the Germans had broken the current French radio code, his indiscretion about the submarine would seem relatively petty. One senses that Kalle must have found her ingenuousness hilarious. Mata Hari said her only reaction in the face of this awkward situation was to offer herself to him again. As she put it in one of her interrogations: "Seeing that I had him under control once more [*Le voyant redevenu soumis*] I precipitated matters. I said 'Oh well, who cares?' [*Ma foi, tant pis!*] and I let him do with me as he wished."

Kalle's apparent indiscretions about the submarine and the French code were what is called in French intelligence slang *intoxication*, poisoning the enemy with false or stale information. After making love, Kalle told her that the Germans knew about the French pilot who had been dropping spies behind the German lines in France. The French, we learn later, apparently knew that the Germans already knew about this. Kalle also told her that German spies carried crystals under their nails, crystals that could be used to make invisible ink. This was clearly also *intoxication*.

Some of these "indiscretions" seem less to have been planted to see what was getting back to the French—he must have known that everything was—and more intended to reassure this very naïve probationer-spy that she had fooled him into thinking that she was on the German side at heart. Being Mata Hari, she attributed his apparently unguarded remarks to her extraordinary powers of seduction.

By then, it seems, Kalle had also told her that he had made inquiries about her and had discovered that she had been approached by the honorary German consul in Amsterdam before she had left for Paris that year and had been asked to work for Germany in France. Much later, she would admit that she had agreed with Kalle that this was so. Indeed, it is conceivable that she had already volunteered this information to Kalle herself in order to ingratiate herself with the German major, at the same time that she had told him about opposition to Briand, the Greek princess scandal, the expected spring offensive, and so on. Still anxious to imply that she had kept her ears open for the Germans while she had been in Paris, she now told him that she had learned of shortages of food supplies in some areas, of poor morale in the trenches, and similar stories—information she was culling from Paris gossip or from recollections of what she had read in the French press. Apparently unable to recognize *intoxication* when she heard it, she was as capable as any dissimulator of creating it. She was to claim that, before she left him, Kalle had offered her a ring and that she had said she did not like it, so he had given her 3,500 pesetas from his desk. We are entitled to doubt this explanation of why he gave her the pesetas, which seems more probably to have been another form of *intoxication*—payment for her "intelligence reports" on France. At least she now had money for the hotel bill.

Back at the Ritz, Mata Hari wrote a letter of twelve pages—she puts only about fifty or so words on a page, because of her singular writing—and sent it to Denvignes in Paris by giving the missive the next day to a French attaché called Mr. Henri, the Marquis de Paladines being absent from his office.

She had by then been a French spy for three afternoons and had, she thought, discovered two major pieces of intelligence: that the Germans had broken the French code and that they were infiltrating Morocco with German and Turkish officers, along with some tidbits such as Berlin's knowledge of French landings behind the lines and the spy role of the German consul-general in Barcelona. That seemed about the maximum she could expect to accomplish in Madrid. It was time to go back to Paris for some payment for what she thought of as her swift successes, and fresh instructions. It was time to head for Moritz von Bissing, presumably via Switzerland and Germany, where she could now, she felt, cite Kalle as a reference that she was a sympathizer with the Central Powers.

She stayed on in Madrid for another week, apparently to give Ladoux time, after Christmas, to evaluate her letter, the "intelligence information" brought to Paris by Denvignes, and the information passed on via Paladines' assistant.

To help handle her financial problems, she had accommodated a Spanish royal chamberlain called Diego de Leon and one of his political friends, a senator called Emilio Junoy. This relationship could well have been fortunate for her if she had known how to profit from its sequel. She soon received a letter from Junoy, who had returned to his home city, Barcelona. He told her that he and the chamberlain had been visited by a "French agent" from Cerbère, just across the border, who had asked them why the two men had been seen in Madrid in the company of someone suspected of being "hostile to the Entente," the Anglo-French alliance.

"We told him that we knew you as a charming, intelligent, spiritual woman, and that no word of politics had crossed our lips," Junoy wrote. The two politicians had found the French agent's visit "surprising," and "since we are gentlemen of Spain, we thought we should pass on this warning."

Mata Hari took this letter to the French embassy, where she now found Paladines in. He assured her that he knew nothing about the man from Cerbère and that it must all be a mistake. Her ingenuousness in producing the letter must at least have given the French second thoughts about the indiscreet behavior of their Spanish senatorial friend.

She was now ready to return to Paris and Ladoux. She went from Paladines' office to the French consul-general in the same building, showing him a visiting card from Denvignes, and was at once issued with a French visa on her existing French "passport." She left Madrid three days later on January 2 and arrived in the French capital on the morning of January 4. Kalle, we learn later, having not heard from her since Christmas, was so little aware of her movements that he thought she had left Madrid a few days earlier.

In Paris, her plan was to report as instructed to Colonel Denvignes, who would straighten up the foolish Captain Ladoux, and then she would finally be off to Belgium and her million francs, the price of paradise in Paris with Vadim. Her future, as she put it later, was "all traced out."

Her return to Paris, however, was to prove to be a more mistaken journey than all the others that this rash and foolhardy woman took.

5. The Arrest

THERE CAN SCARCELY HAVE BEEN a less rational time for a woman in Mata Hari's compromised and unprotected situation to return to Paris than early 1917, the beginning of a year of desperation for the Allies and especially for France.

The war remained stalemated and the outlook was not good. Ladoux's protector, General Joffre, who had been chief of staff since 1911, had been replaced on December 12, 1916, while Mata Hari was in Spain, by General Robert-Georges Nivelle, who was in turn replaced on May 15, 1917, by General Philippe Pétain, the hero of the Verdun salient; but he too was soon to be moved aside by General Ferdinand Foch. In short, France had four overall commanders in the space of a year.

The political world was in equal disarray. Aristide Briand, whose flirtation with a Greek princess was to figure in Mata Hari's alleged spying for Germany, had become prime minister on October 29, 1915. He was to be replaced in March 1917 by the septuagenarian Alexandre Ribot, who in turn would be replaced on September 12 by Paul Painlevé, who lost the post on November 16 to Georges "The Tiger" Clemenceau, who would remain in the position until the victory.

While Mata Hari had been in France in 1916, flirting with the Marquis de Beaufort and others, falling in love with Masloff, and visiting the war zone to be with Vadim in Vittel, France had more serious things on its mind than a courtesan's caprices. A terrible battle to hold Verdun had been fought from February to June of that year; it had been successful, but at a cost of about 350,000 French lives. The only encouraging feature of the year had been the arrival on September 15 of the first examples of Britain's new military invention, the tank, which enabled troops to attack from behind a shield of moving armor.

Two inspectors—not Monier and Tarlet—followed Mata Hari as she left the Orsay station that morning for the Hôtel d'Iéna on the avenue of that name. Did she choose it because it was a short walk from the Guimet Museum, the original source of her fame on the place d'Iéna? While her taxi waited in front of the hotel with her luggage, she went inside. She soon reemerged. Possibly because the Iéna turned out to be too expensive, she took the taxi on to the Hôtel du Palais, on the cours la Reine, then went from there to the Plaza-Athénée in the Champs-Elysées district, where she took a suite for thirty francs a day. This presumably included *pension*—the *déjeuner* and the *dîner*—since, as noted earlier, a woman could not eat unescorted in restaurants. At the price, it was quite a bargain. Then as now, hotels in France as elsewhere charged less to wealthy show-business personalities than they did to poor tourists because of the publicity value of a "star" presence; it rather looks as though Mata Hari—forgetting for the moment that she was supposed to be the granddaughter of a Javanese princess—was shopping for the best discount. Although she must have been looking out for a *filature*, the inspectors said in their first report that she did not seem to have spotted her "shadows."

Having taken over her suite, she then went to a salon, the policemen noted, to have her slightly graying hair dyed back to its normal color. She was preparing herself not for a lover but for Ladoux. At 5:00 P.M., she went to his office and was told that he wasn't in. She asked for Colonel Denvignes, whom she had tried unsuccessfully to call earlier. She was informed that he was now at the Grand Hôtel d'Orsay, next to the railroad station where she had arrived that morning, and whence the colonel would be taking the 9:40 for Madrid.

"Tell him I must see him!" she later recalled ordering the tall young lieutenant who had given her this information. Then, for once showing a little discretion in her new profession, she added: "Tell him it's his cousin from Madrid."

Just to be sure, she telephoned Denvignes' hotel from a café, and by 5:55, the inspectors reported, she was taking a taxi to the Orsay. The colonel was not in, so she returned to the Centralized Intelligence Section. Still no Ladoux. She was back at the Grand Hôtel d'Orsay by 8:30. Denvignes had just left. She walked next door to the railroad station to find that the Madrid express was about to pull out; it was almost nine o'clock. Ladoux's young lieutenant had gotten his time wrong—it was a 9:40 from the Austerlitz station, not the Orsay one. A station official suggested that she try the Austerlitz station, a couple of miles away, where the express would pick up the rest of its passengers, luggage, and mail before setting out for Spain, and where it would be *en gare* for about half an hour. She taxied there, found the express, and got a conductor to go through the train asking for "the French military attaché in Madrid"—she presumably thought the title would inspire the conductor to be more assiduous than if she had just said "Colonel Denvignes."

The colonel stepped down from a car. He seemed embarrassed. She was to recall the conversation on the station platform in one of her later interrogations.

Yes, he had said, he had passed on the message she had given him to give to Ladoux, but he had only seen the prickly captain briefly. He had been more involved with Ladoux's superior, Colonel Antoine Goubet.

"What did he say?" she asked, referring to Goubet.

"He said your pieces of information interested him very much, especially the first"—a reference to the Moroccan landings—"and that you were an intelligent woman."

"That's all?"

Denvignes seemed evasive.

"He asked me if I was aware of whom you were dealing with and I answered no."

"Why did you lie?" she recalled exclaiming.

Clearly something had gone badly wrong. Denvignes was no longer the besotted lover. As the whistle blew, he climbed back into the train, saying to her plaintively: "My child! My child!" (*Mon petit! Mon petit!*)

What could all this mean? She was soon back at the hotel where, the inspectors reported, she wrote a letter to Captain de Masloff and to "a colonel in the ministry of war." The policemen had apparently not heard of Vadim before, and their report does not identify the colonel. Was it Goubet? Or was it a letter to Denvignes, for forwarding by diplomatic pouch?

The next day, she sent a telegram to Baron van der Capellen. This is curious; usually, out of discretion, all her correspondence with this married man went via Anna Lintjens. The inspectors said the telegram was addressed to The Hague, although his home was in Amsterdam. Perhaps she telegraphed the Dutch colonel at the war ministry, or perhaps she addressed the telegram to him at her house in the Nieuwe Uitleg. The inspectors' report does not say.

The rather curt message, in French, said: "Have arrived in Paris. Inform Anna. All well—Marguérite." There was no more explanation than before of why she had returned to Spain and France.

She also sent a card to Anna, but not at Mata Hari's own Hague residence. Anna was apparently at her home village near Roermond. The card said:

Dear Anna,
   I await your telegram. I have arrived here safely. I have telegraphed the Baron. Did he pass on my regards?

Madame

Her letter to Vadim of the night before was now followed by a card:

My darling,
   Will I soon have news from you? Can you come?

Kisses
your Marina

The same day, January 5, finds her sending another letter to Vadim and one to a man in Barcelona called Camprubi. The report gives no details. Then the inspectors followed her on a visit to a dentist and to a fortune-teller. That evening, she returned to Ladoux's office, filled in a slip requesting him to see her, and got it back marked "Absent."

Back at the hotel, she told the manager she would soon be moving to her apartment and would have to buy furniture. Apparently she still believed she was on her way to Belgium and that on her return she and Vadim would stay at the flat together.

The next day, she spent an hour in a furniture store, then wrote to Masloff again. She received a letter, marked "Opened by the censorship." The contents are not disclosed, but the inspectors said it had been sent on by the Ritz in Madrid and the Iéna in Paris.

Despite the continual letters to Vadim, she must have presumed that her first letter to him had reached its destination and that he would find a way to come quickly, because that evening she called the Grand Hôtel to ask if he had arrived at her usual residence. She was told he had not.

When she left the hotel later, the two policemen were unable to find a cab to follow. We learn later from the investigation that in fact she went to Ladoux's office on the boulevard Saint-Germain, filled out another request to see him, and got back a blue slip requesting her to return for an appointment the following evening at six.

Not long after she returned to the hotel, the inspectors said, a French sublieutenant arrived and asked for her. He was told she had retired for the night, so he wrote her a short letter and gave it to the concierge. Later, after he had gone, she came down and gave the desk another letter to mail to Masloff and one for Anna. She was clearly getting impatient both for her lover's arrival and for the five thousand francs she had asked the baron to send.

The two new inspectors were by now having as much trouble as their predecessors. Tracking her on foot the following day, they lost her on a crowded street. That evening, they found a taxi moments after she did, but the vehicle wouldn't start. They thus missed her fourth and finally successful attempt to see Ladoux.

She found him, she would tell Bouchardon later, to be less friendly than at their last meeting, before she left for Spain. He said he had not seen much of Denvignes. He reproached her for going openly to the French embassy in Madrid. This was not the proper behavior for a French agent.

"Never forget," she recalled him saying, "that you don't know me and I don't know you." It was, and is, the classic instruction of a controller to his spy.

He denied knowledge of why someone had approached Senator Junoy about her. She said she complained of Ladoux's unfriendly attitude.

"Are these your thanks for my services?"

"What services?" Ladoux is said to have answered. "The information about Baron von Rolland and the submarine?"

"You're forgetting the code, the French aviator, and the secret ink crystals."

"First I've heard of that."

She repeated what she had gleaned from Kalle and passed on to Denvignes. Ladoux said the news that the Germans had broken the French code had to be a bluff. She said she suggested to Ladoux that if there was only a one percent chance that it was true, wasn't it worth checking, and that he replied: "Of course! I'm staggered!" (*Les bras m'en tombent!*)

She said later under interrogation that she told Ladoux that she was out of money and that she wanted to return to Holland. She said he told her to "try to stay on" for another week while he checked with Denvignes.

The inspectors were waiting for her when she returned to the hotel, where she went to her room and picked up the letter from Senator Junoy that she had received in Madrid, and took it back to Ladoux. Then she returned to the Plaza, where she wrote yet again to Masloff, apparently referring to the Twelfth Night celebrations of the Russian church. The inspectors seem to have had trouble with her handwriting in the salutation, as they have it beginning "*Mon Di*," which means nothing at all. Presumably, she wrote "*Mon Dieu*," making Vadim the male equivalent of a lover's "goddess":

> My God,
>   It's your Christmas today. I send you a long, long kiss.
>   See you soon,
>   your Marina

The next day, January 8, she wrote letters to van der Capellen, to Anna, to someone called Bosch Remper in London, to Vadim, and to a certain Lascaret in Vigo; she sent a card to a Lieutenant Kenneth Mackenzie Walker. Later she came down with a letter for Major Ignatieff, a military attaché at the Russian embassy in Paris. Steamed open, this letter apparently asked for news of Masloff: Where is he? Is he all right?

At dinner, the lonely woman in love was seen by the staff to be weeping at her table. The inspectors explained in their report that "she is without news of her fiancé, Captain Masloff." She ate little of the voluminous repast offered and retired at eight-thirty.

The following day, she penned another letter to Vadim, went back to the dentist, and accepted a luncheon invitation from a young French military pilot. Back at the hotel, she asked if there was a letter for her; when one arrived, they should bring it to her at once, she said. She wrote two more letters to Vadim.

On the morning of the tenth, she again wrote to her lover. A letter was brought to her room, which must have caused her palpitations, then disappointment. The inspectors reported that it was a love letter from an ardent French sublieutenant of artillery called Henry. Whether he was the same sublieutenant of January 6 is not clear. The French aviator of the previous day called and took her to dinner at the Restaurant Viel, a famous establishment on the boulevard de la Madeleine.

The next evening, an "ardent sublieutenant" (the earlier letter-writer?) arrived and was admitted to her room "from 8:50 to 10:45," after which he "disappeared in the direction of the Military School." She came down later with yet another missive for Vadim and a letter for "Martial Cazoux" (presumably Cazeaux, but she herself may have spelled it wrong, or misremembered it) in Vigo. She probably asked if the Russians still wanted someone to go to Vienna.

On the twelfth, she went to the Dutch consul-general, where someone reported to the French police that she had complained of "annoyances" (*tracasseries*) being visited upon her because she was a foreigner. All the staff in her hotel must by now have been aware of the police surveillance; since she was foreign, this could only imply that she was a suspected spy. She had asked, the inspectors said, for the "advice and protection of her minister" [head of legation]. An attaché had apparently promised to call on her at the hotel for tea one day, perhaps implying that this would show the staff that the lady was respectable and under the protection of the Dutch government.

She wrote again to Vadim, the inspectors said, and to "Comprabi" in Barcelona, but the report gives no details. The latter addressee must be the "Camprubi" of January 6. On the thirteenth, she was about to take a fiacre to somewhere when she allowed herself to be picked up and invited to lunch by "a French lieutenant-colonel"—later identified as a Belgian, the Count de Laborde. On the fourteenth, she finally received a letter from Vadim. The report noted that it had been "intercepted" and therefore delayed. Another letter came, this one from the Comptoir National d'Escompte, saying the bank had renewed her lease of a strongbox ("vault 147, box 15"). A third letter was from a Madame L. de Hart, of 87 rue de Ranélagh in Paris. The report does not say so, but presumably all the letters had been intercepted by the hotel and given to the Second Bureau, which would explain why they all finally arrived together. The report for the day ends by noting that she had told the hotel staff that she was feeling sick.

By then, she had noticed once more that she was being shadowed. The *filature* could well be among the "annoyances" of which she had complained to the Dutch consulate-general. The police report for the next day, the fifteenth, says she asked the hotel concierge: "Do you see that gentleman who just came in? That's the one who is following me." The report adds that the person in question was not one of the inspectors and does not belong to the police. Even admirers were making her paranoid.

That day, the police noted, she wrote again to Masloff and sent two letters to "shops."

At this point, the surveillance, which had clearly yielded nothing of value except to suggest that she was not spying for anyone in Paris, suddenly ended. There were no more *filature* reports.

That evening, unnoticed by the now-departed inspectors, a telephone message arrived from the Dutch acting consul-general, Otto Bunge, saying her money had arrived at his office. That night, she wrote to Ladoux, urging him to clarify his instructions and get her on her way. She also reminded him that he owed her money for the information from Madrid.

She called the next day at the Dutch consulate-general and picked up five one-thousand franc notes from Bunge. (We learn later that she sent three of them to Masloff.) Then she took her letter for Ladoux—with superb indiscretion—to her old lawyer-lover Edouard Clunet and asked him his advice before mailing it. He told her that he found her style a bit abrupt. Surely he knew that even her letters to her lovers were often a bit that way? Even her later letters from prison to her examining magistrate, often making numerous dramatic points, were mostly models of concision.

The next day—it later came out at the trial—she had an assignation with "Robert" de Marguérie. (Waagenaar, like others, confuses Marguérie with Jules Cambon in relating this tryst.)

Vadim finally arrived in Paris, apparently in late January, and spent some time with his mistress. He brought her the disquieting news that his commanding officer had been instructed by the Russian embassy in Paris to warn him that he was dealing with a notorious "adventuress." There is no mention of this in the trial papers, but it could well be because of her letter to Major Ignatieff, asking for news of Vadim. She herself, we learn later, was to suspect Denvignes of putting the Russians up to denouncing her.

Sometime in early February, she called on Maunoury at the Prefecture and asked him to ask the unresponsive Ladoux for permission for her to leave for Switzerland. He told her, she recalled later, that Ladoux would be "absent for three weeks in the south of France." She was to say under interrogation that she had made three requests for exit papers for Switzerland, the last being on February 12.

Her money was clearly running out again—in part because her Russian gigolo was proving to be expensive—and she was whiling away her time before setting out for the great espionage achievement, the mirage of a million francs, and life with Masloff. She could clearly no longer go by the Channel route, because of the crazy British at Scotland Yard. She was waiting for an exit visa for Switzerland. The Dutch writer Leo Faust recalled seeing her at the Folies-Bergère, watching *Mademoiselle du Far-West* in the company of "a Polish officer." Somewhere around this time, and probably because of the unfriendly attitude of the staff at the Plaza-Athénée, she moved to the Elysée-Palace.

Why had the surveillance stopped? To explain this requires an explanation of codes and ciphers.

In the days of Mazarin and the Three Musketeers, codes were boy-scout simple. If E was G, two letters further along in the alphabet, then F was H and G was I. At the outbreak of World War I, French messages, astonishing as this may seem, were sent in clear. Then codes were introduced, and became more enigmatic; but the principles were similar. For instance, if A was B, one letter away, then B might be D, two letters away, and C could be G, four letters away, and so on. One code might be used in the first and other odd-numbered paragraphs, and a different one in even-numbered paragraphs. There might be an A.M. code and a P.M. code. Letters might be reversed—A for D and D for A, and so on. A code might be devised by placing letters in a circle, as people do when solving an anagram, and lines drawn from one letter to another. These sophistications constituted the "key." Figures were used, as they almost consistently are today. Since there are only ten of them, as opposed to twenty-six letters, this makes the computation—the key—more complicated to devise and more problematic to solve.

Code is a French word meaning "a system of letters." The French word for figure is *chiffre*, which is also the French for cipher. Code and cipher could be mixed. For simplicity's sake, the author will usually use only the word *code*.

Another factor that needs to be known concerns the Eiffel Tower, built by Alexandre Gustave Eiffel for the Paris Exhibition of 1889. This phallic steel pyramid in the middle of a city of classical architecture had been controversial from the start, and when it was not dismantled after the Exposition, there were calls for blowing it up by explosives. Today, nearly a hundred years later, it is more or less accepted by Parisians as a permanent oddity on the city's skyline that brings in tourists from the provinces and from abroad. But whatever its considerable aesthetic faults, its role in World War I justified the decision not to pull it down in 1890.

"Line of sight" is a great help in transmitting radio waves. Perched at the level of low clouds, antennae installed on the Eiffel Tower could pick up traffic over considerable distances. The platform at the top, which is now an expensive restaurant visited mostly by foreigners, was in World War I a listening post where men with earphones captured messages in Morse Code from behind the German lines. Most messages from Madrid to Berlin could also be picked up there in reasonable weather. To make all this valuable, the French had to understand the German code. This was the task of the *déchiffreurs*—the decipherers or cryptographers.

In 1914, British cryptographers had broken the German code. In intelligence, all things being equal, this is the second most important achievement of all. The most important is to keep the enemy in ignorance of the first achievement.

There is a world of spy lore around the breaking of codes. As most readers will know, Britain broke the German code early in World War II and managed to preserve the secret of this "jewel" all through the conflict. Perhaps the most famous anecdote about

this concerns the Luftwaffe's massive bombing of the British industrial city of Coventry. Churchill and the Air Staff knew the
saturation raid was coming, and the temptation to move in extra
antiaircraft guns and "barrage balloons" (blimps) and to prepare
a huge ambush of fighter squadrons was compelling. But to be so
well prepared would have strained credibility; the Germans would
have been sure to guess the reason. Keeping the knowledge that
the German code was broken was more important than Coventry;
so only minimal extra defenses were added, and the city was left
to be put to the torch by the Luftwaffe.

As most readers will also know, the United States possessed the
Japanese code even before Pearl Harbor; apocryphal tales, inspired
by the Coventry story, still circulate, saying that President Franklin
D. Roosevelt knew the Pearl Harbor attack was coming and that,
like Churchill, he dared not take precautions. (This myth in turn
strains credibility: some of the ships could have put to sea on a
desultory exercise, some aircraft put in the air, and the command
in Hawaii warned of what was coming, without breaking the secret
of the breaking of the code. But all that belongs in a different
book.)

The Allies had scored the second most important achievement
early in the war, but the most important had eluded them. Perhaps
the prospect of appalling death tolls in the trenches from an im-
pending major German offensive had been too much to contem-
plate, and the French and their Allies had prepared too well. Since
the British learned from their intercepts of the treasonal 1914 visit
to Germany of Sir Roger Casement, and arrested him on his return
to Ireland two years later, this may have given the game away. Or
perhaps British or French intelligence was penetrated. In any event,
the Germans had realized in 1916 that the Allies had cracked their
code, and Berlin had then changed it. Back to square one.

But not long afterward, a dusty report by a French *déchiffreur*
called Edmond Locard reveals, he and his colleagues broke the key
to the new code, and the Allies managed to keep this knowledge
secret all through the rest of the war.

Usefully, Locard later explained how the earlier code had been
broken. Berlin had sent a message in clear, perhaps to one of its
intelligence offices abroad or perhaps to the military at the Front—
his explanation does not say. The message said: *"Was ist Circourt?"*

The British recognized the word as the second half of the name of a French village in the battle area, Xivry-Circourt. The village was so named on the French maps used by the Allies, but on captured German maps—the ones used in Berlin—the village had been simply marked "Xivry-C."

The British cryptographers went back to previous German messages to look for a hyphenated name in which the second part contained eight letters. Having thus found the code for "Circourt," they had already broken seven letters (the word has two Cs), as well as X, V, and Y. This broke the "key." The actual codes changed frequently; but if you possessed the key, Locard says, it only took about two hours to break each new code.

Now, back to Mata Hari. On December 13, 1916, while the lady was still cooling her two-inch heels in Madrid, someone from the Eiffel Tower brought a message to Ladoux that Kalle, the German military attaché in the Spanish capital, had sent to Berlin. According to the "Eiffel Tower" originals in the justice file, it said:

> H 21 informs us: Princess George of Greece, Marie Bonaparte, is using her "intimate relations" with Briand to get French support for her husband's access to the Greek throne.
> She says Briand's enemies would welcome further defeats in the war to overthrow him.
> Britain has political and military control of France. French are afraid to speak up. General offensive planned for next spring.

Ladoux must have deduced correctly that surely this scuttlebutt could have come only from Mata Hari. It was indeed exactly the sort of *intoxication* that she would be able to think up, based on Paris gossip. (Aristide Briand was the French prime minister. Both sides were always expected to launch offensives in the spring, when the weather improved. King Constantine of Greece was married to the Kaiser's sister; although his country was under attack by Austria, Germany's ally, he was pro-German. Constantine was in fact to be overthrown the following year, but the throne went not to his son George, the Franco-Greek princess's husband, but to their son Alexander.) However, what must have pricked up Ladoux's ears was the prefix. The Germans had given her a code number: H 21.

Since her freelance assignment involved her being accepted by the Germans, this was not in itself a bad thing. Indeed, for a French agent, it would be an achievement. But for the code number to be understood in Berlin, she would have to have received it earlier—before she arrived in Spain from Liverpool.

On December 20, the Eiffel Tower people brought in another message that Kalle had radioed to Berlin, asking for a rapid response to his earlier one. On the twenty-second, there was another radio from Kalle, querying an error in a message from Berlin that is not now in the file and which the Eiffel Tower may or may not have received. Reading the traffic, there is yet another message from Kalle, identified in a much later internal memorandum as being dated December 18, that is also missing. One of Bouchardon's interrogations of Mata Hari implied that these may have referred to possible plans for an Allied landing at the mouth of the Escaut, which Colonel Goubet was to testify to Bouchardon was common gossip, and to the transportation problems of French officers in getting to the Front, which could well have figured in Mata Hari's attempts at passing *intoxication* to Kalle. This leaves unexplained, however, why these "pieces of intelligence" were separated from the rest and raises the question as to whether they were ever in Kalle's original traffic.

On Christmas Day, the French picked up a message from Berlin that said:

> Give H 21 3,000 francs and tell her [or him—the words are the same in French and are in translation in the files, although they would not be the same in the original German] that:
>
> (1) The results obtained are not satisfactory;
>
> (2) The ink which H 21 received cannot be developed by the French if the correspondence paper is treated in conformity with instructions before and after the use of invisible ink;
>
> (3) If, in spite of that, H 21 does not want to work with invisible ink, the agent should come to Switzerland and, from there, communicate her [or his] address to A.

Reading the files, it is not clear if "A" is a French discretion for someone known to French intelligence or if it refers to Antwerp, from where German espionage for French-speaking countries was controlled. Switzerland is, of course, both French- and German-speaking, and Mata Hari, who spoke both languages, would—had she spied for Germany—have used German.

The next day, December 26, the Eiffel Tower reported another Morse Code radio message from Kalle. He is complaining that he has had no reply to his messages of December 13 and December 20. He says he has given "H 21" 3,500 pesetas. This would appear to make it crystally clear that the message refers to Mata Hari. It continues:

> She will request, by a telegram from the Dutch consul in Paris, that a further sum of money be made available to her domestic servants [sic] in Roermond [Roermonde in the French text] and she requests you to advise consul Kroemer in Amsterdam about this.

On the twenty-eighth, Kalle got a reply from Berlin, agreeing that there had been an error in the message he had queried on the twenty-second.

The same day, the Eiffel Tower picked up Kalle's response, saying in the translation that it was addressed to "Headquarters Berlin." It said:

> H 21 will arrive tomorrow in Paris. She will ask to be sent at once, by telegram, through Consul Kroemer in Amsterdam and her servant Anna Lintjens in Ruremond [sic], 5,000 francs to the Comptoir National d'Escompte de Paris, to be handed over, in that city, to the Dutch consul Bunge.

He says "H 21" has bills to pay in Paris and will "certainly" travel on to Holland via Switzerland. (By implication, this would mean by Germany also.)

On December 29, the Tower listeners picked up a message from Kalle referring to the Christmas Day message from Berlin, and saying that "agent H 21 has already left."

On January 5, shortly after Mata Hari's arrival in Paris, the Tower intercepted a message from Berlin to Kalle, querying a detail in the report about the Franco-Greek princess.

In the light of all this, it is not hard to understand why Ladoux was not anxious to put Mata Hari definitively on his payroll, and why he was reluctant to receive her when she first called at the boulevard Saint-Germain on her return from Spain—and why he was brusque with her when he finally gave her an appointment.

He was waiting for instructions from the examining magistrate to whom he reported for legal purposes—Bouchardon.

Ladoux, the trial papers reveal, had sent a report to Bouchardon as soon as Mata Hari checked in at her hotel. In it, he covered himself for having sent an apparent German spy already detected by the British on a mission to the German general staff in Belgium; and in it he also carefully did not mention that his men at the Spanish border had shooed the prey away from the trap that she had unwittingly set for herself when they had tried to deny her entry into France the year before.

To give Ladoux his due, it is true that he had still been suspicious, because of the British reports, and in spite of the fact that months of his surveillance in France had yielded nothing to support them. There seems no reason to doubt his later claim that, when he allowed her to leave the country instead of having her arrested, he was testing her for loyalty as well as for efficiency. But his report to Bouchardon leaves any reader—including, presumably, Bouchardon—with the impression that the woman whom the British thought was AF 44 had been identified long ago by Ladoux himself as someone called H 21, the code number Kalle used. But at this point he did not pass the Eiffel Tower traffic on to the army magistrate.

The information obtained through the excellent work in the Tower and the brilliant deciphering of the cryptographers seems to be the very stuff of great intelligence work. What a coup! All Ladoux has had to do is behave as a wily civil servant and fudge things a bit, covering his rear for not having resisted the temptation to use ''H 21'' to work for France by allowing her to ''escape'' in November and pretending to have had more knowledge than he has. For the moment, the surveillance continued, so that she could be arrested whenever he wished and to see if, despite all the blank results of the previous year, she would lead the two inspectors chasing after her fiacres to a whole network of German spies in Paris.

It is thanks to Locard's report that we know what brought Ladoux's dreams down and led to the lifting of the surveillance—just before she took time off with the French diplomat who handled codes and ciphers at the Quai d'Orsay, and later had her last idyll with Vadim. Sometime in the middle of January—it was presumably late on the fourteenth or early on the fifteenth, the date the surveillance was called off before the end of the working day— one of Locard's colleagues brought something to Ladoux's attention that, in the Keystone-Cops world of World War I intelligence, had not been reported a month earlier as it should have been: all Kalle's messages and Berlin's responses were in the old code that the British had broken earlier and that the Germans knew that the Allies possessed. *They were therefore meant to be read by the French.*

Using the old code was also a signal to Berlin that the messages were *intoxication* for Paris and that suitable responses should be sent back in the same broken code. The whole traffic between Madrid and Berlin about "H 21"—who is clearly Mata Hari—was therefore a gigantic bluff meant to persuade the French to arrest their probationer-spy and shoot her.

Locard says in his report that the German military attaché had "specifically used an old cipher which he knew was cracked."

Kalle had put Mata Hari's prattlings to good use, constructing a plausible exchange. Her twaddle about the Greek princess and about French tolerance of British direction justified Berlin's "complaint" that H 21's results were inadequate. Her reluctance to use invisible ink anywhere, perhaps learned from German penetration of Ladoux's service (see the penultimate chapter of this book) and from knowledge of her conversation with Ladoux the previous year, had been given a German context and made a part of the reason for her (already existing) desire to go home via Switzerland this time. There are believable messages about a transmission error, and all Mata Hari's open-mail telegrams and letters from the Ritz concerning money expected from van der Capellen, and by which means, had been cunningly used to talk of funds being sent by the German spy-consul in Amsterdam.

To anyone probing the Mata Hari story, little seems sympathetic about Georges Ladoux. But this officer out of Saint-Cyr, a protégé of General Joffre, who was still a captain at forty-two in spite of the war, had suddenly, he thought, hit the jackpot; then it turned out that it was all a mistake. For a moment, at least, it is hard not to feel sorry for him.

He called off the surveillance.

*   *   *

But the world of intelligence, then as now, had its own momentum. Indeed, given the quasi-universal acceptance of secrecy's overcoming the rule of law, there was not much that you could *not* do with documents if you wanted to—especially if testimony to their falsity would never be presented to a trial behind closed doors by the lowly world of noncommissioned cryptographers. Urged on by the British suspicions, Ladoux had had a long, exhaustive, expensive *filature* conducted on Mata Hari, and he must have been naturally reluctant to concede that it had all been a waste of time and money. Moreover, the pressure was coming all the way from the President's palace to catch more spies.

Exactly four weeks after the surveillance ended, to wit on Tuesday, February 13, 1917, Mata Hari was arrested in her bedroom at the hotel.

Captain Pierre Bouchardon, the investigative lawyer of the Third War Council (military court) to whom Ladoux was reporting and who would have had to obtain the order for the arrest, had done so. He gave Commissioner Albert Priolet a warrant to go to "103 avénue des Champs-Elysées." The warrant read:

> Woman Zelle, Marguérite, known as Mata Hari, residing at the Palace Hotel, of the Protestant religion, born in Holland August 7, 1876, 1 meter 75 centimeters tall, able to read and write, is arrested for espionage, attempted espionage, complicity in espionage, and intelligence with the enemy, in his favor [*dans le but de favoriser ses enterprises*].

Even her Hinduism had been denied her. And Ladoux was to keep Kalle's spurious radiograms from Madrid under lock and key for more than three months longer, in the hope that Bouchardon could construct a case without them or with no more than arcane references to material that Ladoux claimed he had.

6. The Pretrial—
1: "Marking Time"

Commissioner Priolet took Mata Hari straight to Pierre Bouchardon's tiny office on the quai de l'Horloge. The forty-six-year-old captain, with his thin face, cropped moustache, querulous eyebrows, and what contemporaries described as "beady" eyes, was an experienced prosecutor who was to spend his entire working life in that specialty. He had been a prosecuting attorney in Rouen before coming to Paris and had become an army examining magistrate in the first days of the war. He had, by all accounts, a blistering temper and the Norman's reputation for craftiness. She found him sitting in a straight-backed chair at a tiny table. He gestured to her to take a similar seat. At another small table sat Sergeant-clerk Emmanuel Baudouin, who copied everything down in shorthand—a facile skill that all clerical staff in Europe, then as now, were required to know—and transliterated into his florid penmanship.

To Bouchardon's first question—had she read the warrant?—she answered that she was innocent and that someone was playing games. He asked her to speak slowly and explained that her responses would be recorded. She then signed a statement that reads: "I am innocent. Someone is playing with me—French counter-espionage, since I am in its service, and I have only acted on its instructions."

Bouchardon told her that she had a right to have a lawyer present, and her statement adds the words "I do not need a lawyer." The jurist was aware that this excited reaction might not satisfy legal process, so he asked her if she was prepared to waive her right to the assistance of an attorney at this first appearance.

This stratagem, often used, equally often works, because arrested persons do not want to spend a day or so in prison arranging for a lawyer. In the American grand jury system, a defending attorney may be present but may not ask questions; he at least knows everything that is said, what mistakes his client has made, and what advice to give between one session and another. In the system Mata Hari faced, a defense counsel could be present only at the first appearance—which thus usually became a formality, with questions about identity and perhaps an explanation of the accusations—and at the last, when it was learned whether the case was to go to trial. Most writers have assumed that Edouard Clunet was present at the February 13 appearance, and Waagenaar explicitly says that this was so. In fact, in her panic, she gave up her right to counsel's presence, allowing Bouchardon, if he chose to, to extend the interrogation into the facts of the case. While he methodically chewed his fingernails—his most famous tic; he even chewed them in court—she signed a paper handwritten by Sergeant Baudouin that said:

> I expressly renounce for the present interrogatory all formalities of the law as it concerns the assistance of a counsel and the [illegible] of the procedure at his disposition [or *its* disposition, if the illegible word referred to the law].

She signed "M. G. Zelle McLeod" (instead of MacLeod). Bouchardon countersigned with his own distinctive signature, in which the final "n" becomes a downward-sweeping, sinister hook.

The lawyer-captain does not seem, however, to have taken advantage of Mata Hari's mistake; but she was startled to learn that she could not go back to her hotel. She would be taken to prison, he said; he would see her again "in a few days."

Weeping and shaking with a combination of fear and rage, she was driven to the Saint-Lazare women's jail, where she was placed in a padded cell—a frequent precaution with new prisoners, to avoid suicide. The cell had only a mattress, one weak gaslight, and one tiny window near the ceiling. By evening, the temperature was to fall below freezing point, and Saint-Lazare had no heating. She was examined by the prison doctor, Léon Bizard, who recommended that she be given a better cell as soon as possible. Bizard, whose later memoirs contain the only account of her prison conditions and her life in captivity, says he asked her if there was anything she needed. She replied that she needed to take a bath and use a telephone. He told her the prison had no baths and that he did not have the authority to allow her to make telephone calls.

Bouchardon called her in on the fifteenth, two days later.

Like confessions, based on questions and answers and written by police for an accused to sign, Sergeant Baudouin's version of what Mata Hari said under this first full interrogation, and the later ones, is often stilted and terse and seems to be his synopsis rather than her words. Bouchardon started by asking her to trace her life, while the beady eyes watched for signs of dissimulation and the fingernails disappeared, calcic chip by calcic chip, down the captain's throat.

She recounted her childhood. She said she had been educated at Leeuwarden until she was twelve. When her mother died, her father had sent her to a girls' boarding school in Leyden until she was seventeen. She thus avoided mention of the quarrels and ultimate separation between her parents by advancing her mother's death by about three years, rehabilitated Adam as a good father, and eliminated the experience of being farmed out, along with her brothers, to relatives. These dissimulations were innocent and irrelevant to the case, but they were in her character; she had not yet realized that, if there were ever a time to tell the whole truth, it was now.

On March 30, 1895, she said, she had "been engaged to" Rudolf MacLeod, whom she had married on July 11. This implied that the match had been arranged by her father, instead of her own responsibility, thus delivering her from blame for the union's failure. What was virtually an elopement with a rake by a headstrong and unconventional teenager became a marital tie imposed by a conservative Dutch burgher on an innocent. Even the short six-week space between engagement and marriage had been stretched to a more respectable four months. It was another harmless and irrelevant tinkering with the truth that demonstrates how unprepared she was for the ordeal ahead. Throughout the interrogations, there are similarly "Suzy Wong" attempts by the famous courtesan to cloak herself in respectability.

She said her son was poisoned "by the wife of a native soldier" in the Indies and that the poison was intended for her husband and herself as well, which seems to make the crime more plausible.

She had left her husband in 1904 because of his drinking. She thus left out the real separation the previous year and the 1903 trip to Paris. She said she had done some modeling (which was actually in 1903), then turned to dancing.

She had herself dancing at the Kursaal in Madrid in 1904 and in Monte Carlo in February 1905. This implies earlier success than the reality, but she may have merely transposed 1904 for 1905 and 1905 for 1906 because of her faulty memory. She said she met Kiepert in Monte Carlo and went to live with him for "three years" in Berlin. This, of course, implies a much more stable and enduring relationship than the reality—an on-and-off affair over eighteen months. She said correctly that she was in Vienna from December 1906 to January 1907. She admitted that Kiepert's family had disapproved of his maintaining a foreign mistress and that he had finally paid her off with 300,000 marks.

This, we can recall, had taken place at the end of 1907. She said she returned to Paris and became the mistress of the banker Rousseau (whom she did not actually meet until 1910). She said Rousseau was now "presumably dead." Whether she said this in order that he should not be bothered or because she believed it to be true, we cannot tell. Although Rousseau was in fact alive—in 1917, he was only forty-three—his "death" was never questioned by the military investigation. Rousseau, she went on, had gone bankrupt, and she had "returned to the theater" in 1912. She thus extended her liaison with Rousseau from about two years to five.

In January 1914, she continued, she had gone to Milan, where the Duke of Visconti, the "owner of the Scala," had suggested that she dance in Berlin. This had led to the contract at the Metropol to dance there for 48,000 marks "until September 15." In reality, it was for two engagements of two weeks each, spread over a five-month period.

She had had lovers in Berlin in 1914, the most permanent one being a married Frenchman, Constant Bezet, whom she described as the director of the *Caisse de Banques et de Depôts* (Fund of Banks and Deposits). This is an odd title for a private banking institution; another witness was to tell the investigation that Bezet was actually the director of the German subsidiary of the big French bank Société Générale.

She said she had briefly renewed contact with Kiepert, who had visited her but had said he could no longer be seen with her in public because of his family. Mrs. Kiepert is usually described by writers as a beautiful Hungarian, but Mata Hari says she was in fact Austrian. Kiepert had told his mistress that it would be easier for the two of them to associate again when he was in Paris, where he would soon see her. She said she had pointed out that her Metropol engagement would keep her in Berlin until September, but she said Kiepert had responded: "You'll be in Paris sooner, and so will I."

She had at once written to Colonel Messimy, a former lover who was then the French minister of war, to pass on this apparent revelation of German invasion plans. (She referred to him, of course, as "de Messimy" and later as the "Marquis de Messimy.") She had suggested (rather naïvely) that Messimy come to Berlin to investigate the situation. Messimy had responded, thanking her for passing on Kiepert's menacing remark but saying that his cabinet post precluded him from dropping in on Berlin just like that.

In May or June 1914, she said, she had become the mistress of a German naval officer called Captain-Lieutenant Renitzer, who was the commander of the seaplane base at "Putsig" (Sergeant Baudouin's spelling; this must be the Baltic naval base at Putzig. The German archives give the officer's name as Paul Kuntze. Since, apart from ennobling them, Mata Hari was unlikely to misremember the names of her lovers, this is presumably Baudouin's mistake as well.) Like Kiepert, the naval commander had prophesied that he would soon be in Paris, so she had passed on this information by letter to Henri Capférer (Sergeant Baudouin's spelling), whom she described as the pilot who had "flown over Paris." This man—actually Henry Rapférer, of whom more later—had not replied. (Rapférer was the president of the Astra company, which built airships, or zeppelins.)

The Austrian attack on Serbia had taken place (on July 28) and she had had her dinner "late in July" with Griebl in a private room at a restaurant. According to the transcript, Mata Hari described Griebl as "chief of police," thus perhaps making herself responsible for the subsequent French official confusion between Griebl and his superior, Traugott von Jagow.

This was the time when the German police "treated all foreigners like animals," when she had been arrested in the streets "several times," when she had tried to break her theatrical contract to get home to Paris, when the dressmaker had seized her furs and jewelry to collect his debt, and when the bank had frozen her account. "I was told that because I had lived in France for about ten years, I would be treated as French," she told Bouchardon. The property of all enemy nationals had been seized.

Griebl had offered what help he could, and she had set off for France via Switzerland "around August 6." She had been held up at the border, but the train, including the baggage car with her luggage, had gone on to Basle. She had returned to Berlin on the seventh and been blocked in Germany, she said, until the seventeenth (actually the fifteenth).

She explained that, on her return to Holland, she had thought of "the Baron Colonel van der Capellen of the 2nd Hussars" as a possible protector almost at once, but that he was not the man to approach in shabby clothes and exhausted; so she had reconstituted her wardrobe while she was the mistress of the banker van der Schalk, who had believed her to be Russian and had thought at first that he was "showing her Holland." When he had discovered her true identity, he had sent a lawyer to Berlin to recuperate the funds in her bank account and her jewelry.

After leaving van der Schalk for van der Capellen, she had written to the Maple warehouse at 29 rue de la Jonquière in Paris to ask them to send ten large wooden crates of silverware, linen, and saddlery. She had received a response asking for back payments on the rented space. It had been van der Capellen who had suggested that she go to Paris and handle the Maple people in person.

She recalled the visit to Paris as "May 1915"—apparently confusing the date with the May 1916 trip. She said she stayed in Paris for "three months"—it was actually closer to three weeks. Presumably, under the long questioning, she was getting tired and, perhaps, irritable.

She recounted her meeting with the Marquis de Beaufort, who was staying, as she was, at the Grand Hôtel, and whose mistress she had become. She had wanted to return home to Holland via England, the way she had come, but because of troop movements this route was closed. The Dutch consul had recommended that she travel via Spain, which she had done—bringing her precious crates with her.

The interrogation had gone on for several hours; Sergeant Baudouin must have been getting writer's cramp. Bouchardon called a halt, and she was returned to prison.

A few days later, she was moved from her padded redoubt to an ordinary cell in another building at Saint-Lazare, known to prisoners as the Animal House (*la Ménagerie*). This stood at the corner of the rue du Faubourg Saint-Denis and the boulevard Magenta; the building no longer exists. She was eventually to write scores of letters to Bouchardon in her huge, proud handwriting, and the early ones were full of complaints about the dreadful food and foul wine served up by Sister Auréa, the prison cook, and the general filth of prison conditions. She protested the refusal to supply her with the clean changes of clothing and the toiletries that she had left at the hotel; she appealed for her laundry to be delivered from the Elysée-Palace, along with her blue leather bedroom slippers. Ever mindful of the minutiae of her existence, she also asked that a coat under repair be collected from a dressmaker's, and a boa feather from a cleaner's. Eventually, if belatedly, all these simple requests were to be attended to, but her most poignant appeal—to be able to write to Masloff—was turned down. Her arrest was a secret.

Bizard recounts that she was a "well-behaved" prisoner; contrary to what has been said in most books on Mata Hari, which are highly fictionalized, she made no special requests. Unlike other prisoners, she rarely complained of the bitter cold that winter. At first she was not allowed out of the cell except to visit the vile toilet down the corridor; but in time Bizard obtained permission for her to take about fifteen minutes of exercise each day, as the other prisoners did; she had to take hers alone, however. Perhaps, since she was accused of being a German spy, this was for her own protection from other inmates. Her only occasional companions were the two nuns who brought her food and a small bowl to wash in; but there were brief calls by Bizard, his assistant Jean Bralez, Pastor Jules Arboux, and the prison's Catholic chaplain, Father Dommergue, as well as an almost daily visit from her lawyer, Clunet.

The seventy-four-year-old attorney was singularly unsuited to defend a criminal case in court, especially in a military court. He was regarded as France's greatest expert on international corporate laws and published an authoritative newsletter on the subject, known familiarly to lawyers as "the Clunet." But he had not pleaded in court for years. She had chosen him because he was still be-musedly in love with her and had been her regular attorney for eleven years.

On February 10, just before her arrest, an unsigned report was made, which appears in the files. It was from the ministry of war to the military governor of Paris, for the attention of the staff headquarters (*état-major*) of the army, Fifth Bureau. This was the bureau dealing with military justice.

The document—number 1 of the 437 pieces of the Mata Hari dossier—summarizes briefly the reasons why someone (Ladoux? Goubet?) was asking for her arrest.

It says "Zelle is strongly suspected of being an agent in the service of Germany." This statement of mere suspicion is bizarrely followed by a statement of fact: that she "belongs to the Cologne intelligence center, where she is listed under the designation of H 21." If this was so, why was she only a suspect?

It says Zelle had made two wartime visits to France (actually, the present one was her third) and that she had "offered" to work for the French. It says she was "turned back" by the British on her way to Holland and that she had been in contact with the military attachés of both France and Germany in Madrid.

There, she had passed on information to the German military attaché that was sent to staff headquarters in Berlin.

A "secret document emanating from the German military at-taché shows that she received, in Paris, 5,000 francs from the German intelligence service." The military governor—and Bou-chardon, the ultimate recipient—are not told what the document is. There is no mention of intercepts, with their implication of code-breaking.

The money, the report says, had come through the Dutch consul-general in Paris, who had received it from "the German consul in Amsterdam." She had picked it up on January 16, 1917. A receipt for the money, signed by "G. Bunge, Dutch Consul," had been given to the Comptoir National d'Escompte de Paris, 2 place de l'Opéra. (Bunge's initial seems to be a typical French mistake with

a foreign name: had the author of the memo consulted the diplomatic list, he would have seen that the acting Dutch consul-
general was Otto David Eduard Bunge.)

There is no explanation of why someone who belongs to the
"Cologne intelligence center" was sending information to Berlin.
This memo, however, appears to be the basis upon which Bou-
chardon was expected to construct a case.

Six days passed before Bouchardon recalled Mata Hari to the
quai de l'Horloge. After a week out of contact with the world, a
prisoner is no longer so confident or self-assertive, and is therefore
more pliable. Bouchardon, in any event, was noted for his bullying
style and his nervous habit of constantly standing up and pacing
his tiny, eight-foot-wide office.

Stiffly, he invited her to sit down. She must have found his
fireplace a welcome sight, but he would recall later that she told
him that she found his manners irritating: as usual, he was tapping
a pencil on his table, peering at his fingernails, and biting them to
make them match.

In this February 21 "interrogatory," Bouchardon began by drawing
her out about the reasons for her 1916 trip to Paris. She now
corrected the date of the earlier, 1915 visit from May to December.
She talked of her life in The Hague, where she said she had a
comfortable (*jolie*) situation; but van der Capellen was mostly at
the frontier with his unit, leaving her bored. She had needed new
clothes. Beaufort, she said, had invited her to Paris.

She told the story, already recounted in this book, of the trip to
Vigo aboard the *Zeelandia* and her misadventures with the supposed
British agent Hoedemaker. She recalled her problems at the border
post at Hendaye and her interrogation there by "three gentlemen,"
her days with Beaufort, and her early frequentation of Vadim and
his fellow Russian, Gasfield, in Mrs. Dangeville's salon. Vadim, she
said, had come to Paris "often" after Beaufort had left. She recounted her problems in getting to Vittel to see him, and how her
old friend Jean Hallaure, now a lieutenant of dragoons, had arranged for her to visit 282 boulevard Saint-Germain. This explained
how she had met Ladoux, who had asked her to spy for France.
She digressed about her time in Spain and her friendship there
with the court chamberlain, Diego de Leon.

Bouchardon brought her back to her talk with Ladoux. She recalled his asking her about Capellen's sympathies and the discussion of the baron's card with its mention "Marguérite, you who love France so much. . . . " She recounted Ladoux's joking request that she not strike up relationships with French officers in Vittel, and her promise not to do so because "I know a Russian with whom I am too much in love."

The third major interrogation—her fourth *comparution*, or appearance—was two days later, on February 23. Bouchardon, tapping his pencil, marching up and down in the confined space, chewing his nails, seems deliberately to have moved around in areas of questioning to confuse his victim.

First they discussed her initial meeting with Kalle, who had remarked on her Dutch identity because of the *Vrouwe* (Mrs.) on her calling card. But soon Bouchardon was back to her meeting with Ladoux before her trip to Vittel.

Here, as often happened, she confused events and their times. She told Bouchardon that she had gone straight from Ladoux's office to Marguérie's at the Quai d'Orsay to discuss with him whether she should accept the request to spy for France. The *filature* record—which Bouchardon of course had—showed the foreign ministry call as coming later and that, after seeing Ladoux, she had in fact gone to the police for her *carnet* for Vittel. She said she had told Marguérie that she did not think Ladoux fully understood the value of the services that she could render.

She told Bouchardon that, after discussing things with Marguérie, she had returned to Ladoux the next day and said: "Captain, in principle, I accept." To which Ladoux had replied: "Let's chat a bit. Can you go to Germany and Belgium? Have you a plan?"

This account obviously telescoped time, but she did recall telling Ladoux that she wanted to go to Vittel first, where only two weeks remained of the season. At that discussion—there seems no reason to disbelieve Ladoux on this—she had not yet accepted his assignment.

She talked of Vadim's wounds, his possible total blindness, her acceptance of his marriage proposal, of her life "clearly traced out"—the Ladoux mission in Belgium, the generous payment for her services, the moving of her furniture from The Hague to Paris, then marriage to the youth of her dreams. "I would be the happiest woman on earth," she told Bouchardon.

She recounted her later discussion with Ladoux of how she would get to Wurfbein and von Bissing, of her asking for a million francs, of Ladoux's saying that they had once paid two and a half millions to an agent. She recalled the discussion as to whether she had ever been to Antwerp. She said Ladoux had offered her a choice between missions in Belgium and Germany, but had said that Belgium would interest his service more.

The next interrogation was the following day, February 24. She recalled how she had written to Ladoux for an advance of funds to buy clothes "to impress von Bissing" and to furnish her Paris apartment for her return, so that she could entertain Vadim in her home. She told Bouchardon she had regretted not having asked about an advance earlier, but Ladoux had told her he had been ordered not to give her any money until she had proved her skills. She recalled that he had said: "You'll have your million, don't worry."

Ladoux had asked her if she would write from Brussels with invisible ink, and she had turned that process down as "trickery." She recalled Ladoux's orders to her to wait in The Hague for "about two weeks," until someone would come to her with instructions. She recalled also how Ladoux had asked her if she was not a German spy known as AF 44.

Maunoury, at the "Prefecture" (she means the commissariat in the rue Taitbout) had suggested that traveling through Switzerland and Germany would be quicker than going through Spain; but, like Ladoux, she had preferred the Iberian route, she said.

Bouchardon then took her through the trip to Hendaye on November 6 and Vigo on November 9, the misadventure at Falmouth, and her captivity at Scotland Yard.

She described the four days of interrogations by "three gentlemen in uniform" who had used a Belgian man to interpret to and from Dutch. The interpreter, she said, had "visibly detested the people of my country." He had spoken Dutch "like a filthy Fleming" and had had "the audacity to tell those three gentlemen that I had a German accent."

On the fourth day, she told Bouchardon, the three English *mes-*

sieurs had said that "We now know that you are not Clara Benedix" but that they were refusing permission to all Dutch citizens coming up the Channel to proceed to Holland. She had left Liverpool on December 1 and arrived in Vigo on December 6.

Her sixth *comparution* and fifth interrogation was on February 28. She described her time in Vigo, Cazeaux's prospection of her as a potential spy for Russia, and her arrival in Madrid, where she had met Diego de Leon and, through him, Senator Junoy. She talked of her lunch and dinner with "de With" and the other Dutch consul in the Spanish capital. She described in great detail her meetings with Kalle and Denvignes, recalling how the latter had said: "I never saw anything so harmonious as your entry into the Palace Hotel yesterday." She talked of Denvignes' flirtation, the discussion with him about her first meeting with Kalle, his sending her back to the German attaché for more information about the submarine landings, the business with the violets and the ribbon from her *cache-corset*, and her last encounter with Kalle after Denvignes had left for Paris.

At her next interrogation, on March 1, she described her receiving of the Junoy letter, her problems with Denvignes on her arrival in France, and Denvignes' assurance, on the station platform, that Goubet had found her submarine information interesting.

She gave a few more precisions about her efforts to collar Denvignes before he returned to Madrid. She talked of writing a note in the conductor's office at the Orsay station, as the train was about to pull out, telling the colonel she was expecting him to meet her at the Austerlitz stop, of buying a ticket for a suburban station to get onto the platform there, and of sending a conductor through the train in search of the "French military attaché in Madrid."

She recalled the problems with the evasive Ladoux, discussing her letter to him with Clunet, later discussing with Maunoury whether his earlier suggestion of going through Switzerland to reach Holland might not make more sense, and asking Maunoury to suggest this to Ladoux. In Switzerland, she said, she had reasoned that she could get a German attaché to talk by seducing him, as she had done with Kalle.

She confirmed that the five thousand francs from Holland had been sent by the Baron van der Capellen. She noted that she had received a letter from the baron saying that he had sent the money but could not keep up the house if she did not return soon. There had also been a confirming letter from Anna about the money and telling her that "the Baron misses you."

Bouchardon showed her some copies of the letters she had received from the baron and from Anna, with those from the baron being in French. She agreed that they were accurate copies. In the files, the baron's read like the sort of missives a mature man would write to his absent "kitten."

Also in the dossier is a telegram from Anna, which apparently arrived after her arrest, asking if Madame had received the money sent to her at the Paris bank.

Around this time, Bouchardon, relying partly on Mata Hari and partly on other resources, inserted into the record a brief biography of the prisoner, starting from her "first arrival" in Paris in "1904." He says she had first stayed at a *pension de famille* at 91 rue Lecourbe, then in a furnished hotel at 7 rue Nouvelle, where she had paid 150 francs a month for board and lodging.

This information was presumably gleaned from the *Service des garnis* of the Paris police. Actually, she must have paid for food and lodging at the *pension*, not the hotel, since the sort of modest hotel at which she stayed in the rue Nouvelle would not have served meals; and all this, of course, refers to her 1903 visit, not to the second arrival the following year. (She herself had given a wrong date at her first "interrogatory.")

Bouchardon says she posed for painters and also used her body for less moral purposes (*s'est lancée dans la galanterie*). He is now running 1903 and 1904 together. Under questioning, he continues, she had explained that she had been forced to sell herself to men because she had "debt problems with a jeweler." This sounds like Mata Hari excusing her fall from grace by the sort of lifestyle problem she could only indulge much later.

He sums up her career with almost comic concision by saying she danced at the Musée Guimet in 1905 and "later" at the Folies-Bergère, and appeared in private salons. She had had "several addresses in Paris and Berlin."

She had met "the banker Rousseau" in "1909." (He is one year out, but two years closer to accuracy than Mata Hari's own account.) Bouchardon omits her life as a chatelaine in the countryside and says Rousseau had given her a "private mansion" at 11 rue Windsor, where the annual rent was 5,500 francs. Rousseau had been unable to keep up this expense and the couple had parted "at the end of 1913 or early in 1914." It was actually, of course, early in 1912. The errors are of no consequence in the case, but they illustrate the general carelessness about fact in the investigation.

Bouchardon notes, no doubt correctly, that she had left Neuilly for Berlin without paying several bills. We learn that Rousseau was sentenced on July 1, 1914, to a year's imprisonment and a five-hundred-franc fine for a confidence trick. (Here as elsewhere, there seems no evidence that Rousseau actually served time: most French first offenders, especially for white-collar crime, receive suspended sentences, which they serve only if reconvicted later for another offense.)

Bouchardon had, it seemed, questioned her about her life as a courtesan, and she apparently admitted that she had entertained men at 5 rue de Galilée, 86 avénue Kléber, and 14 rue Lord-Byron—all high-class *maisons closes* with a staff of ladies of easy virtue, and which rented rooms to the escorts of part-timers like Mata Hari. She had primly said she had done this to "pay off jewelry and other debts." Curiously, none of this appears in Sergeant Baudouin's transcript of the interrogation about her early biography.

The Bouchardon version of this then jumps to her first wartime return to Paris in 1915 and her stay at the Grand Hôtel until "January 7, 1916" (actually January 4), when she had left for Spain and Holland. He says she had returned again in "July, 1916." Actually she had returned on June 16.

We learn that she had agreed to pay an annual rent of three thousand francs for the apartment at 33 avenue Henri-Martin but had never furnished or lived in it.

For some reason, Bouchardon throws in a police informer's anecdote. Since her arrest, he says, the hotel manicurist has reported that Mata Hari had told her that the battle of Verdun had cost one hundred thousand French lives; she had said that the

Dutch lady had blamed this on inadequate support from the British and the Belgians, whom she seemed to "hate."

This insertion in the files ends by noting her arrest at the Elysée-Palace hotel, the address of which is now given as 39 rue Bassano.

On March 6, 1917, the Eiffel Tower picked up a radio message to Madrid from Berlin, but signed "Antwerp." It asked Kalle if "H 21" had been informed that she should use invisible ink and should return to Holland via Switzerland (by implication, through Germany). This message differed from the rest of the traffic of the day in being, once again, in the broken code.

On March 8, once again using the redundant cipher, Kalle replied:

> A response has already been sent to Berlin's 3B of December 25, 1916, noting that H 21 has already left, and that in consequence one cannot make the communication in question to her.

This exchange must have confirmed for Ladoux that the whole Kalle traffic was *intoxication*; but it must also have put Bouchardon, when he was finally informed about the messages—without knowing about the use of a redundant code—in a quandary. If Mata Hari had actually been working for the Germans, there was no way that Berlin would not have known at least the Paris hotel gossip that she had been arrested. Why would they be seeking to contact her in Madrid two months after her departure from there?

Possessed as we are of more knowledge than Bouchardon had, we can similarly ask the reason for the exchange. It could only have been either because her arrest had not appeared in the press and the Germans were still trying to prod the French (by using the code they knew was broken) into going after her, or because—more believably—they knew of the arrest and were seeking to "load" the case against her. Kalle's answer to Berlin made perfect sense, of course, since it served to remind the French that "H 21" was in Paris where, had they not arrested her already, it was time to do so. Most probably, the exchange had two purposes: to "load" the case and to try to "intoxicate" the French into believing that the Germans were so inefficient that they did not know of the arrest of "their" spy.

However, for the moment, none of this *intoxication* traffic had been made known to Bouchardon, obviously partly because it could not be used unless Bouchardon could present it as not being *intoxication* at all—which would be easiest if he himself were never told about the use of the redundant code.

By March 5, Mata Hari had been in the rat-infested prison for three weeks. Her lawyer, Edouard Clunet, penned a letter to Bouchardon in his neat and almost childish script, asking for provisional liberty for his client or, at the very least, her hospitalization.

"There is an accident to be feared," he wrote.

Two days later, Dr. Bizard reported that she was "crying all the time," suffering from headaches. He noted pedantically that her "nervousness is very accentuated." That day, Clunet, in hospital himself following an accident, wrote to Bouchardon again to complain that she was still confined.

Sometime that week, Mata Hari herself wrote to the captain in her broad sweeping hand:

> You have made me suffer too much. I am completely mad. I beg of you, put an end to this. I am a woman. I cannot support [what is] above my strength.

But Bouchardon knew from experience in Rouen and Paris that even the innocent will often confess if held in prison long enough. Habeas corpus barely exists in France, where even today an accused may often languish in confinement for two or three years awaiting trial, even in simple cases.

On March 9, she wrote to him saying that she was too sick to appear that day. Her eighth appearance and seventh interrogation took place instead on March 12, when she was examined about the identities of the visiting cards found in her purse.

By the sixteenth, Clunet was out of hospital and able to visit his client again. He wrote to Bouchardon that she was "spitting blood." This is, however, the only reference in the files to a drastic medical condition, and one senses a little Mata Hari hyperbole. Perhaps, since she persistently had dental problems, her gums were bleeding.

Dr. Socquet, the military physician, examined her and apparently found that, however tortured her mind might be, her robust Frisian peasant body was in good order. On March 21, he refused to recommend hospitalization. Clunet asked for a second opinion by a civilian doctor and renewed the request again on the twenty-sixth, but to no avail.

The next interrogation did not take place until a month later, on April 12. Bouchardon began it by asking her: "When you came to 282 boulevard Saint-Germain to offer your services, did you belong to German espionage?"

She answered: "No, I went there to get permission to visit Vittel."

He asked again for a list of her lovers in Berlin. Then he asked why she had dealt with Kalle in Madrid. She said that since she had failed to reach Holland, she was still awaiting instructions and doing the best she could. She said she had concealed from Kalle the fact that she had a Russian lover, since this would have given away the fact that her claim to be pro-German was a pretense.

Had she given Kalle any military or diplomatic information? Bouchardon asked. She said she had not. The interrogation ended with him asking her to describe the uses of the contents of her toiletry kit—the medicines, the hair pommade, the skin potions. These cosmetics included powder for "lightening skin" and a Javanese perfume for "throwing on the fire" (incense?). The following day, everything in the toiletry bag was to be returned to her except for two products held for testing as possible invisible inks.

She asked to be released, pointing out that she could not leave the country and would obviously be under constant surveillance. Bouchardon said he wanted to question her further first. In fact, she was never to see freedom again.

That month, Mata Hari began a long series of letters to Bouchardon, explaining over and over again what had happened in Madrid.

She had, she recalled in a letter of April 13, given five pieces of information to Denvignes, saying to him "I tell you this as it was told to me," and recommending that he verify the facts. Although Kalle had spoken of having seen her at the Silesian maneuvers and at the Carlton Hotel in Berlin, she had not consciously known who he was when she had found his name in the hotel copy of the Madrid diplomatic list.

For Bouchardon to accuse her of pro-German sympathies was absurd, she noted. At the outbreak of war, the Germans had seized her furs, worth "sixty thousand to eighty thousand francs." To her, that was a good enough reason to hate *les Boches*; to the reader, it is certainly an indication that she was under no official protection in Germany, as she would have been if she had been their agent. Although a neutral Dutch citizen, she had been treated as a French resident and therefore as an enemy. She pointed out that it was only with the help of the Dutch legation and a lawyer (supplied by van der Schalk) that she had been able to recover some of her property after leaving the country. She had had no desire to travel to Holland via Germany, she insisted, before being turned back by Britain; only Ladoux and Maunoury had suggested that as a possible route.

The following day, the faithful Clunet was at the prison again to pick up another letter for Bouchardon. In it, she assured the captain that she knew nothing about the war beyond what she read in the papers. She had given no intelligence to the Germans because she knew nothing to give. She recalled that she had, however, given two pieces of intelligence about the Germans to Ladoux by mail and three to Denvignes in person.

Later the same day, mulling over Bouchardon's questions of two months before, she wrote to the captain again to stress that all her affairs with Germans dated from before the war. She had had no contact with Germany since leaving Berlin in August 1914. If some of her information from Kalle had proven to be inaccurate, she had simply passed it on "as it was told to me," she said again.

From Bouchardon, there was only silence. He knew that if there was anything for her to confess, keeping her locked up in frustration was the best way to persuade her to talk. If there was nothing, as seemed more and more likely to be the case, leaving her in captivity would do no harm to France.

On the sixteenth, she was writing again:

> I beg of you, stop making me suffer in this prison. I am so weakened by this system and the cell is driving me mad. I have not done any espionage in France, and there is nothing bad in my luggage, in my [toiletry] bottles or my strongbox.
>
> Let me have provisional liberty. Don't torture me here.

The next day, she was back to her pen and inkpot again. The handwriting, throughout this long monologue by correspondence, remains racy and proud, even domineering, with the usual generous spaces between the letters and the words and the strange absence of sensuality—almost no downstrokes below where the lines would be on lined paper. One is tempted, since one knows who the author is, to say that this is the unromantic calligraphy of a courtesan, who closes her eyes and her mind as she opens her legs; but above all, it is clearly the handwriting taught at a "school for young ladies." All over Europe, there were and are private schools that teach a distinctive script, always recognizable anywhere in alumni and alumnae. It is also the writing of a gushing, extrovertive woman (her own word for her character was "spontaneous") but nonetheless one with a secretive, nonsharing nature: the downward and upward strokes of her letter *v*, for instance, overlap and retrace each other, making her *v* like a printed lowercase *r*. For someone enduring such a Kafkaesque experience, and clearly at her wit's end, it is also astonishing how calm and undemented she becomes when she sits down to write, despite her passionate appeals.

This time she asks him plaintively: "Why are you turning my Madrid visit against me?" Had she not worked for France there? To get the sort of information that Ladoux wanted, "it was obviously necessary to address oneself to a German." Had not her conduct in Paris and Vittel been "impeccable"?

By now Clunet, who visited her almost daily, had a fairly clear picture of what she had been asked and how she had responded, even though she had not been allowed to be assisted by counsel during any of the interrogations. Clunet also knew the contents of her letters to Bouchardon, for which he was the mailman. On April 23, Clunet wrote to the captain, asking him to expedite the pretrial process. Clunet noted that two months had passed and that "no proof has been furnished against her to support this indictment."

Clunet was her only contact with a saner world. She was forbidden to write to friends, including Masloff; even Clunet was not allowed, under wartime security laws, to contact the young Russian on her behalf. Bouchardon wanted his investigators to get to him first.

On April 28, Mata Hari wrote solicitously to the lawyer-captain, complaining that the questioning of Masloff in connection with her case could hurt his military career, while forbidding Clunet to make contact with him would mean that Vadim might not know why she had not written.

"He does not deserve to suffer on my account in any way," she said.

Bouchardon was biding his time. He had not even questioned Denvignes. At this point, Mata Hari herself had apparently said nothing self-incriminating. When Clunet met Bouchardon in his office one day, the magistrate chewed his fingernails with irritation and admitted to the prisoner's counsel that "the pretrial is marking time" (*l'instruction piétine*).

On the twenty-ninth, convinced that the only thing that would get her out of prison would be a trial, Mata Hari wrote to Bouchardon insisting that Denvignes and Hallaure be called upon to testify. The latter would confirm that she had only gone to Ladoux's office at all at his suggestion; Denvignes could testify that she had brought him the news that the Germans had broken the French radio code, that the Germans knew the French were landing spies behind their lines from aircraft, that German agents could carry invisible ink crystals under their nails, and so on.

However, by then, Ladoux had decided to give the investigation a push. He would reveal the Madrid-Berlin messages to Bouchardon but leave out all mention of the use of a redundant code, thereby labeling them as meant to be taken seriously in Berlin.

7. The Pretrial— 2: Gilding the Evidence

ON APRIL 21, Ladoux had sent a report to Lieutenant-General Dubail, the military governor of Paris, revealing the existence of "fourteen messages" between Kalle and Berlin. The summaries given to Dubail by Ladoux corresponded to what was then inserted—typed this time—into the dossier. The Second Bureau did not explain—to the general who had been asked to order Mata Hari's arrest—why it had been sitting on this traffic for over three months.

Around the same time, Ladoux wrote directly to Bouchardon with his blockbuster offering. His memo to the lawyer-captain began in a deceptively historical way. Ladoux detailed the long barren months of surveillance and noted "numerous indications of the indiscreet curiosity of Mata Hari, but no proof that she belonged to the German intelligence service."

On the question of "proof," he went on: "It was necessary, for that, to make her trust us again [*la remettre en confiance*] and to offer her a mission for the French."

Ladoux thus made the Belgian mission not a test of her skills as an amateur spy, as he admitted in his memoirs that it had been—and for which he could have been held remiss in the light of her arrest as an enemy agent—but solely and exclusively as part of a trap. He was, he implied, simply giving her enough rope to hang herself. He did not say how this would have been done if the subject had known she was under surveillance at all times, or what could have been done about it if the British suspicions were realized but she remained abroad.

He agreed that he discussed her surveillance in France with her and that Mata Hari had expressed irritation about it. He ignored the point that, had she been a German agent, the long surveillance would have clearly informed her that she was "surfaced"—or "burned," as the French said then. He said he tried to "diminish" any fears that she might have felt because of the surveillance.

The "mission," he said, was coordinated with the British, which would imply that it had always been Ladoux's intention that she end up in Spain, "where she was in fact brought." Thomson, however, insists in his own memoirs that there was no coordination until after he had telegraphed Ladoux with her assertions that she worked for French intelligence.

Ladoux noted that she left Vigo for Holland on the ship "without making contact with the German services in Madrid." (She had, of course, no reason to do so, since her mission was Belgium, not Spain. She only went to the Germans in Madrid, in the way Ladoux had authorized her to do in Belgium, after the British experience—which emphasized how much surveillance she was under, and the fact that she could probably not do anything without Ladoux knowing of it.)

Ladoux's report then referred dramatically to the enclosure of "nine" intercepted messages (as compared to fourteen in his memo to the general) between Madrid and Berlin. He gave a brief description of what Bouchardon would find when he read each of the enclosures.

These "enclosures," however, except for the first, are not in the files—either addended to Ladoux's memo or anywhere else—and the descriptions in Ladoux's memo *do not conform to the "Eiffel Tower" messages which actually are in the dossier*. (These were related on pages 139–41.) Nor are they identical with the larger number sent to Dubail, which are in the files.

Ladoux noted that the originals were in "the German cipher" and that therefore, "in passing these documents to the pretrial phase [*à l'instruction*], I draw your attention to their importance and to the grave inconveniences which their divulgation would present for the National Defense." He asked that the military court be instructed accordingly and that its hearings be *in camera*. He thus already appeared confident that there would be a trial.

The German message listed as first in the "Eiffel Tower" originals is the one of December 13, 1916, about the Franco-Greek princess, Briand, and British "control" of France. In Ladoux's memo, the first is said to be a "radio telegram from Kalle to Berlin, dated

December 31, 1916." There is no message of such a date in the files. This is the first indication of a fabrication.

As Ladoux tells Bouchardon, this was how it began:

> The Agent H 21 of the intelligence centralization sector of Cologne, sent in March for the second time in France, has arrived here.

What have we here? The head of French counterespionage should have remembered that Mata Hari's second trip to Paris during the war had taken place in May 1916, not in March. Was this a mistake of Kalle's, taken from one of the later "missing" messages in the sequence—a mistake that Ladoux was making his own, without checking, since he had claimed in an earlier memo to Bouchardon that the Second Bureau knew that Mata Hari was H 21? Or was it pure fabrication? Everything points to fabrication: why would Kalle, having identified an agent by code number, jeopardize the anonymity this was meant to confer by going into extraneous details about which "centralization" sector in Germany controlled the agent, the number of past assignments and where they were, when Berlin would know all this from the code number? Ladoux's version for Bouchardon of the "first Kalle message" goes on:

> She pretended to accept offers by the French intelligence service and to undertake two trial trips to Belgium for this service.

Two? He continues:

> She wished, with the assent of the French service, to go from Spain to Holland aboard the *Hollandia*, offering to take advantage of this trip to renew contact [*renouer des intelligences*] with the Cologne center.

There had never, of course, been mention of the "Cologne center." Why would the Germans control intelligence in Belgium, her assignment, from Cologne and not from Antwerp, a Belgian city? Clearly, Ladoux, apparently believing that "H" meant Cologne, sought to pretend not only greater knowledge than he had, both in January 1917 and in the previous year, but knowledge of something quite wrong. His version of Kalle's message goes on:

> Although in possession of French papers, she was arrested at Falmouth on November 11, because she was erroneously thought

to be a German woman whom I know about and who is in Madrid; when the British recognized their error, she was sent back to Spain because the British persisted in thinking her suspect.

Ladoux thus makes Kalle make Mata Hari make Thomson responsible for sending her back to Spain, although Thomson says this was on Ladoux's instructions. He also makes Kalle take a superfluous risk with the cover of Clara Benedix. The "Kalle" message continues:

> She now intends to go to Holland via Paris and Switzerland.
> She has furnished very complete reports on the enclosed subjects,
> by letters and by telegrams.

Leaving aside the bizarre suggestion that a radiogram can enclose letters and telegrams—this is presumably just a badly written sentence—the reference to her Madrid reports to Kalle are incriminatingly flattering. The message concludes:

> She received 5,000 francs in Paris in November and is now
> asking for 10,000.
> Please give me instructions rapidly.

Why the five thousand francs that she was awaiting from the Dutch baron had become ten thousand is not clear; perhaps it was a genuine error on Ladoux's part.

Ladoux's second enclosure to Boucardon is described as another Kalle message "containing information brought in by Zelle." No date is given, but this would have to have been after December 31. The only true Kalle message in the "Eiffel Tower" files containing "information brought in by Zelle" is that of December 13. According to these files, by December 28 Kalle was telling Berlin that "H 21" would be in Paris "tomorrow." On December 29, he sent a reply to a Berlin message saying that "Agent H 21 has already left." The only message in the files after that is Berlin's of January 5, 1917, querying a detail in her report about the Greek princess and Briand. The message listed as second in the "Eiffel Tower" files is Kalle's request of December 20 for a response to his message of December 13.

This would seem to invalidate the possibility that Ladoux transposed two digits accidentally and wrote "December 31" instead of

"December 13." The report is handwritten, not typed, making such errors unlikely in any event.

Ladoux describes his third enclosure for Bouchardon as containing more information based on Kalle's talk with "H 21," while the fourth enclosure is described as a "response from the 3rd Bureau of German staff headquarters." In the files, the "real" third and fourth messages are missing, as is indicated by a break in the archival file numbering system.

Ladoux describes his fifth enclosure as a follow-up to an earlier message. In the original file, the fifth is Kalle's message querying an error, which would fit Ladoux's description. Ladoux says his sixth enclosure is a query from Kalle about the fourth. This could also be a fitting description for the fifth message in the files, but not for the sixth, which is the Berlin message instructing Kalle to give "H 21" three thousand francs, criticizing her unsatisfactory work, and giving her orders about what to do in Switzerland.

Ladoux tells Bouchardon that his seventh enclosure is a radio telegram "from Antwerp" about H 21. In the files, the seventh message is a complaint from Kalle that he has not received answers to two of his earlier messages, and is the message in which he asks that money be sent to H 21 in Paris from Amsterdam. And why, if Ladoux's reasoning is right, does the "message from Antwerp" not refer to the agent as AF 44?

Ladoux says his eighth enclosure is a message from Kalle saying he had advised H 21 that it was time to leave Spain. Since Ladoux's enclosures indicate that the intercepted traffic started on December 31, the eighth enclosure would be well into January, by which time Mata Hari was already in contact with Ladoux in Paris. In the original files, the eighth message is from Berlin to Kalle and confirms that there had in fact been an error in one of their earlier messages.

Ladoux's ninth enclosure for Bouchardon is described as a Berlin message replying to an unidentified earlier query from Kalle. In the files, the ninth is Kalle's, saying that "Agent H 21 has already left."

There is also a tenth message in the "Eiffel Tower" files, the one dated January 5: this is Berlin querying H 21's information in Kalle's message of December 13 about the Greek princess and so on. This is the only message in the original files that postdates

December 31—when Ladoux claimed the traffic concerning H 21 began—except for the two March radio telegrams, related in the previous chapter.

What does all this mean? Assuming Ladoux was sending Bouchardon a dossier of false and more incriminating messages between Kalle and Berlin, were these simply "translations," with no spurious originals in the German cipher, or were there also fabricated messages in the current German code, instead of the old one, to steer the investigation away from any question of *intoxication*? Was Bouchardon not told of the cryptographers' report, or was he Ladoux's accomplice? (There would seem to be no reason for suspecting him in this way. There would have been little point in Ladoux confiding in Bouchardon and asking a member of the bar, however enthusiastic and even maniacal a prosecutor as Bouchardon clearly was, to help in subverting justice.) And finally, how did the traffic which Kalle began on December 13 and which— except for his belief that she had left for Paris a few days earlier than was the case—corresponds to the real dates of his conversations with her get into the file? Were the messages put back into the dossier in the course of Ladoux's own later troubles (which will be explained in due course)? It would appear that when these were inserted into the files, Ladoux's own spurious "intercepts" were removed at the same time, perhaps to form part of his own dossier—but not his summary descriptions of them, nor the subsequent interrogatory in which Bouchardon apparently quotes from some of them. (Also, as noted, the first of the nine remains in the dossier—presumably bureaucratic carelessness.)

Regarding the two messages that are missing from the original "Eiffel Tower" set—and also from the longer set sent by Ladoux to General Dubail—there is a note in the files saying that their absence was discovered on January 6, 1962. An addendum to this note reads: "And on November 19, 1970, I bear witness that these items 238 and 239, which are of capital interest, have never been returned to their place."

This addendum is signed "Lt.-Col. du Chesne, head of the Old Section." *Section ancienne* refers to older, inactive military justice files.

Also in the dossier is a much more recent addendum dated

September 21, 1978. This is from Magistrate-General Le Gallois to the Army Historical Service (the conservators of the secret military justice files) enclosing a report dated from six days before.

This report notes that "Dispatch No. 9515–SCR 2/11 of April 21, 1917, from the Second Bureau to the Military Government of Paris" is a covering note that speaks of "fourteen telegrams." (These were the ones sent, typewritten, to General Dubail, which we will come to later.) The report enclosed by General Le Gallois notes that numbers 238 and 239 are missing. (These numbers are the archival *côte* or reference numbers in the historical files and do not refer to any original denumeration used by the SCR—the *Service de Centralisation des Renseignements* run by Colonel Goubet.)

Le Gallois' 1978 report points out that "C237" (*côte* 237), which is in the files, is Kalle's message of December 13, 1916, to "staff headquarters in Berlin" with information that "H 21 brought back to Holland [*sic*] from her journey to France." It notes that "C238" had contained information additional to that found in "C237" and had been dated December 14, 1916, while "C239" was a message of December 18 of that year in which the Third Bureau of the German general staff had "replied telegraphically."

The fact that "C238" and "C239" were missing had been discovered (on the above-mentioned 1962 date) by a certain Alain Presles, the report concluded.

Incidentally, another paper inserted into the file in 1962 is a copy of the response, dated November 21 of that year, from the officer-clerk, chief of deposited materials, Central Archives of Military Justice, to the late Sam Waagenaar; he was then staying at the Amstel Hotel in Amsterdam but gave a Rome address on his calling card (also filed) and described himself as "Photographer, Author and Journalist."

Waagenaar, who became interested in the case of a fellow Parisian Dutch citizen while he was employed by MGM to publicize the Greta Garbo film about Mata Hari in 1931, was told: "In application of the rules in force, I can only send to you a copy of the judgment, and it is not possible, without the authorization of the Minister of the Armies, to send you other copies of the process [*procédure*] nor indeed any full accounting of the written materials or the decision of the Paris Council of Revision."

If Waagenaar, after thirty years of efforts, had not met with this rebuff, there would have been little apparent need for the present writer or anyone else to reopen the case.

The latest insertion in the file is a letter from the minister of defense, authorizing this writer to consult the whole dossier. In keeping with the honored French tradition of mangling foreign names, the writer is referred to not as Mr. Howe, but as Mr. Russel (with one *l*).

In a deposition to Bouchardon recorded by a Sergeant Louis Guillaume, and made shortly after Bouchardon got the report from Ladoux with the "enclosures," Ladoux "authenticated" these as messages passed between Kalle and Berlin. He said these made it clear that "H 21" must be the same person whom the British arrested at Falmouth in mistake for "Clara Bénédict." He said the five thousand francs that Mata Hari received in January must have come from "Consul Krämer" and through "Anna Luitjens" (*sic*). He was obviously referring, in the first name, to Kroemer, the German honorary consul in Amsterdam.

Ladoux, apparently in response to a question from Bouchardon, said he had given Mata Hari no names of persons to make contact with in Holland but had told her that someone would get in touch with her there. This confirms Mata Hari's own statement. (Bouchardon and Massard, in their memoirs, tell a bizarrely different but probably fictitious story, as will be related later.)

Although Ladoux answered questions about the Kalle messages and said that Mata Hari and "H 21" must be the same person, he also referred to her as "AF 44" and said one of his agents believed he had seen her in Antwerp.

Apparently in answer to a question about Vittel, he said: "She was under surveillance, but there, too, no proof of her guilt could be found." In answer to some further question, he said, "She is suspect, but we have no proof." At this point, therefore, we have the sole indication on the record from Ladoux himself that the Madrid-Berlin traffic was accepted for what it was—an *intoxication*. But he could not tell Bouchardon that at this late stage.

Bouchardon then sent a memo to Colonel Goubet (presumably—it is written "Gaboulet" in the files) to ask for his evaluation of the information given by Mata Hari to the Germans, as reported in the "enhanced" Ladoux version of Kalle's first message.

Goubet responded that it was roughly true that the British were in charge, "but not of the French army."

Bouchardon asked if Kalle's information to Mata Hari that the French were landing spies behind the German lines by aircraft was correct. Goubet said it was, noting that the people landed were French, not pro-French Germans.

The magistrate said he had information that Mata Hari had spoken of plans for an Allied landing at the mouth of the Escaut River (also known by its Flemish name, the Scheldt). Is this from the "real" number-three message from Kalle, which is missing in the files? Goubet said this was a common rumor, implying that the Germans must have heard it also.

Now Bouchardon, after waiting eighteen days, decided to call Mata Hari in for another "interrogatory" on May 1. This was her tenth appearance since her arrest, and her ninth real grilling.

The questioning began by going over old ground. Even if the information that she had given to Kalle had been out of date, Bouchardon said, might it not still have been useful? He was reminding her that she was in what we would today call a catch-22 situation. She had been told to speak to the Germans but had not been authorized to "talk" to them.

Mata Hari responded that "I repeat that I went to see von Kalle because Captain Ladoux had asked for proof of my loyalty and capacities.

"Turned back to Madrid after my adventure at Falmouth, receiving no instructions, deprived of aid, I said to myself: If I just went ahead [*si je devançais les choses*], and if I made contact with the Germans, the captain would pay me when I passed through Paris.

"Take note of the fact that I did not act secretly [*en cachette*], since I wrote to Captain Ladoux. . . .

"What is more, I told everything to Colonel Denvignes."

Bouchardon then referred mysteriously to a December 14, 1916, German message—presumably Ladoux's version of one of the two missing from the files—in which he said Kalle had reported her as saying that the French knew how to develop German invisible ink and as discussing the transportation problems of French officers trying to rejoin their units after leave. She denied having discussed these subjects with Kalle.

She was asked about German knowledge of French landings behind the German lines. She pointed out that it was Kalle who had spoken of this and that she had passed the information on to Denvignes. She admitted that she had told "everyone" about Allard, the alleged British agent aboard the *Araguya*, because his identification was common gossip. She denied talking about a possible Allied landing at the mouth of the Escaut. She said this was the first time she had heard of the subject.

She said she suspected that Denvignes had passed along the information about the invisible ink crystals, about German knowledge of French aviators operating behind German lines, and about Kalle's "revelation" of the breaking of the key of the French radio code, without mentioning that he had received the information from her.

Bouchardon told her the French had discovered a developer for German invisible ink only as late as October 9, 1916, implying that any information she might have given Kalle along these lines would not be coffee-shop rumor but intelligence. He presumably would not have talked about the October 9 achievement if it had been true or unless the Germans already knew about the French breakthrough. He talked more about German messages in invisible ink. Was he making this up? We are left wondering what was in the real December 14 message. Did it exist? Was Bouchardon, perhaps prompted by Ladoux, on a fishing expedition because the Second Bureau did not have Kalle's letters to Berlin, only his radiograms? There is a confusion of deceit here. Like most intelligence services, was France's in 1917 deceiving itself as well?

Bouchardon summed up her arguments, tapping his pencil on the table and occasionally, one imagines, pausing to chew his nails and look up in her direction. Then he revealed the information about the intercepted traffic between Kalle and Berlin. To cover the fact that nothing had been said to him about this when the intercepts had been made four months before, he pretended that the traffic had only just become known by French intelligence.

What he said was this: "However, we have had in the dossier

for a few days material proof that, not only with our counterespionage service but with us [i.e., Bouchardon and Sergeant Baudouin] you have played the most audacious comedy. You are Agent H 21 of the intelligence centralization section of Cologne, sent for the second time in France in May 1916. You pretended to accept the offers of Captain Ladoux and to accomplish a journey in Belgium on behalf of his service. You received, from Germany, five thousand francs in Paris during November 1916, and finally you have supplied von Kalle with very complete information on a certain number of political, diplomatic and military subjects."

Bouchardon skipped over the fact that she was only in Madrid because the British turned her back, that she did not make contact with Germans to pass on the "political, diplomatic and military information" while in Madrid on her way to Vigo and Holland a month earlier, and that, had she been a German agent, she would have passed the information to Cologne in some way from Paris instead of waiting several weeks to do so on her second stopover in Madrid.

Mata Hari responded: "You are now doing exactly what Captain Ladoux did, when he wanted me to be Agent AF 44 of the Antwerp center and what England did when they wanted me to be Clara Bénédict [*sic*—Baudouin's transcript]. You are taking me for someone else. . . .

"Captain Ladoux and England also claimed to have proofs and they were obliged to face facts. What is more, I repeat to you that it was not my idea to go to 282 boulevard Saint-Germain."

Bouchardon came back with: "We have the full text of a communication sent on December 13, 1916, by von Kalle to staff headquarters in Berlin."

This corrected Ladoux's "December 31" date; but the message he then read to her was longer than Kalle's actual message of December 13 in the "Eiffel Tower" files and implied that she was not an unexpected caller in Madrid in December, but on a mission. The "text" he read was as follows:

> Agent H 21 of the intelligence centralization section of Cologne, sent in March [*sic*] for the second time in France, has arrived here. She has pretended to accept offers from the French intelligence services and to carry out trial trips in Belgium on behalf of that

service. She wanted to go from Spain to Holland aboard the *Hollandia*, but she was arrested at Falmouth on November 11 because she was mistaken for another. When the error was recognized, she was sent back to Spain because the English persisted in considering her suspicious.

This is similar to the wording of the "Ladoux" message cited earlier but is not quite the same. "Two trips" have become "trial trips" of indefinite number. Kalle's mention of knowing the identity of Clara Benedix and her present residence are omitted. Neither version bears any resemblance to the original "Eiffel Tower" intercept.

The beady eyes looked up from the page he was reading, and Bouchardon rasped: "That's certainly you, is it not?"

Having said that Kalle had recalled that Cologne had twice sent her to France, he must have been looking for some revealing sign of distress in her eyes, but we are not told by the files what her reaction, if any, was.

The April 21 letter from Ladoux to Dubail, which refers to fourteen messages, describes the first as dated December 13, 1916, and as saying that "H 21 cannot carry out her mission." The message enclosed for the general to fit that description makes it clear that the mission in question was the one for the French that was fatally jeopardized by her expulsion from Britain back to Spain. This version refers to "two trips" to Belgium for the French and contains the reference to Kalle being able to identify the woman for whom Mata Hari had been mistaken at Falmouth. It is, in short, identical with the first "Ladoux" message of which Bouchardon apparently used a revised version in his interrogation.

Bouchardon told Mata Hari that there was a "second message" in which Kalle had recommended that she be paid ten thousand francs, another from Berlin authorizing him to give her three thousand francs, and another from Kalle saying she had been given 3,500 pesetas. What information had she given that Kalle had valued at ten thousand francs? Had she had a lawyer present, the jurist would presumably have said that the information in question must surely be in the original message from Kalle. She said she had assumed that Kalle had checked on her, since he must have had informers in the Ritz Hotel, and that he had read her mail or had had it read.

"Spain is full of German spies," she said.

Bouchardon shot back: "But the H 21 referred to by von Kalle had a maid called Anna Lintjens in Holland."

Mata Hari pointed out that both sides clearly had access to the public and diplomatic mails she used in France and the public mails she used in Spain, so it would not have been difficult for Kalle to give details such as the name of her servant. Her telegram to Anna from Madrid had been carried to the post office by a hotel porter.

She went on: "In any case, I am not Agent H 21, von Kalle never gave me a penny and the five thousand francs that I received in November and another five thousand francs that I received in January of this year came from my lover, the Baron van der Capellen."

She was, of course, dissimulating when she said Kalle never gave her a penny; clearly she was afraid that if she admitted that he had given her some local money (3,500 pesetas) after making love to her on two or three occasions, this would weaken her case. Of course, telling the lie had just that undesired effect.

Bouchardon said that they had a second intercepted communication of December 20 and a third of December 28. The real message of December 20 was Kalle's asking Berlin for a reply to his message of December 13. However, Bouchardon read out the following message as being that of December 20:

> H 21 will request by a telegram from the Dutch Consul in Paris that a new draft of funds be made to her servants [sic] at Roermonde [sic] and requests you to inform Consul Krämer [sic] in Amsterdam on this subject.

This is almost textually the same as Kalle's true message of December 26, and the confusion of dates suggests that Ladoux, in composing his own set of intercepts, and building on the "Eiffel Tower" originals, was obliged to change the sequence. The most obvious giveaway here is: why would a German intelligence officer referring to another describe Kroemer as "Krämer"? The misspelling of the foreign name is an obvious French "signature."

Bouchardon then read what appears to be the correct message from Kalle of December 28. For recollection, this was: "H 21 will arrive tomorrow in Paris. She will ask to be sent at once, by telegram, through Consul Kroemer in Amsterdam and her servant in Ruremonde [*sic*], 5,000 francs to the Comptoir National d'Escompte de Paris, to be handed over, in that city, to the Dutch consul Bunge."

A lawyer would have asked why, since headquarters in Berlin was apparently paying her (three thousand francs), a minor intelligence functionary like Kroemer in Amsterdam was being asked to pay her also. He would also have questioned why a man who was supposed to be her controller in Madrid was announcing her arrival in Paris for December 29 instead of January 3 or 4. There is no evidence in the files that Mata Hari, who was always terrible about dates herself, noticed this slip, but Kalle's error makes it clear that he was not planning her movements.

Bouchardon pushed on, telling her that, in the space of two and a half months, she had received ten thousand francs (from Holland) and 3,500 pesetas "coming from German espionage." Anna Lintjens, he said, was clearly an accomplice.

"All those letters in which she may announce to you the dispatch of funds from van der Capellen are only stage directions and comedy!" he roared.

Mata Hari said that because van der Capellen was married and Holland was a small state "where moral disapproval [*censure*] is excessively severe," van der Capellen had asked her never to write him directly any letters "in which there was any question of tenderness or money." All communications to the baron went through her servant, whom she said she had had for eight years (actually, twelve).

After Vittel, she had been short of money. Ladoux had not offered an advance of funds, so "what is there surprising in that, under these conditions, I asked my protector to help me?"

Since we are dealing with three sets of what are meant to be the same messages—the twelve intercepts by the Eiffel Tower, the nine given by Ladoux to Bouchardon, and the fourteen given by Ladoux to Dubail—it is time to look at the latter group, which are in the files, and of which the first has been described.

In the set apparently crafted by Ladoux for the general, the second message is said to be dated December 13, the same as the first, and to contain information "brought to Holland [*sic*] from her journey to France."

The accompanying "copy" is a message about the Paris scuttlebutt that Mata Hari agreed she had passed to Kalle: this concerned Marie Bonaparte using Briand to try to get her husband on to the Greek throne, a party being formed to oust Briand from office, Britain's "absolute" political and military domination of France, and the expected spring offensive.

The third message is said to be dated from December 14 and to contain "additional information," while the fourth is said to be a reply on December 18 from Berlin's Third Bureau. As noted, these two elements in the "Dubail set" are also missing in the files.

The fifth message is described as coming from Kalle on December 20 and asking for a response. In the enclosed "copy," Kalle in fact is quoted as saying that Berlin should reply soon or "H 21's" journey to France would be "compromised." Kalle does not make this point in any of the "Eiffel Tower" originals.

The sixth message is said to be from Kalle on December 22, querying Berlin's (missing) message of December 18 and asking about mention of a Third Bureau director who does not exist.

The enclosed "copy" has Kalle asking scathingly: "I cannot begin to understand what the 'EST' chief of 3B [the Third Bureau, in the French initialese translation] has got to do with my telegram of December 13."

The seventh message, as described to Dubail, is said to be dated on Christmas Day and is "Antwerp" giving details about "H 21."

The justifying "copy" is from Berlin, which says it is passing on an Antwerp telegram of December 23. This instructs Kalle to pay H 21 three thousand francs, complains that her work is unsatisfactory and says that she should use invisible ink. If unwilling, she should get in touch with "A" while in Switzerland.

It is thus clear that some of the fourteen messages sent to Dubail (of which two are missing) are similar to the nine given to Bouchardon (of which two are also missing) and to the twelve "Eiffel Tower" originals (again with two missing), but that there are minor and also highly significant differences between all three versions, as well as changes of sequences and date.

The eighth message in the set supplied to Dubail is described in the Ladoux summary as being dated December 26 and containing a warning from Kalle that H 21 should not stay in Spain too long. This corresponds to what Bouchardon has described as the second message and to number seven in the "Eiffel Tower" originals (in which number eight is a message from Berlin about the "EST" error queried by Kalle).

In the "Dubail" version, Kalle is still complaining about not getting replies to his messages of December 13 and 20. He says he has given "H 21" 3,500 pesetas because she is "unwilling to go to France" if delayed much longer in Madrid. This point is an addition to the "Eiffel Tower" original. The "Dubail" version uses the same or similar wording about Mata Hari requesting, by a "telegram from the Dutch consul in Paris," that more money be made available to "her domestics" at "Roermonde" and asks Berlin to inform "Consul Krämer" in Amsterdam. Once again, Kalle is made to misspell his colleague's name.

In the "Dubail set," message number nine is described as answering Kalle's query about the transmission error. The "copy," dated December 28, has Berlin agreeing that "EST" means the head of the Third Bureau on the Eastern Front and says that the telegram was a mistake.

Dubail's number ten (we are now beyond, in enumeration, the nine given to Bouchardon) resembles number nine in the "Eiffel Tower" originals. Dated December 28, like the previous "Dubail" one, it "complements" Kalle's radiogram of December 26 and says H 21 "will be in Paris tomorrow." There she would ask for five thousand francs to be sent "through Consul Krämer and . . . Anna Lintjens." It now adds that she needs the money "urgently." Once again, Kalle is made to misspell the consul's name.

Message number eleven in the "Dubail set" is dated December 31 and is summarized as noting that "Agent H 21 has already left." It corresponds to number ten in the "Eiffel Tower" originals, which was one of the best examples that the original Kalle messages were *intoxication*, since it indicates that the major did not know that his subject was still in Madrid.

Dubail's number twelve, dated January 5, also corresponds to an "Eiffel Tower" original. It is from Berlin and concerns "your report No. 4300 of December 15," with an "extract of a report from Agent H 21." It goes on: "No. 176, Secret, to which you allude in the first paragraph, has not arrived." This appears to refer to Kalle's message of December 14, not December 15, since the December 14 message is missing in all the versions.

Dubail's messages numbered thirteen and fourteen are the "Eiffel Tower" originals of the last exchange about "H 21," sent on March 6 and March 8, and which imply Berlin's ignorance of her arrest.

Bouchardon's set of nine messages was of course less prolific than the general's fourteen, and he did not read all of them to Mata Hari during the May 1 interrogatory. But he did show her a translation of Kalle's message about Marie Bonaparte, in which the German major is apparently quoting her. Bouchardon reminded her that there was "more" in Kalle's dispatch. The lawyer-captain was trying to build a case that she had offered to work for the French on the orders of the Germans. To give him his due, he almost certainly did not know that there were three versions of the Kalle traffic or that the originals had been purposely sent in a redundant code. Mata Hari, equally ignorant of all this, was trying to defend herself logically against an illogical force: she reminded Bouchardon constantly that the suggestion of working for the French had come from Ladoux, at a time when he had a hold on her— it was up to him to decide whether she could rejoin Vadim in Vittel—and that she had only accepted after returning from Vittel, nearly a month later.

"Since I was to be paid only after a success, I didn't take anything from the captain," she said. She seems to have been arguing from the point of view of a courtesan: if her services were not as valuable as she herself thought, she had, after all, not accepted payment in advance. Bouchardon, not surprisingly, was not impressed with this reasoning.

What about the story of invisible ink? Bouchardon asked.

She said: "As far as ink is concerned, I swear to you that I know absolutely nothing."

Bouchardon read her Berlin's message of March 6, which—in all the versions—says that she is supposed to go to Switzerland and to use invisible ink. She insisted that she had never possessed invisible ink.

"Where would I have put it, when the British went through all my belongings? And I am not H 21." As it turned out later, she was telling the truth in spirit but not quite in fact—her sempiternal error of character.

Bouchardon retorted that she had had to pretend to work for the French because the French knew that she was in touch with the Germans.

Said Mata Hari: "I did not offer myself to France, I say this once more, and I am not an expert in spying, since I never thought of that before Captain Ladoux spoke to me of it. I don't know how to go about it. [*J'ignore comment on fait et comment on doit faire.*] I said to him: 'Captain, when I give you information, verify it always before using it, I [will] give it to you as I hear it.' "

She reminded Bouchardon that she had refused Ladoux's offer of French invisible ink: "That was a fine gift to bring to Germany if I had served that country."

She had, she said, deliberately refused to accept secrets from Ladoux. She claimed she had told him: " 'I want no secrets from you. Let me do as I please, and I ask of you only one thing: don't argue about my methods.' We shook hands on that."

Bouchardon replied: "I find it hard to believe that you do not recognize the exactitude of the information which von Kalle has scrupulously transmitted to Berlin." He pointed out that Kalle knew about Anna, the exact sum she was requesting from Holland, the correct bank, the name of Consul Krämer [*sic*], and so on.

He said: "It must mean that you informed him exactly and that he faithfully passed on your request to Germany."

"I telegraphed from London and from Madrid to Anna Lintjens to ask the Baron van der Capellen to help me," she replied.

She repeated that there had been a number of ways for Kalle to know the contents of her telegrams.

"Spain is full of German spies," she said again. "In each message [*dépêche*] there are possible errors. It is very possible that von Kalle sought to know who I was and with whom I have relationships. He could have asked the personnel of the Hotel Ritz, have my correspondence read and have very complete information about me."

On the question of German spies, she said Beaufort had told her that a German woman had been arrested on the *Hollandia* on an earlier voyage. (A note in the files says that Colonel Goubet had confirmed this, adding: "It was Ilse Blüme, born April 21, 1893, on her way from Berlin to Madrid on the *Hollandia* on December 15, 1916, arrested at Falmouth.")

Bouchardon, riffling through his papers, now noted that Kalle had spoken of H 21's "mission" in March and observed that she had not left Holland until May 12, but he used the error to suggest that Kalle must have received the information from her.

"You often get your dates wrong, don't you?"

Bouchardon must have queried Goubet on the point, because there is an undated note in the files from the colonel saying that she may "simply have left Holland late."

This concludes those interrogations which were based mainly on confronting Mata Hari with the Ladoux versions of the Kalle-Madrid traffic. One major question remains unanswered: Why did Ladoux invent two different versions to replace the "Eiffel Tower" originals?

There is a vain temptation, in writing books of this nature, to try to solve everything; but this writer concedes that no incontrovertible reason is apparent as to why there are two sets of Ladoux variations—fourteen for Dubail, nine for Bouchardon. That there *are* two spurious versions is sure, since the files contain descriptions of Bouchardon's nine and the full texts of the general's fourteen. Clearly, both are intended to be even more incriminating than the intentionally incriminating *intoxication* messages exchanged by Kalle and Berlin, in the redundant code, to try to fool the French. Both spurious versions help to buttress the case against Mata Hari.

It is legitimate to presume that the two sets were written on two different occasions. Was the "Dubail set" the first, and the shorter "Bouchardon set" a refinement? Such a theory would be based on the assumption that a general gets first whack at something rather than a captain. Were Dubail's messages more numerous than the originals because it is usually easier to fake a case with more incriminating "evidence" than less? Why then was Bouchardon given a shorter set? Although the falsifications vary, neither of the two spurious versions seems profoundly more incriminating than the other. The author confesses to being unable to solve this riddle. The answer may lie in the congenital contradictions within intelligence services. Perhaps, for instance, Goubet read the "Dubail set" and insisted that the number of messages should be closer to the number intercepted by the Eiffel Tower, in case the court president demanded to see the coded originals; and Ladoux, being a captain, executed his colonel's orders.

But where are Anna Lintjens and Eduard van der Capellen in all this? Given Bouchardon's problems in trying to build a case out of intercepted messages intentionally sent in a code the Germans knew the French could decipher—even assuming, in the worst case, that Ladoux had actually taken Bouchardon into his confidence—his reluctance to deal with these two key witnesses is understandable. But otherwise, if only Ladoux was cognizant, which seems almost sure, and Bouchardon was ignorant of the truth about the redundant code, why was he not seeking for confirmation of the origin of the two drafts of five thousand francs in November and January? He couldn't call Kroemer; but if the maidservant was an accomplice and knew that when Madame said "the Baron" she really meant "Consul Kroemer," surely the Dutch police, working in a neutral country sympathetic to Belgium and France and constantly on guard against a German invasion, could have pumped it out of her? Surely van der Capellen could have been discreetly questioned and his bank account examined for evidence of what money he had withdrawn for Anna to send to "Marguérite" in Paris? If Bouchardon had tried, through the French legation in The Hague, to get a deposition from Anna, and the woman had been too frightened to present herself, or if the Dutch authorities had said that this was going too far, could Bouchardon not have usefully insinuated that her nonappearance implied guilt?

Clunet obviously must have wanted to have van der Capellen and Anna questioned, but he was forbidden under wartime security rules to contact any witnesses. He could not even inform the baron and Anna that Madame was in prison. Under the laws of war, the only witnesses who could be called were those whom the French army would permit to be acquainted with the case. All except one of the witnesses allowed at the trial were to be members of the French military or other disciplined services; the one permitted civilian was someone cleared to read the most confidential material. The two key defense witnesses—who would have been the key prosecution witnesses if Bouchardon's case had been genuine—were intended, like the rest of the "public," to be kept ignorant of Mata Hari's arrest until after her execution was announced, even though her arrest was salon gossip all over Paris.

Actually, on April 11, van der Capellen, made anxious by Marguérite's silence and her failure to return to Holland, had the Dutch foreign minister, Loudon, send a message to the head of the Dutch legation in Paris, saying:

> Please communicate by telegram the present address of Margaretha Zelle alias Mata Hari. Last known address Plaza Hotel, 25 rue Montaigne. Please ask if she intends to return soon.

The Paris legation replied to The Hague on April 23, saying the minister in charge had been "semiofficially" informed by the Quai d'Orsay that Mata Hari was in Saint-Lazare prison charged with espionage.

She herself had tried to get this message out by insisting on her right to contact her legation. The diplomatic question had gone to the highest authority in the Quai d'Orsay—her old friend, Jules Cambon. The secretary general had written to the minister of war on April 4, saying:

> I esteem it not to be possible to prevent the accused from addressing an appeal to the Representative of her country. We would [otherwise] expose ourselves, when the situation of this Dutchwoman is finally known, to reclamations from the legation of the Netherlands and from the Dutch Government.

But it was not until early in May, more than two months after her arrest, that the minister of war finally allowed her to write to the Dutch minister, whom Clunet had been forbidden to contact. She wrote that she had been imprisoned at Saint-Lazare for espionage but that she was innocent. This letter and two others for the legation passed through Cambon's hands. A letter to Anna and another to a "Monsier Otto," a painter who had portrayed her in pastel, both enclosed with the first letter to the legation, were removed by Cambon, so in one of the letters to the Dutch mission she asked the consulate-general to get in touch with her servant, "without speaking too much about an arrest, *but saying I have difficulty getting out of France and above all that she should not worry*" (underlined in the original). She gave Anna Lintjens' address—Mata Hari's own house in The Hague—and told the consul-general: "I assure you that I am half crazy with chagrin."

She asked the diplomat to ask her friend the Count van Limburg Styrum, an embassy attaché, to do what he could for her.

The consul-general wrote to Anna along the cautious lines she had requested. (The letters turned back and Cambon's letter are in the military justice files. The details of the permitted correspondence with the legation come from Waagenaar, who read them in Holland.)

She was not allowed to reveal any details of her case to anyone. Capellen remained ignorant of the fact that he could prove the supposedly key charge against his mistress false by testifying that it was he who had sent the drafts of funds, through Anna, to Marguérite.

Curiously, a memo in the files records that a letter of Mata Hari's of March 15 to Anna had in fact been forwarded to her on March 30—after being tested for invisible ink!—because it specifically did not mention that she was under arrest. This letter points out that the three-year lease on her house, which was signed on October 31, 1914, required a six-month notice of renewal. This should therefore be done by the baron not later than April 30, she told Anna. The official memo, recording the contents of the letter, notes the necessity to keep Mata Hari's arrest secret because it is still *"not known to the Germans"* (underlined in the original). This could hardly have been true, but it was of course suggested by the Berlin message in the redundant code sent on March 6 and by Kalle's reply of March 8.

There is an undated note in the files that appears to have been written in May, after the interrogation just related, in which Bouchardon asks Goubet for the French legation in The Hague to provide "information" on van der Capellen and the banker van der Schalk—"lovers of Zelle MacLeod"—and on Wurfbein, whom Bouchardon spells "Wurfbain," using a Gallic suffix instead of the Germanic one. Goubet's answer ignores Bouchardon's request and says simply that Mata Hari was the mistress of "Crémer" (meaning Consul Kroemer) who is "associated with Wurfbain" (*sic*), who is, he says, the Amsterdam representative of the Deutschbank.

*   *   *

On May 3, Bouchardon also received written answers from Ladoux concerning some of Mata Hari's responses and the points she had made. Ladoux said that, previous to the prisoner's statement, "the Germans in Spain were worried about the surveillance exercised by the French concerning possible departures of German submarines for Morocco, and their military and naval attachés had telegraphed Berlin to warn them that their cipher might be broken; as a point of fact, they modified it later. It is possible that von Kalle wanted, in passing on this information [about the submarine landings] through his agent [i.e., Mata Hari] to try to obtain from her some more precise details in this regard."

Ladoux then told Bouchardon more explicitly that he had planned for her *refoulement* by Britain back to Spain, so that German intelligence there would have to send messages about her. This is presumably false: if Ladoux had prearranged her *refoulement* by the British, they could have sent her back from Falmouth; they would hardly have questioned her for days in London and involved themselves in unnecessary problems with the Dutch legation. Ladoux also carefully did not tell Bouchardon about Kalle's use of the old code, which he conceded that the Germans had changed out of awareness that it had been broken. This at least told Bouchardon that the present code was also broken, since he must have assumed that that was the code that Kalle used for the messages which he had been given. Ladoux also thereby implied that the Germans did not know that their current code was also broken, thereby defending his (untrue) need for secrecy about the reading of the traffic (in the redundant code) about Mata Hari.

Ladoux also insisted that he did not offer "Zelle" the "secret" of French invisible ink. He did not, however, say that he did not offer her the option of using it.

He said again that he gave her no addresses in Belgium to contact and raised again the suspicion that she had been to Antwerp: he said a French double agent pretending to work for Germany's Antwerp center, and "today no longer with us," had once seen "Zelle" in the lobby of that city's Grand Hôtel.

On May 4, Clunet wrote Bouchardon that he had the right to be present at all interrogations under a law signed on June 15, 1899. Bouchardon sent the letter the next day to the chief military prosecutor, Major Jullien, noting that a wartime decree of April 27, 1916, had suspended the right to which Clunet referred.

Bouchardon argued strongly that the dossier showed that French intelligence could read the German code from Madrid. "The least indiscretion could be fraught with consequences," he insisted, and he was afraid that Clunet would insist on seeing the Madrid messages.

Bouchardon told Jullien that Clunet was "an old and rather naïve admirer of the dancer that Mrs. Zelle once was," adding: "He brings to the defense of his client the ardor of a neophyte and he shows concerns for her that I have difficulty in understanding since he knows that on the eve of the war, the accused was, in Berlin itself, the mistress of two officers and of the chief of the police. It is Mrs. Zelle who has said this."

Clunet, he concluded, could not be trusted with the news of France's code-breaking skills.

Bouchardon also told Jullien that he had taken the precaution of getting support for his position from the current head (*bâtonnier*) of the Paris bar, Henri Robert. Jullien wrote the same day, May 5, to the military governor of Paris, General Dubail, supporting Bouchardon, and Clunet's demand was rejected.

We can note that Bouchardon was still confused between Griebl and von Jagow, thus making her relationship with Griebl more significant. And no one seems to have noted that Clunet would learn about the code-breaking once all the interrogations were communicated to him so that he could prepare for the trial.

8. *The Pretrial—*
3: The Honorary Consul
and the Fortune-teller

A PARALLEL INVESTIGATION was being conducted by the French police. Much further on in the files, one finds the report of a "rogatory commission" by Commissioner Albert Priolet, the man who had arrested Mata Hari in the company of five police inspectors, whom we learn were called Mercadier, Curnier, Desloyères, Génélin, and Frisou. He gave her address as "103 Champs-Elysées, Room 131 with private bathroom." To someone like Priolet, who would almost certainly not have had a bath in his home at all, this must have seemed the summit of extravagance for someone merely spending a few weeks in a hotel.

Priolet had taken possession of her passport for France, valid for one year and delivered by the French legation in The Hague on November 27, 1915. This was the one marked NOT VALID FOR THE WAR ZONE. Priolet noted that this document showed that she had had it stamped, after her last arrival in Paris, on "January 4, 1916." (Priolet was wrong: the visa stamp says, of course, "1917.") Priolet did not mention, and no one seems to have noticed, that this passport had expired while she was in London, and this fact was never mentioned in the pretrial investigation or at the trial. The document bears a visa from the British consulate-general in Rotterdam enabling her to pass through England on the 1915 journey. There is a French visa, issued in London, permitting her to travel to Paris via Dieppe, and a January 4, 1916, French stamp authorizing her to return home from her December 1915 visit via Spain and Portugal.

The French passport describes her as "Mme. Zelle Marguérite

Gertrude, divorced spouse of M. MacLeod, dancer under the name of Matahari [*sic*], of Dutch nationality." She has signed it "M. G. Zelle McLeod" [*sic*] and added the second signature "Mata Hari." A fiscal stamp bears witness that she paid nine florins and twenty cents for the document.

The passport gives her age as thirty-nine, her height as one meter seventy-five centimeters (five feet nine inches), and her hair and eyebrows as brown. Had she dyed her graying black hair and even the eyebrows, giving up the color that was part of her "Javanese" image?

Her eyes, brown in childhood, must have become hazel (for which a perfectly good French word exists) because they are described as "green, veering on brown." Her brow is described as "high," just possibly indicating that she was losing some hair, her nose as "regular," her chin as round, and her face as oval. Her complexion is described as pale. As well as dying her black hair brown, was she covering her famous olive skin with the powder discovered in her toiletry kit?

Priolet listed among other objects seized her *carnet d'étranger* No. 1408, dated August 23, 1916, and valid until September 20, permitting her to go to Vittel; page one of this document specifies that she can spend three weeks at the spa for "reasons of health." The booklet is stamped for her arrival in and departure from Vittel, and for her return to the "Grand Hôtel, rue Scribe."

The commissioner also listed an earlier *carnet* issued on December 13, 1915, in Paris, an "extract from the register of foreigners," her Dutch passport No. 312 with the pretty photograph, dated May 12, 1916, and issued in The Hague, and an "annex of passport 312 visa-ed in London on December 2, 1915, and in Hendaye on January 11, 1916." (Actually, there are far more visas on it than that, including one for Dieppe on December 3, 1915.)

Despite the six folds, the Dutch passport is still in mint condition in the files. There are several signatures by Bunge, "Acting Consul-General of Holland," all confirming her dates of arrival in and departure from Paris. Contrary to what has often been written, there are no signs of any tampering with dates in any of the documents.

There are papers related to her strongbox, to her account, and to her lease of the apartment in the avenue Henri-Martin. There is her Crédit Lyonnais checkbook, showing her account number to have been 147045. (Later information revealed a meager balance of fourteen francs and thirty-five centimes.)

The police had also found fourteen photographs (although the accompanying document says thirteen), and these are in the files. Some at least seem to have been taken in Vittel, and Vadim appears in nearly all of them. They had also seized fifty-three calling cards, which were to give them a mountain of mostly useless work.

One of the photos is a studio portrait of Vadim and Marina. He is in uniform, with the long patch across his left eye stylishly tied around his head with what looks like a dark ribbon. She is dressed to the nines. With her one-and-a-half-inch heels, they are about the same height, and he is youthfully handsome. Together, they look like an eighteen-year-old with a rather "fun" mother. There is also a head-and-shoulders studio portrait of herself, taken when she was much younger, with her hair in a fringe.

The rest appear to be snapshots or postcards taken by street photographers. Two of them show Vadim in uniform on horseback, while a third has him holding the bridle of his horse. This one is dedicated "to my dear little Marina—your Vadim." One photo shows a group of Russian enlisted men lining up for a meal. It is hand-captioned "*La bonne soupe.*" Another group photo has Vadim and some fellow officers apparently toasting her as she snaps them. Someone has interpreted their supposed sentiments in French on the back: "Long live Marina, and we'll get them!" (*On les aura*— "we'll get them"—was the slogan of the French army facing the Germans.) The writing resembles Vadim's. One snap shows Masloff and a fellow officer knee-deep in water; a trench and casemate are in the background. This one, like the group shots, was presumably not taken at Vittel.

The police had also taken a suitcase containing books, brochures, and theater programs. There was a toiletry bag, a small pendulum clock in a glass case, and a box of "various objects" that was waiting to be sent to Holland. It was addressed to "her servant," Priolet said.

Her purse had contained six one-hundred-franc notes, one sixty-florin note, one forty-florin note, and a Russian note. We know she gave generous sums to Vadim; while waiting to leave the country, she appears, from the state of her bank account, to have been spending—with Vadim's help—about one thousand francs a week.

Then there were, of course, the last cards from Vadim to the Elysée-Palace, and from these we learn clearly that his French was far from perfect. He had apparently moved to a military hospital at Epernay.

The first card in the files, to "my dear little Marina," says that (apparently before her arrival in Madrid) he had had a throat operation at the "Michlé" (presumably Michelet) hospital in Paris and that the operation had gone well. In the address section, he gives his name as "Capitaine V. de Masloff" and his address as "Hôpital 24, Epernay."

Another card begs her to come to Epernay, where he says the Grand Hôtel is good. He asks her to reply by telegram. The last card, dated February 18, just after her arrest, complains that she has not written. (Unfortunately, the file does not of course contain the numerous letters and cards that she wrote to him in those final weeks before her arrest.) He says he is expecting to come to Paris "this week." The sign-off, in a mixture of Spanish and French, reads: "Many kisses from your Vadim who loves you madly" (*Muchos basos de ton Vadime qui t'aime à la folie*). None of these cards are dated, but all were sent after her move to the Elysée-Palace.

There is also an undated letter that presumably was sent before the cards and that also contains a few words in Spanish announcing his arrival in Epernay and asking her to come.

There are some translations of letters in Dutch that had been found at her hotel. One is an October 25, 1916, letter from Anna to Madame, saying that she had contacted the baron, who had received Madame's letter in which she had said that she expected to return around November 19. There is another missive, dated December 15, 1916, from Anna to Mata Hari saying the writer is sorry to learn that her employer is encountering difficulties in returning to Holland. The baron, Anna wrote, had asked if Madame had received the five thousand francs he had sent through the consulate-general of the Netherlands. Anna added that "the Baron found the house beautiful but sad, for it is still Madame who is missing."

There is a November 28, 1916, letter to Mata Hari at the Savoy Hotel in London, where she was staying while waiting to be put aboard the *Araguya* in Liverpool. This is from Egbert Willem de Jong, the London correspondent of the Dutch newspaper *Algemeen Handelsblad*, asking for an interview. She must have replied at once, because there is a further letter from the reporter dated November 30, asking to be received on December 4 at 11:30 A.M., then yet another letter from him of December 1 asking to change the appointment time to 3:00 P.M. because of a conflicting engagement in the morning. The Savoy was not blessed with room telephones at the time. By December 1, Mata Hari was already in Liverpool. The December 1 letter was sent on by the Savoy to the Ritz in Madrid and from there to her hotel in Paris.

Similarly sent on from Madrid was a letter from Lieutenant Kenneth Mackenzie Walker of the 1st Wiltshire Regiment, with the British Expeditionary Force in France. He was on leave and gave his address as the family firm: Walker Brothers & Company, Oporto, Portugal. He invited her to visit him on his port wine vineyard there. This was presumably the letter to which she replied from Paris shortly before her arrest.

Also forwarded by the Ritz was a telegram from Juan Camprubi, to which, we can recall, she also replied. He asked her to come to Barcelona for "two or three days." He had arranged respectable accommodation with a "Miss Carola."

Priolet, who already had the receipt signed by Bunge at the bank, had by now also seized the receipt that she gave the acting Dutch consul-general for the five thousand francs. It is signed "M. G. Zelle." He noted that the bank had seized her strongbox on January 16. This was four weeks before her arrest; should it be February 16? The box had been found to contain only an empty leather bag. Curiously, Priolet said the inspectors doing the *filature* had found no evidence of any telegram sent by Mata Hari.

Priolet also reported that he had been asked to discover why Mata Hari went so often to a jewelry shop on the boulevard des Capucines called Au Collier d'Ambre and to check out a modest address that she had visited in the suburb of Le Raincy. Neither turned out to be a spy "drop." Priolet said the jewelry store yielded "nothing of interest." At Le Raincy, the commissioner's men made the acquaintance of Eugénie Soreuil née Bazin, a fifty-year-old woman who read futures in cards and who was married to a retired streetsweeper. Mrs. Soreuil said she had given Mata Hari two "consultations" for five francs each and that the lady had apparently come back for a third reading but had found the *cartomancienne* out.

Whether the Paris police told Mrs. Soreuil the reason for their visit, we do not know, but the card-reader would have realized that the visit implied that her customer was in trouble; in any event, Mata Hari's arrest was widely known in the city. It appears that Mata Hari had posed specific questions about her future. Mrs. Soreuil told the police that she had given her customer (whether at the first or second consultation, or on both occasions, is not clear) some startling news—and news not connected, as one might have expected, to affairs of the heart:

"Mrs. Soreuil told her that she would not make the trip she planned, and that the million [francs] to which she had alluded would not be collected [*perçu*] and that she would be shot first."

Assuming that Mrs. Soreuil was not prompted by the police and had not thrown in her prediction of execution because she knew that that was what happened to spies, she emerges as a woman who believed in her craft and was not afraid to predict the worst for her customers, however much a more satisfying prediction might have assured her a more grateful fee.

The French had to make a case that Mata Hari had more money than she had admitted receiving from the Dutch baron. Priolet calculated that she had spent about thirteen thousand francs in Paris hotels and stores and on meals, taxi fares, and miscellaneous purchases. He apparently did not know about or include her remittances to Vadim. The commissioner had found that the news of her arrest as a Dutch spy for the Germans was well known and that hotel and restaurant staffs were full of disobliging remarks about her. She had left many unpaid bills. Not surprisingly, one of her strongest revilers was the manager of the Hôtel Meurice, the man who had had to get a court order to obtain partial payment of an old bill.

We learn that he was Johannes-Frederick (Friedrich?) Schwenker, a Swiss, and Priolet noted that he had been a spy for the French in his native Switzerland, where he had procured the formula for "German poison gas."

A separate report by Priolet goes into the contents of her toiletry bag. This contained "five face powders, three pommades, a bar of soap, a stick of lip-rouge, a stick of mascara, two brushes for applying these products, seven liquids (perfumes and toilet waters), a small bottle of benzine and six therapeutic products."

She clearly never used a toothbrush, which was then something of a novelty. Even without this, the collection constitutes a curiously modest set of cosmetics for a lady of the time who was so consumed with her appearance and with the need to repair the ravages of time. The benzine may indicate that she was using the latest gadget, a cigarette lighter, but was more probably for removing food stains from clothes. Most of the "therapeutic products" were presumably headache pills and the like, but two were sent for further examination.

One, said to come from "Roberts & Co., 5 rue de la Paix," which must have been an English pharmacy, was issued on the prescription of a Dr. Verne. It was said to be composed of one part *biïodure de mercure*, seven parts *iodure de potassium*, and one hundred parts water. This, Priolet's chemists had found, would make a "first class invisible ink if stretched with forty to fifty times its volume of water."

The second, whose bottle was said to bear a Spanish label, contained pills of what is described in French as *oxycyanure de mercure*. The mercury compound is called a "common antiseptic" but one that is "unobtainable in France without a prescription." Dissolved in five hundred times their volume of water, the pills would be an "excellent invisible ink."

Dr. Verne's prescription is in the files but has now faded to the point of being illegible—an ironic fate for something linked to invisible ink. But the Spanish label from the bottle of pills confirms that they are a soluble antiseptic.

This interesting discovery—that two of her "therapeutic products" could be used to make *encre sympathique*—was not mentioned at the trial. Invisible ink (the writing becomes invisible when the "ink" dries and visible again when the page is heated) can be a number of products or even natural liquids. Lemon juice or milk, for instance, will do perfectly well. The prosecution did not claim that they had discovered anything written by Mata Hari in invisible ink, and the German spymasters, in their later books, described having used sophisticated mixtures that could not be "developed" by heat alone but had to be brushed with or immersed in other chemical compounds of which they had the secret. Locard, well after the war, said the German inks were a mixture of "silver salts and hypersulfite." The British, who had pioneered sophisticated invisible inks, also reportedly had a fluid that the Germans could not "develop."

However, perhaps the best reason why the mercury and potassium mixture provided to Mata Hari by the British pharmacy in the heart of the French capital's classy bordello district was not mentioned at the trial was because it was a spermicide used by almost every prostitute and courtesan in Paris when they went to the bidet. The mercury pills from Spain were presumably the Iberian equivalent and were intended to ensure that Mata Hari did not arrive for her nuptials with Vadim heavy with Kalle's infant.

The proof, if still needed, that the Kalle-Berlin traffic was *intoxication* had been completed by the Berlin and Madrid radiograms of March 6 and March 8, with both centers reverting to the redundant code and with Berlin implying unawareness that its purported agent had left Spain two months before. Ladoux now had uncomfortable extra evidence that the French military justice system had an innocent captive on its hands; but there still seems no reason to believe that Bouchardon was ever told that the Allies had broken the key to two codes, not one, that the Germans only knew about the first success, and that Kalle had sent his messages in the code he knew the French could read. For Ladoux, there were two options: he could either level with Bouchardon about the codes, so that Bouchardon could release her and send her off to Switzerland or Spain to find her own way home (or to wait for Vadim in Paris, supporting herself on the toils of her flesh); or he could let Bouchardon continue to use the spurious traffic and anything else that could be found to build a case. Everyone from President Poincaré on down was still insisting that the Second Bureau help the war effort against "defeatism" by catching more spies. Not to comply by adding Mata Hari to the list would be to concede that the captain, the police, and the military legal service had spent a small fortune in money, personnel, and time in simply investigating a courtesan on vacation.

Bouchardon was apparently left with his half-knowledge, and it was decided to try to interview as many people who had known her as possible, including, ideally, all the people whose names appeared on the fifty-three calling cards found in her purse. This task was not made easier by the fact that traditional French calling cards do not bear addresses.

Meanwhile, Bouchardon was having other witnesses questioned as well. The first was Berthe Boucher née Guilloton, the thirty-one-year-old manicurist at the Plaza. She said she had done Madame's nails four or five times.

Mrs. Boucher was asked about her earlier report that Mata Hari had discussed the battle of Verdun and that she distrusted the British and the Belgians. The manicurist now embellished the story. Mata Hari had said that she hated the British, who were a heap of imbeciles, while the Belgians were "a filthy race, worthless." The 100,000 dead at Verdun had now become "200,000" (actually, even this was a wild underestimate).

Madame must clearly have been in a rotten mood that day. If one knew the date of the manicure session, it would be interesting to go back to the inspectors' *filature* reports to discover whether she had not entertained a Belgian lieutenant the night before and to wonder whether the fellow had not been wearing dirty underwear and to have found himself unable to meet her usual honorarium.

The Boucher woman said Mata Hari had told her that she was trying to get in touch with her Russian fiancé at the Front and had asked the manicurist if she knew where the Russians were fighting.

Next, her hotel chambermaid, Anna Baron, remembered Madame saying that she doubted if the British would ever give back the territory they now occupied in France.

Was Mata Hari spreading gloom and despondency or simply showing how much she shared the prejudices of the French?

More important, testimony was taken from someone she had asked to be cited as a defense witness, if she were tried. Lieutenant Henri Mège was questioned on April 10. Mège was officially described as an "engineer" in the "Inventions Service" of the ministry of war; but according to the author René Masson, this was a cover title for his real job as a code and cipher expert. He appears to have been one of the escorts she acquired during the long summer and fall of 1916.

He described his first meeting with the "tall, elegant woman" and says he saw her three times in the course of about two weeks. One of the meetings had been at the Restaurant Larue where he had invited her to dine. He said she had not discussed anything military or asked any "unacceptable" questions except to inquire if the Russians were fighting in the Verdun salient. She had said she was anxious to know the whereabouts of Captain de Masloff, for whose safety she was concerned.

Finally, testimony was taken from Denvignes. The "old colonel" described by Mata Hari turns out to have been barely older than she. He was fifty.

Staff Colonel Joseph-Cyrille Denvignes recounted that he had met the lady at a social occasion in Madrid. After revealing that she, like he, was working for French intelligence, she had discussed her plan to renew contact with the German Crown Prince, whom she had described as "an imbecile with whom I can do anything I like." More important, she had said, would be for her to seduce the Kaiser Wilhelm's son-in-law, the British Duke of Cumberland, who had stayed in Germany after the outbreak of war and had been stripped of his title by Britain. (His father-in-law, the Kaiser, was, as noted earlier, Queen Victoria's grandson.)

She had told him, Denvignes said, how the British had taken her for "a certain Clara Bénédict." She had had other problems: she had said that "I fear Colonel Goubet has no confidence in me." If the head of all French intelligence felt like this, she had wondered, how could she get any sense out of his unimaginative counterespionage subordinate, Captain Ladoux? Denvignes did not say so, but he should have been puzzled as to why a French spy outside France was working for the head of *counter*espionage.

She had told him that, because of the Falmouth problem, she would have to proceed on her mission by going through Switzerland. Then he quoted her as saying: "They don't know how to use me; they ask me to denounce spying agents or more or less dubious people of little importance. That's not my specialty, and you'll see in what circles I can, above all, render services to you."

According to Denvignes, she went on: "What's more, your service is shadowing me in every hotel in which I stay; I always notice it right away; all this simply vexes me by showing me that they don't understand how to use me [*la partie qu'on peut tirer de moi*]."

Apparently responding to his plea for her to live with him and "brighten my home," he said she told him that she was prepared to stay in Spain, but that she would prefer to return to Paris and resume the mission Ladoux had given her. If she stayed in Spain, she was prepared to go on working on "von Kalle," whom she had learned had met her many years before when she was watching the Silesian maneuvers and he was a cavalry captain. She had said she had a more or less open invitation to call on the German major either at the embassy or at his home.

"I think I can see him again whenever I want," he quoted her as saying.

Denvignes confirmed that he had asked her to go back to Kalle and try to get more details about the Moroccan landings, such as, were these on the southwest coast, and how many German and Turkish officers were involved? He had asked her for "precise" details, and she had promised to see Kalle the next afternoon.

He said he next saw her "four or five days" later at the Ritz, which suggests that the head of French espionage in Spain was none too good at remembering dates either. She had said that she had seen Major Kalle and could only confirm what she had told Denvignes before—that there had been landings on the Moroccan coast.

He said he insisted to "MacLeod" that more detail was necessary, so that a future landing could be prevented. At their "third meeting," Mrs. MacLeod had said that Kalle was becoming suspicious. Denvignes said he had expressed dissatisfaction with the absence of detail.

The only other elements of that conversation that the colonel remembered were her assurances of her love for France and her intention to live there after the war, to resume her career as a dancer.

Denvignes said he left Madrid "on the 22nd or the 23rd" to report to Colonel Goubet. Mrs. MacLeod had continued to send him information through his Madrid office. There had been "four or five very true pieces of information but which had only a very secondary interest for us."

He listed these as the ink-crystals-under-fingernails story, the supposed breaking by the Germans of "one of our codes," and their discovery of French landings by aircraft behind the German lines. He said Goubet had told him that "all this was known already."

The French consulate-general had issued her with a "passport for Paris" (actually a visa on her existing passport, which the French consuls did not notice had expired), and she had arrived in the French capital "in the early days of January." He himself had left Paris "on January 4 or 5." At the Orsay station a *Wagons-lits* employee had told him that Mata Hari wanted to see him and "I did not reply." (The *filature* inspectors said that when she arrived at the Orsay station, the train had gone, but both Mata Hari's and Denvignes' testimonies indicate that it was simply on the point of departure.) When the train had stopped at the Austerlitz station, another employee "said a lady was waiting to speak to me, and then I saw Mrs. MacLeod at the door of the car." She had wanted to know what she was supposed to do and what Goubet and Ladoux thought of her.

Denvignes testified that he had replied: "Madame, they take you for a very intelligent woman, capable of succeeding in the most difficult operations."

She had responded, he said, with: "Well, then, what should I do?"

He said he had told her to "put yourself at their disposal." She had said she would do so the following day.

Then came the kicker: "My absolute conviction is that MacLeod is in the service of German espionage." Since she was aware that her visits to "von Kalle" were known to French espionage (i.e., to Denvignes), she had, "as an intelligent professional," he said, "pretended" she was going to Kalle's house on France's behalf. He thought the Germans had passed her false or outdated information. On this latter point, of course, he was undoubtedly right.

On May 7, at three o'clock—a rare precision about time in the files—a deposition was taken from Adam Wieniawski, the delegate in Paris of the Russian Red Cross. Wieniawski said he had known of Mata Hari as a dancer. She had written to him in January, asking to work with a Russian ambulance team so that she could be with Masloff, whom he knew personally. She had shown him her snapshots of him, which bore "very amorous dedications."

She had asked him if Masloff had been wounded at Verdun, which was then the battle that had reaped the most ink in the French press. The question shows how little she knew about the war, since Russian troops were not involved in the Verdun battle— as Masloff himself could have told her. Wieniawski had promised to let her know if "anything serious" happened to Masloff. He had also promised to recommend that Vadim be given convalescent leave in Paris; but "a general" had since warned him off Mata Hari, saying: "I have very bad information about her." The lady had later telegraphed him at Châlons, where he was based; she had sought news of her lover.

On May 5, Clunet, having been forbidden to question Capellen or Anna, demanded in writing that his client be confronted with Lieutenant Hallaure, Captain Ladoux, and Colonel Denvignes. The confrontations with Denvignes and Hallaure were denied, and it was decided that she could see Ladoux again only if she had something new to say to *him*. Otherwise, she would have to deal with Bouchardon. In a note bearing the mention "Wednesday" but no date (May 9?), she asked if she could use money from her bank account to pay for her transportation to interrogations in a taxi instead of the police van. This request was granted.

Jean-Hélie Hallaure was in fact questioned by somebody on May 9. The twenty-seven-year-old dragoon lieutenant recounted how they had met in his circus days, confirmed that he had sent her to Ladoux because she needed permission to go to Vittel, and certified that she had never asked him any military questions.

The same day, a twenty-eight-year-old Plaza waiter, Louis Ghiga, was also questioned. He said she had offered him a postwar job as her butler. He thought she was married to a "British count." She had talked to him about her "Indian dancing" and had told him of her appearance at the Guimet Museum. He had seen her with "her Russian captain." She had never spoken to him about the war. She had left the hotel without tipping him.

Also that day, a forty-five-year-old moneychanger called Henri Liévin said he had known her while she was living in the house Rousseau had provided in Neuilly. He had no information about her to offer, however.

A forty-four-year-old lady with "no profession" called Louise-

Elisabeth-Emma Eydoux was questioned the following day. She said she had met Mata Hari in Vigo in November, when Mrs. Eydoux was on her way home from Rio de Janeiro. Mata Hari had told her that she was engaged to a Russian officer and had shown her Masloff's photo. At the hotel, Mata Hari had played the piano and sung. She had told Eydoux she was on her way home to Holland on the *Hollandia*. She was going to "collect her papers" there and return to Paris to "marry her Russian."

Ghiga, Liévin, and Eydoux were names found on the calling cards in Mata Hari's purse when it was seized at her arrest. So were many of the other persons questioned that month.

Also on May 10, for instance, a thirty-six-year-old sublieutenant called Emile-Louis Thiry said he had met Mata Hari at the Molier circus before the war and again more recently. She had never asked him any military questions. The next day, "Henri Raphérer," described as a forty-six-year-old engineer and reserve lieutenant, testified that he had met Mata Hari at a reception at the Palais d'Orsay before the war. Since "Raphérer" had lived in Java and Sumatra, he was interested in her "Javanese dancing." She had invited him to Neuilly, where they had had dinner alone and gone to bed. He had given her two hundred francs. She had later written him from Berlin and asked him to look her up if he ever visited the German capital.

This can only be the "Henri Rapférer, *aéronaute*" who had made the headlines by flying a dirigible over Paris and to whom she had written from Berlin about German invasion plans. She was to try, unsuccessfully, to have him produced at the trial to give evidence on her behalf. In his deposition, we can note that he was specifically not asked if Mata Hari had written him from Berlin about the indiscretions of her naval commander–lover, "Renitzer" (Kuntze?), and that he does not appear to have volunteered this information himself.

That day, Hallaure was recalled for more questioning about his help in getting her to Vittel. No, he said, he didn't think she was visiting the spa because she was sick; he thought she wanted to rejoin Masloff. It was true, however, he noted, that Vittel water was noted for problems of the liver, and "she had a limber hand with the fork, and would eat everything."

*   *   *

On May 19, a gendarme officer finally spoke to Masloff. The files contain a "rogatory commission" from the commander of the Gendarmerie in the Breton capital of Rennes, where Vadim was then a patient at Military Hospital 114. The interview was conducted by a gendarme captain, Louis Pineau.

"The subject says he met the accused in late August 1916, at the Grand Hôtel, in Paris, where they were introduced by a French Hussar officer," Pineau reported.

Had she told him the story of her life? Yes, of course. Masloff recalled her telling him that she had been born in The Hague and had lost both her parents while still young. She had been raised by an aunt until she was sixteen, then married off to a British officer in the Dutch army.

The slight liberties with the truth all sound like vintage Mata Hari—The Hague sounds better than her obscure village, killing both her parents off early enhances her plight, and being married off at sixteen, rather than married of her own free will at eighteen, also makes her more pitiful.

The twenty-one-year-old Russian said she had blamed the breakup of her marriage on the difference of age between her and her husband. (Since she was nineteen years older than Masloff, and the age difference is more accentuated when the older partner is the woman, this would seem to have been an ill-chosen excuse.) She had, Masloff said, spoken of her travels in Europe, of being blocked in Berlin by the outbreak of war, of having settled in Holland, and of having come to Paris to collect "her clothes."

Pineau asked: "Did she ever discuss military questions with you?"

Masloff answered: "She asked only to know on what part of the Front I was serving so that she could follow my problems in the papers."

He had spent three days with her, he said, then reported back to his unit. He had been with her again in September and October 1916 and again in January 1917. She had told him about her attempt to go to Holland. She had recounted that she had returned to Paris because the British had told her that if she went to Holland, she would not be able to get back to France until after the war. In short, she had flattered Vadim by saying that she had abandoned her trip to The Hague because it would have cut her off from him.

At this point, it is worth recalling that she had claimed, under interrogation, that Sir Basil Thomson's men had told her that the British were not allowing any Dutch citizens to return to Holland, which sounds implausible. Was she confusedly trying to say that they had told her that, once in Holland, she would not be allowed to traipse back and forth through the Channel on visits to Paris and would have to stay at home until the end of the war? In such an event, she might well have consented to the British sending her back to Spain—the road to Paris, to Vadim. Or was she simply telling Vadim a lie, and something more flattering to him, and less alarming than revealing that the British suspected her of being a German spy?

Masloff said he had been treated for diphtheria at the Epernay hospital and discharged in March. He had at once gone to the Elysée-Palace, where he was told that she had left and had given no forwarding address. Back at the Front, he had received the last of her letters. In one, he said, she had asked him if he could spare any money; but, even if he had had any, he would not have known where to send it, he noted. (We learn later that she had loaned him money to pay a debt.)

Pineau then said: "Were you asked by your general and others to be prudent?"

Masloff answered: "True. Was asked if I intended to marry this woman. In January, the general called me in again and told me to cease all relations with this lady who was regarded as an adventuress."

So why did he rush to Paris as soon as he left hospital in March? He answered rather ingenuously that he had gone there to break off the affair.

He said again that she had never discussed with him anything remotely military. He had been "very astonished" to learn that she had been charged with espionage. The deposition ends with Masloff's childish signature.

On May 15, Mata Hari again wrote Bouchardon an imploring letter, complaining that she had been "three months in a cell" and that "I am here because of a misunderstanding." There were only "appearances" that she had done something wrong. He had remained "deaf" because he expected confessions. There were no confessions to make. If she were set free, she promised to talk to no one of what had happened in Paris. She had only agreed to work for France in the first place in order to make enough money to sustain her marriage to Vadim. The letter is very repetitive, which is unusual for Mata Hari and suggests that she was breaking down emotionally.

Two days later, Clunet wrote to Bouchardon, pleading with him to give his distracted client provisional liberty and again demanding that she be confronted by her accusers. Once again, both captive and lawyer were told that she could "confront" only Ladoux, and then only if she had something new to reveal to *him*.

In his book *Les chasseurs d'espions*, Ladoux says that, at some point after her arrest, Mata Hari asked to see him personally. This is true. There is a letter, apparently written just after the rebuff to Clunet, and taken by Clunet to Ladoux. She started it: "Dear Captain [*Mon capitaine*], Yes, I have some very serious things to say to you."

She asked to meet him alone, or with Clunet, or Bouchardon, or all together. She continued:

> I desire to inform you that I did not come to France to harm you in any way at all.
> I have never attempted the least espionage [in France], and I do not have on my conscience the death of any soldier, French or otherwise.

She agreed that "appearances" might make it look otherwise. Then she added intriguingly:

> I hope that this time I will have the courage to tell you what I have to tell you.
> Perhaps the moment had not yet come, until now, and you wouldn't have wanted to believe me, or even admit the possibility of the things which I will tell you now.

In his book, Ladoux says she had been brought to his office and he had asked her: "What can I do for you?" She had countered with: "What am I supposed to have done?"

Then he says he told her: "If you will tell me all the truth, I will not use it against you. I will even do the impossible to rescue you from the stake." Was Ladoux actually having pricklings of conscience?

He says that she asked for assurances on this point and that he had gone at once to the office of the *rapporteur*—Bouchardon—who had refused any deal.

Mata Hari had been returned to prison while Ladoux went to see Bouchardon. She was brought back to the boulevard Saint-Germain the next day. Her first words had been "I am thirsty." The implication Ladoux seems to want to impart is that she appeared to be getting ready to talk at length. A member of the Republican Guard was sent for water, which was brought in a soldier's carafe. Meanwhile, Ladoux says, he told her the news:

"It is impossible for me to give you my word as a soldier that you will not be shot."

"Fine," he says she responded, "have them take me back to prison; I will say nothing more."

According to the trial papers, the truth was dramatically different.

On May 21, she was in fact received by Ladoux, with Bouchardon also present and eventually doing most of the questioning.

She began with the following statement: "I have decided today to tell you the truth. If I have not said it completely up till now, it is because I felt certain feelings of doubt which I will explain to you in a moment."

She then recounted that in May 1916, late one night, when her servant Anna was already in bed, she had received an unexpected caller at her house in the Nieuwe Uitleg in The Hague—Kroemer, the German consul in Amsterdam. He had told her that he knew that she had just asked for a passport for France.

There was chitchat, she said. She had told him about her trip to Paris five months before and how the French were sick of the insolent manner of the British in France and concerned that the British would take over the country. Kroemer had responded with a startling suggestion: Would she gather information for the Germans? He was, he said, authorized to offer her twenty thousand francs.

She had answered that the sum was not much, and he had said that she would have to prove her abilities before getting more. She said he added that "then, you can have all you want." She had asked for time to think about it.

She had reminded herself that the Germans had "stolen" her

furs and had concluded that "it would be fair enough [*de bonne guerre*] to take from them what I could."

In consequence, she had told Kroemer a few days later that she would accept the assignment, and he had come back with twenty thousand French francs in cash. He had offered her invisible ink and told her to sign herself as "H 21." He had given her three small flasks numbered one, two, and three. The first and third were white, the second a "bluish-green, absinthe color." He showed her how the first could be used to dampen the paper, the second to write, and the third to efface the text.

He had told her to send letters to him at the Hôtel de l'Europe in Amsterdam, where he maintained a suite. Since Kroemer was a common name, he said, this would not attract attention.

As her ship sailed through the channel between Amsterdam port and the sea, she had thrown the flasks overboard. She was sure that the French had access to Kroemer's mail in Amsterdam and that they would know that she had never written to him, with or without invisible ink.

Turning to Bouchardon, she said she had not revealed all this to Ladoux the previous year because she had intended to make it—her recruitment into the German intelligence service—her first coup after returning to Holland: "I could not release my secret to him and give away my game play [*grand jeu*] for nothing."

She said that when she had told Ladoux that she would prefer to return to Holland via England rather than through Germany, it was because she had "accounts to render" in Germany, having taken the twenty thousand francs and done nothing in return.

That the Germans had sent radiograms in a broken code that the French were meant to act on had raised one question that her revelations now explained: if they wanted to get the French to kill one of their own agents (in return, as it appeared later, for a similar trick pulled off by the French earlier at the Germans' expense), why had they selected the bumbling Mata Hari, who would always be useful as a pipeline for false information to the French, and not some more skilled French operator? Now the reason was evident: the hussy had taken the Kaiser's shilling—and a handsome shilling at that—done nothing, and gone to the French. Authorized, in his broken-code traffic with Berlin, to pay her three thousand francs—

thus, it was hoped, convincing the French even more that she was a German agent—Kalle had taken his sexual pleasure with the bawd, paid her like a tart in local pesetas, then sent her off to the death that he had planned for her and that he clearly thought she richly deserved. It was not only a great coup against the French but a just reward for someone who thought she could fool Germany out of twenty thousand francs.

Mata Hari, probably using a dose of her usual hyperbole, had claimed that the furs the Germans had taken from her (on the pretext that, although the Dutch were neutral, she was not) were worth three or four times the money Kroemer had produced. It may well be, however, that the sum was closer to the furs' real worth. She was clearly justified in repaying the Germans in their own coin for their dishonesty. Where her naïveté shows is in accepting the money from, of all sources, German intelligence. If she had held up the Deutschbank's Amsterdam office at gunpoint, the French would undoubtedly have applauded. What Bouchardon at once noted was that, in accepting the money—even though, so far as they could determine, she had done nothing in return except her prattling about such things as Briand and the Greek princess—she had committed the felony of "intelligence with the enemy."

The mystery that remains is how she managed to spend such a sum, in addition to what she received from the baron and what she earned in bed, in such a short time, and even run up debts as well. Commissioner Priolet had obviously underestimated when he suggested that she had spent about thirteen thousand francs in all; it must have been closer to thirty thousand—more, if the unpaid debts are factored in. Since the hotel cost only nine hundred francs a month and many of her meals were paid for by escorts, friends, and lovers, the money had clearly been spent where she found it easiest to spend it—at clothiers and in jewelry shops, and of course on Vadim.

How much twenty thousand francs was worth, then, can best be calculated in terms of what could be bought for it. It would, for instance, have paid for her discounted hotel suite (i.e., room with bath) for nearly two years. It was a generous advance, by the standards of the time, but hardly excessive for a luxury-living celebrity of the entertainment world who was being asked to risk her life for a foreign country to which she owed no allegiance.

What would the Russians offer, in time of war, to a Swedish film star, to sleep her way into the White House staff or the higher echelons of the Pentagon? Certainly more than they would offer a White House staffer or a lady colonel. Bizard, who claims specialist knowledge because of his experience as a medical inspector of *maisons closes*, says her fee for a night or an afternoon was probably a thousand francs—although, as mentioned earlier, Rapférer claimed to have paid only one-fifth of that.

Mata Hari said that if, at the time she accepted to work for Ladoux, "I had had anything on my conscience with regard to France, I would have accepted his suggestion that I travel to Germany. Once turned back to Madrid, circumstances obliged me to do what you know."

With Kalle, she said, she not only had to give him some gossip to make him talk, but she also had to pretend to offer him something for her advance of funds; even if he did not know her as "H 21" when she first called, he would certainly have made inquiries about her. If she was going to have to go through Germany to Holland because the British were barring the Channel route, she would have to be in good standing with their intelligence people.

"I composed for him, based on my newpaper readings and my recollections, certain pieces of information or certain analyses [*appréciations*] which have no other significance and which in any event could do you no harm," she said.

Kalle had, it was true, asked Berlin for permission to give her more money. He had told her that Berlin had said no, but that he would give her 3,500 pesetas from his own pocket (which was presumably where the three thousand francs authorized by Berlin in the radio message went).

The payoff had seemed believable to her, because "in his study, he had had some very intimate moments [*de grandes intimités*] with me, and had offered me a ring. As I don't like that sort of jewelry, I declined it, and I suppose the 3,500 pesetas were a replacement gift."

Now apparently confident that her revelation would close the case, she said it was just possible that the two five-thousand-franc payments had actually come from Kroemer, because she had told Anna Lintjens that, if she were ever unable to see the baron, she could fall back on Kroemer at the Hôtel de l'Europe. She added:

"It was well understood, however, that she should never have recourse to this unless the Baron van der Capellen, for whatever reason, could not receive her. . . .

"Nevertheless, I doubt that Anna would have needed to have recourse to Kroemer, and I believe that the money quite simply came from the Baron. That is, after all, what she wrote to me."

If Kalle's messages had not been in the wrong code, Ladoux would presumably have questioned whether Kroemer could not have told Anna to write anything he dictated. Bouchardon, in ignorance of the use of a redundant code, had suggested that anyway when he had called Anna an accomplice. As it was, Bouchardon apparently decided that he might now be able to make a credible case solely out of her own statements. Why, he asked skillfully, had she concealed her relationship with Kroemer from Ladoux but had told Kalle that she had pretended to work for French intelligence?

She answered: "If my attitude was different toward the French and toward the Germans, it was because I wanted to harm the latter—an intention which I brought off—while I only wanted to do well by the French, an intention which I similarly brought about." In order to be able to go through Germany safely for the French, she had had to prove to the Germans that she had access to Ladoux.

Bouchardon insisted that it was the French whom she was out to deceive.

She conceded that she had acted recklessly. She was not, she reminded them, a professional spy—"I had never done spying before. I have always lived for love and pleasure."

In that case, Bouchardon asked, how had she expected to bring off an espionage coup in Belgium that would be worth a million francs to the French?

It was a very valid question, and the answer must certainly be that it is highly unlikely that she would have lasted long in Belgium. Mata Hari riposted that it was Ladoux who had suggested that she pretend to work for the Germans and to become that most difficult spy of all, a double agent.

Bouchardon and Ladoux now knew how she would have proceeded with Kroemer, had she reached Amsterdam: she would have fed him the same trivialities she had fed Kalle and would have expected that this would persuade the German consul to launch her on the road to von Bissing.

Bouchardon, however, was still looking for some evidence that she had actually done something—anything—in return for the Kaiser's money. Riffling through the reports of the *filature* inspectors, he noted that on August 6, 1916, she had dined at the Lyon station—a famous rococo restaurant that still exists—with a staff captain called Gerbaud who was about to leave for Chambéry. Why?

Said Mata Hari: "I love officers. I have loved them all my life. I prefer being the mistress of a poor officer than of a rich banker. . . . And I like to compare nations."

The officers, she said, sought relief from the horrors of the Front. "They went away happy, without ever having spoken to me of the war and without my asking anything indiscreet of them. The only one I held on to was Masloff, because I adored him." She was to ask for Gerbaud as a witness.

In the hope of finding that she had spied on an officer, somewhere, Bouchardon took the conversation back to Vittel. Why had she told van der Capellen that she was in good health before she left for the "cure" there? Said Mata Hari: "You are talking of a man before whom one must never admit to being sick. He needs a cheerful, healthy mistress in lacy clothes."

She admitted to the trips to Raincy to consult a fortune-teller. She was asked about the American, Moore, who had said he was a munitions merchant. He had made advances, she said, but she had rejected him because of his table manners.

She was also asked about some scuttlebutt passed on by Hallaure. She denied that, after Rousseau, she had been maintained in Neuilly by a "foreigner." She had had many different lovers, she said. She also denied that she had left the Molier circus because her act was a flop; she had left to take a contract at the Folies-Bergère. (This must surely be a lapse of memory; and Hallaure, like many others, must have presumed her guilt and was seeking to distance himself from her by disobliging remarks.)

"I worked against the Germans in the hope of gaining my independence and my happiness with Masloff, but I did not feel any aversion toward the German people," she said candidly. "I played a money trick on them for the furs I lost, and that's all. In any case, once in Paris, I never wrote to Kroemer, and I have done nothing against France."

The next day, May 22, Bouchardon called her in again to ask once more why "Krämer" would give her twenty thousand francs without any proof that she was worth it. Surely she had worked earlier for the enemy? He asked why she preferred to send letters by the diplomatic pouch to sending them through the wartime mails. He was clearly still anxious to make a case but seems to have been running out of questions.

Ladoux was also there again. He said it was true that he had told her that, for the right sort of information from German head-quarters, France would not hesitate to pay a million francs, or fifty times what Kroemer gave as an advance. She in turn admitted that, having failed to say at the start that Kroemer had given her the "H 21" number, she had feared to reveal it later.

Now Bouchardon was repeating himself. Why had she returned to France from Spain? She said it was because that was the only way of getting to Holland through Switzerland and Germany and completing her assignment in Belgium.

Ladoux chipped in that he had never really "assigned" her, because he had not spelled out the mission, or given her a number, a means of communication, or money. He had told her to await instructions in Holland.

Said Mata Hari to Bouchardon: "The captain was more affirm-ative than that. How do you think I would have gone along if he had limited himself to what he says? He knew perfectly well that I was going to frequent [German] staff headquarters in Belgium." She forgot to mention that, despite his remark, he had in fact also offered her a "means of communication"—invisible ink.

Bouchardon complained again that she had said nothing about "Krämer" before. She answered: "I told you nothing [of this] because you didn't want to pay me and so I didn't feel obliged to furnish you too soon with my great secret."

Ladoux said something about "intelligence with the enemy" being the same as "supplying information to the enemy." He did not say what he had hoped that she would do at German staff headquarters.

Mata Hari returned to her prison, leaving the two men alone.

Bouchardon then questioned Ladoux on Mata Hari's testimony about choosing to go to Holland via Spain instead of Germany. Ladoux was evasive, saying most people preferred to go via Spain because the luggage was handled "in a more practical manner" on that route. Bouchardon asked about Mata Hari's quotation from Denvignes, saying Goubet had found her information interesting. Ladoux said he knew nothing of that. Then Ladoux, following up on Bouchardon's question to the prisoner, added one of his most curious remarks: he said he could see no good reason why anyone would want to take advantage of being able to use a diplomatic pouch. He found her failure to use the slow and frequently ineffective wartime mail system "suspicious."

The next day, May 23, she was asked for more details of her discussion with Kroemer. What had she said to persuade him of her German sympathies? She said again that she had recounted how British officers were behaving badly in Paris and being impolite toward the French. She had told him the French story about how the British would never go home after the war but would hold on to the territories where they had troops. (One wonders if this was not a disinformation line put out by the Germans.) This area of conversation reminded her to tell Bouchardon that there was an error in one of Kalle's radiograms—the one in which he says "March" for "May."

She complained that Denvignes had "deformed" his testimony to hide the fact that "he ran after me, making himself ridiculous." He had offered to marry her, but she had never actually slept with him. She cautioned: "A man of the rank of Colonel Denvignes should not throw the first stone at a woman in her misfortune, the more so since he had asked me to become his mistress, to which I replied that I was in love with a Russian captain whom I intended to marry." She was obviously implying that Denvignes had been spiteful out of jealousy. If Denvignes had really suspected that she worked for German espionage, she added, would he have courted her so assiduously in public, bringing her violets and untying the ribbon at her bosom?

It certainly seemed as if the colonel's testimony had been less than candid.

9. The Pretrial—
4: The Trap Closes

THE THIRTEEN APPEARANCES and twelve mostly heavy interrogation sessions had not seemed to change the attitude of Ladoux and Bouchardon. They appeared determined to press on, and put her on trial. On May 24, she must have awoken with a strong sense of persecution. After her ablutions, she perched paper and inkwell on the washstand and wrote a bitter letter to Bouchardon.

Some person or persons, she knew, were out to get her. Accusing Ladoux or Bouchardon themselves would get her nowhere. Whom had she antagonized? In her letter, she concentrated on Denvignes, the absent and flirtatious colonel whom the two overworked captains knew was not without his weaknesses.

She said she thought that Denvignes must have been behind the letter that the Russian military attaché in Paris had written to Masloff's commander to try to ensure that the two lovers no longer met. Denvignes was clearly acting out of "vengeance and amorous spite," because she had rejected him and had said that she was going to marry a Russian. Hell, in short, hath no fury like a colonel scorned in favor of a foreign junior officer.

The trial that was being prepared, she wrote, was "half vengeance and half the fatality of appearances." She concluded that "I have truly never, never done any espionage."

Bouchardon invited her to give her own version, in writing and in detail, of her relationship with Denvignes. She sat down to write again, and this time her version was more detailed.

She explained once more that, a few days after arriving in Madrid, she had been dining at the hotel with the Dutch consul de Witt (she wrote "de With") and his colleague, Baron van Aerssen.

214

A "gentleman in civilian clothes" had asked to be presented. This was Denvignes.

He had turned up at the hotel the next morning while she was reading in the lobby. His first question had been: "Can you guess, Madame, why I have come?"

Mata Hari had responded, coyly: "For me, perhaps?"

Said Denvignes: "Yes. I have never seen anything as harmonious as you, yesterday evening, entering in evening dress, in the hall of the hotel. It was a vision that I shall never forget. Where are you dining this evening?"

She had said that she was attending a gala dinner at the Ritz with the same Dutch diplomats. Denvignes had said that he would come to the gala later. That was the occasion when she had warded off the lovelorn officer's attentions by talking of professional matters and telling him about her conversation with Kalle.

All the first moves, she pointed out, had been made by the colonel, who had implied in his testimony that the tawny siren had seduced him. (Bouchardon and Ladoux, in their memoirs, believe Mata Hari.)

Sitting apart with Denvignes on a canapé sofa, she had had the impression that the submarine story was news to him. As she recalls it, it was while she was in the hotel reading room the following day that he had returned and asked her to check further into the story. He had returned for tea, but she had reported that she had been unable to draw out Kalle any further. It was the day after that, as she remembered, that Denvignes had told her that he was going to Paris with General Lyautey. They had discussed her relationships with prewar Germans, including the Crown Prince. She had said Kalle claimed to have met her at the Silesian maneuvers and in the Carlton Hotel in Berlin, but that she had had no recollection of him. She had told Denvignes that she had raised with Ladoux the prospect of seducing the Duke of Cumberland.

Then, she said, "the colonel was very friendly toward me and asked me if I would like to be more intimate with him." He had suggested that they leave their hotels and take a house: "You will brighten my home," he had said. She had explained that she had "given my heart" to a Russian captain, whom she had promised to marry. He had asked for the captain's name, and she had told him.

She said Denvignes had agreed to ask Ladoux and Goubet for a cash advance for her and that he had told her to continue reporting to him, Denvignes, at 282 boulevard Saint-Germain, handing the letters to the French embassy.

"He gave me a small bouquet of violets, which he asked me to wear between my breasts during the day. He would come and take one of them in the evening," she wrote. When he had returned on his romantic mission, he had disentwined a ribbon from her *cache-corset* and had asked for her perfumed handkerchief. They had kissed. She had agreed that they would meet in Paris, as soon as she had her French visa and could travel. He had told her to find him at the Grand Hôtel d'Orsay, and she had agreed to have dinner with him there.

It was on a Sunday (December 31?), she recalled, that she had given a letter for him to the delegation; it contained the information about invisible ink crystals, the landings behind the German lines, and German knowledge of the French radio code key.

Denvignes had already given her his visiting card to use at the frontier in case of difficulty. She had arrived in Paris "on about January 4."

She redescribed the difficulties in meeting him and how they had finally met at the Austerlitz station. She recounted the conversation like the script of a play:

> Mata Hari: You're leaving like that, without saying anything to me?
> Denvignes: Yes, what do you expect? I must return to Madrid.
> Mata Hari: Did you at least have the time to talk to Captain Ladoux and settle my affairs?
> Denvignes: I didn't see the captain much, but I spoke to his superior, Colonel Goubet.
> Mata Hari: What did he say?
> Denvignes: He said you were an intelligent woman to whom a dangerous mission could be entrusted.
> Mata Hari: Is that all?
> Denvignes: I told him you were well introduced to Madrid society and that I had met you through the attachés of your legation. He asked me if I knew about your *démarches* with the German attaché. I said I knew nothing.
> Mata Hari: Colonel, why did you lie?
> Denvignes: Ah, my child! My child!

She said she was left "astonished" on the platform. Denvignes had seemed embarrassed, no longer amorous, quite different from his manner in Madrid.

The police were still questioning the names on the calling cards. On May 19, there had been Ernest Molier, the retired seventy-three-year-old stables and circus owner. He recalled having advised her against seeking a job as a professional horsewoman, an occupation that was passing out of style. He had told her Javanese dancing would be more of an attraction.

Molier said: "She seemed to me remarkably intelligent. . . . She spoke five or six languages, of which three correctly."

On May 23, they questioned Annette Borillot, widow Lelarge, aged sixty, home nurse. She said she had been "Madame Zelle's" cook in Neuilly from May to October of 1912. She claimed no knowledge of her employer's love life or finances but spoke well of her. Madame had tried to get her back later, but by then she had been working for someone else. Madame had been in touch when she returned to Paris in 1916, and she had visited the lady twice at the Grand Hôtel.

The same day came Fernand Bloch, aged forty-four, a businessman at Mulhouse in Alsace-Lorraine, which had become German territory in 1871 but was to be restored to France after World War I. He had met Mata Hari at the Bristol Hotel in Berlin, where she had appeared at the time to be the mistress of the director of the Berlin branch of the French bank, Société Générale, he said. In 1916, he had run into her in a Paris street, chatted, and given her his card.

The police had picked up a tip that a Paris dressmaker called Mrs. Breton had been promised a false Dutch passport by Mata Hari, who had offered to take her, as a maid, to Germany, where the woman could visit her husband, a prisoner of war. This outlandish proposal seemed to fit the activities of a spy, they thought. But why would a German spy want an "enemy" French maid in Germany in wartime? Anyway, they had picked up Julie-Clothilde Breton, née Clotos, aged forty, who was also questioned on May 23.

The woman said that Mata Hari had ordered dresses from her while the dancer was in Holland and that they had exchanged correspondence. When Mata Hari returned to Paris, she had given her more orders in June 1916.

Madame had said that she had had an Indian husband who had beaten her and driven her from the house when he had found her in bed with another man. She had rambled on that her protector was now a Dutch colonel, but that she was staying in Paris with a Belgian officer (Beaufort). Mrs. Breton had discussed the fact that her husband was a prisoner. She confirmed that Mata Hari had suggested the scenario for getting her to Germany to see him but said she had turned the project down.

"When you have a husband who is a prisoner, a brother killed, and another at the Front, you can't go to Germany," she recalled saying. Mata Hari had said: "Don't be angry." Mrs. Breton, as it turned out, was more angry about something else: Mata Hari had tried to lure one of her seamstresses away, to work directly for the Dutchwoman on her wardrobe.

Behind Ladoux, the head of counterespionage, stood a shadowy figure three ranks higher who controlled the whole French intelligence service, the Second Bureau. Colonel Antoine-Joseph-Pierre-Edouard Goubet, aged forty-nine, testified in writing to Bouchardon on May 24. He said he had never met Mata Hari but considered her "one of the most dangerous spies" known to his organization. To get a conviction, he was clearly prepared to say that the Madrid-Berlin radio traffic was genuine and to use the amplified version of the messages supplied by Ladoux.

His statement was penned in his own hand and reads:

"If you will refer to the first radio message of von Kalle, you will notice that, on his own admission, Zelle has been sent twice into France for German espionage: in consequence, she should explain to you, as she has not done, her first trip, which began in June 1915."

Why the great panjandrum of French intelligence should write "June" instead of "December" is not clear: it suggests that he had only studied the dossier briefly. He continued:

"She used that journey so well for an espionage mission, and brought back such interesting information, that Krämer [sic] gave her, all at once, before her recent departure, that of May 1916, the sum of twenty thousand francs."

This, he said, was unthinkable unless an agent had "shown her prowess." There had been another five thousand francs in November.

"If Zelle, through an intermediary at whose identity it is perhaps not difficult to guess, had procured nothing for Krämer, if she had swindled him out of the twenty thousand francs in May without giving him any further sign of existence, this consul would not have sent her another five thousand francs in November through Anna Litjens [*sic*] and Bunge. What is more, Zelle would not have presented herself in December to van Kalée [*sic*], under her number as Agent H 21, thus permitting the military attaché to unmask her and learn of her treason."

Goubet knew he was addressing a captain in the army legal service with no "need to know" about codes and who would accept whatever intelligence told him as genuine. Now the head of the Second Bureau built on the information that Mata Hari had volunteered—that she had taken twenty thousand francs from Kroemer, money that she petulantly felt the German government owed her for her furs. Goubet used this to suggest that her 1915 Christmas idyll with Beaufort was a spying mission for which Kroemer was paying her *half a year later.* Carefully avoiding any suggestion of questioning van der Capellen and Anna Lintjens as to where the two five-thousand-franc drafts came from, he confirmed Bouchardon's assumption (which presumably had been suggested by Ladoux) that they must have been sent by Kroemer. Since Goubet's service had been unable to unearth any sign of spying in France that would justify these "payments," it was up to Bouchardon to find out what she did.

Why, asked Goubet, didn't she tell Ladoux that she had already been recruited by the Germans, when she had told Kalle that she had been recruited by the French? (She had, of course, already explained that when Bouchardon had asked the same question.) For Goubet, "that is the classic manner of the double agent. To keep us confident, she pretended to bring us something," and she had offered to try to get more from Kalle. The information that the head of German espionage in Spain was von Rolland in Barcelona was "deceptive," Goubet said. The real director was "a certain Rueggeberg."

The next day, a statement was taken from Henri Monier, the thirty-three-year-old police inspector who had followed Mata Hari around Paris and Vittel for months with his colleague Tarlet. Bouchardon's questioning only touched on a few points that the examining magistrate needed to build his case.

We learn that Mata Hari "approached men in a way that made it difficult not to enter into conversation with her." She was femininely "provocative."

To another question, Monier answered that he had followed her on six trips to the Dutch consulate-general and that she had told employees at the hotel that she was known to Consul Bunge.

Having established, correctly, that she could use her powers over men and was a frequent visitor to the Dutch mission, Bouchardon needed additional evidence that she frequently made up stories. Monier said that at Vittel she had once told some officers that she was a countess with a château in Touraine.

There was little more. Mata Hari had "extravagant tastes." At Vittel, she had flirted with General de Sancy de Rolland. All of this seems incontrovertible, but Monier did recount a rumor that she had twice delayed her departure from France for Holland because she had been informed that the ship she was to take from Vigo would be torpedoed. This was a story that apparently got about because a ferry *was* torpedoed that year just before she took the *Hollandia*.

There is no testimony from Mrs. Dangeville, whose salon entertained officers; this was where Mata Hari first met Masloff away from the hotel. The police seem to have confused Mrs. Dangeville with Miss Henriette Doyen, a fifty-one-year-old playwright whom Mata Hari occasionally visited while being shadowed. This lady was interviewed on May 26; she said that it was possible that Mata Hari had met Lieutenant Gasfield at her house, but that she had never heard of Masloff.

On May 29, the general from Vittel of whom Inspector Monier had spoken made a statement. He was Jules-Clément Le Loup de Sancy de Rolland, a reserve brigadier of seventy-three. He said he was taking the cure at Vittel when, although he was dressed in civilian clothes, he was saluted by a Russian officer in the hotel dining room. He had noticed the young man before, because the fellow had an eye injury that was now covered by a patch. There was some conversation, then Mata Hari arrived and the Russian presented her as his fiancée.

The brigadier commented: "This person betrayed an age in such disproportion to that of the officer that I scented at once the adventuress." He said he had acted toward her with reserve.

He noted that for six years he had been a military attaché at the French embassy in Berlin and had had plenty of experience with German women spies. Had he made a report? Yes, he had told the special commissioner of the Vittel railroad station that he had found her suspicious. But he conceded that she had never discussed military subjects with him.

A sixty-three-year-old colleague of the brigadier's, Lieutenant-General Maurice-François Baumgarten (whom readers will recall she met in Paris just before she left for Vittel), related being at the spa at the same time as Mata Hari. He had first come across her in the dining room of the Grand Hôtel in Paris.

The hotel conversation had been about horses and about Dutch people who were making money out of the war by representing German firms in the Americas. She had asked no military questions, but she had sought his help in getting in touch with the Russian, Captain de Masloff, whom she thought had been gassed. But she had received a letter from Masloff "the following day" and had left for Vittel a few days later. No, she had not flirted with him, either in Paris or in Vittel, he said.

There were several more interviews with persons she had met at the Paris and Vittel hotels, with shopkeepers, even a nun. All yielded nothing of apparent use to the prosecution.

On May 30, Mata Hari was interrogated once more. Bouchardon took her back over her relations with Denvignes in Madrid. Although he appears to have learned nothing new, he apparently inflamed the lady's enmity for the inadequate colonel.

Back in her cell, she took pen in hand again to write to Bouchardon, saying she wanted to expand on the points she had answered. She referred to her letter of six days before about Denvignes: it seems she mainly wanted to emphasize that she had returned to Kalle solely on Denvignes' instructions, to collect more information about the Moroccan landings.

"He knew nothing about all that," she wrote. "On the contrary, it was I who brought him this information, and he was astonished by it, so astonished that on the following day he returned to see me and asked me to try to have precise details."

She denied, however, that Denvignes had asked her to get a date for a future landing. She also denied, for some reason, a phrase that Bouchardon had said Denvignes had heard her say: "In France, I had an artistic career and in Germany I had a ball." (*En France, je faisais de l'art, et en Allemagne, la noce.*) Perhaps she felt it implied that she had enjoyed Germany more.

The next day, Clunet brought Bouchardon another letter from his client. She complained that Ladoux had never understood what she was trying to tell him. Ladoux had said that France would shoot her unless she revealed her accomplices. She went on, addressing Bouchardon by his military legal title of Reporter (to the court):

> I swear to you, captain Reporter, that I have never had any accomplices, and that I am not coward enough to invent names under the threat of death. . . .
>
> Captain Ladoux and I will never understand each other. Because of my travels, my foreign acquaintances, my life style and situation, I have a grand view of events, and grand methods. With him, it's quite the contrary. He sees everything small; petty. . . . He never knew how to use me. That is his fault and not mine.
>
> As for myself, I have been sincere. My love and my self-interest are the guarantee of that. Today, around me, everything is collapsing, everyone turns his back, even he for whom I would have gone through fire. Never would I have believed in so much human cowardice. Well, so be it. I am alone. I will defend myself and if I must fall it will be with a smile of profound contempt.
>
> Respectfully,
> M. G. Zelle McLeod [*sic*]

The following day, she wrote again, on a more positive if impractical note, asking to be given the opportunity to do what Ladoux had said was all that could save her from the stake:

If Captain Ladoux gives me *immediate liberty* [underscored in the original] and permission to leave for Holland, I will give him within one month what he asked to know yesterday, and of which I know absolutely nothing: details of the organization of German intelligence in France and in Paris.

Captain Ladoux should make it possible for me to go for six months. I cannot do it in a cell.

You can threaten me and make me suffer, but I cannot tell you what I do not know.

This was the same day, June 1, that she was called in by Bouchardon for more repetitive questioning. She denied that "Krämer" had ever been her lover or sought to be. Are they sure they had the name right, she asked plaintively; wasn't it Krömer (an alternative spelling for Kroemer)? In any event, the man was not a powerful figure, she said. He was merely a wealthy businessman in Amsterdam who had been made honorary consul. He had approached her only after she had herself decided to return to France and had already obtained a French visa. Of the invisible ink bottles that she had accepted, she said she felt "purified" of any link to German intelligence after throwing the three flasks into the Amsterdam ship channel.

But the pencil-tapping, nail-chewing Bouchardon was not to be satisfied, and this nervous figure could from time to time turn brutal in his manner. On one occasion, he had crudely questioned the depth of her feelings about Masloff, saying scornfully that he was just another trophy among her multitudinous clientele. Now he questioned again why Kroemer would pay twenty thousand francs without having received any intelligence from Mata Hari before.

"We know German prices!" he rasped.

She responded that she had not approached Kroemer; he had approached her; therefore the asking price was sure to be higher. Moreover, she was a neutral on whom Germany could not call for a patriotic effort, and she was a woman who would be risking her life if she ever did what he was asking.

Bouchardon came back to Kalle's reference to more of "H 21's" information being forwarded by letter. What information would that be?

"Sophisticated chitchat (*Des mondanités*)," Mata Hari answered.

Bouchardon asked about her boast of having a château in Touraine. She said she had been referring to the Château de la Dorée at Eures (probably Baudouin's mistake; actually, it was at Esvres) and briefly recounted her time there with Rousseau.

Back in her cell, she wrote to Bouchardon to add some more details. She had had no contact with any Germans in France during the war, she said. She repeated that she had gone to see Kalle in Madrid to satisfy Ladoux's intelligence needs and to be able to travel safely through Germany to Belgium. Once more she reminded Bouchardon that she had insisted that Ladoux never question her methods.

She recalled that she had been driven to Kalle's house (she says "the German embassy") in the Hôtel Ritz car, so there had been nothing secret about the call. She had written to Captain Ladoux about it the same evening. She had informed Colonel Denvignes "the next day." She had not asked for a French visa until about ten days after that. Since the visa had been granted, she had assumed that Paris was satisfied with her work.

On January 3 (this is a wrong date again, since she left Madrid on the second) she had received the Junoy letter, which she had taken to Paladines, who had told her that she had absolutely nothing to worry about in France.

"A visa is a safe-conduct and, when France gives a safe-conduct, it should not use it to arrest a woman," she complained.

Still grasping for an explanation for her dilemma, she asked if perhaps Ladoux had wanted to use her at first, then had changed his mind after she had been arrested by the British.

The next day, she wrote again to say that both the Marquis d'Aurelles de Paladines and another attaché had assured her that she could trust her French safe-conduct. And how could Ladoux pretend that he had never recruited her?

She added, and underlined: *"I have not betrayed you!"* And she concluded: "When France sends Mata Hari on mission, they must expect her to go to the top. If they want information about the Germans, that means the German embassy."

But the unscrupulous Ladoux and the manipulated Bouchardon were relentlessly building a case that a half-informed panel of officers would not be able to reject. On June 3, Ladoux had passed a note to Bouchardon with a new theory about "H." He said he had never seen a German agent with an "H" number before: surely this indicated *prewar* recruitment. (Marthe Richard later cleared this up. "H," she said, stood for Holland. She herself had had an "S" number—S 32—with the "S" standing for *Spanien*, German for Spain.)

But in bizarre contradiction, Ladoux's memo also said: "In response to your note of June 2, I have the honor to inform you that no element of proof exists to my knowledge that permits the affirmation that Zelle MacLeod was engaged by the German SR [intelligence service, in the French initials] from 1915."

Nevertheless, she was to be accused of working for the Germans in that year and to be found guilty.

On June 5, Mata Hari wrote once more to Bouchardon, stressing her treatment in Berlin at the outbreak of war. All foreign accounts had been frozen, she said once more, but all creditors had brought in their bills. Luggage had been seized. She had been especially roughly treated, she recalled, because she had lived in France for most of the previous decade and because she had wanted to return to France, not to her native Holland. She repeated how the Dutch lawyer and the Dutch legation had finally recovered her money and the jewelry in her strongbox but not her furs. She had been happy to take the German government's money when the opportunity presented itself:

> I have encountered in this world riff-raff and good people. I lose. I win. I defend myself when I am attacked. I take when someone has taken from me.
>
> But I beg you to believe me; I have never done an act of espionage against France. Never. Never.

There are more letters on June 6, June 8, and June 9, explaining what she was doing during her 1915 trip. She had spent most of the time with the "Marquis" de Marguérie. He had taken her to the station when she had left to return to Holland. She had seen both Marguérie and Beaufort in 1916 and had discussed Ladoux's proposals with Marguérie, whom she had not slept with again after falling in love with Masloff.

In the letter of the eighth, she noted that Bouchardon had told her that one of the intercepted messages had referred to her arrest at Falmouth on November 11. Actually, it must have been November 18, she said, because her passport would show that she had been in Hendaye on November 11. (She did not know this, of course, but she was referring to a Kalle message that never existed or that had been rewritten by Ladoux; and her memory was wrong—she had passed through Hendaye on November 6.)

Until then, she had assumed that the Kalle traffic was genuine and that it reflected her success in fooling the Germans into thinking she was the H 21 whom Kroemer had wanted her to be. Now, knowing nothing about Locard and code-breaking and the game of *intoxication* that the cryptographers had pointed out, and getting the dates of some of Kalle's messages confused, she hit on the truth, but only out of suspicion:

> Since, knowing me to be in Paris, how is it possible that he [Kalle] continues to telegraph Berlin for two more months, as you have told me? Might it not be possible that the Germans themselves threw French intelligence on a false track, to permit some true woman agent to be left unbothered?
>
> I never gave sign of life to the consul [Kroemer]. Is it that this affair could only be a revenge on their part? It cannot be otherwise.
>
> Fate put me in the presence of the German military attaché in Madrid, from whom I truly succeeded in taking information. There is perhaps vengeance on their part; the dispatches which you have intercepted, are you sure that they don't know that these dispatches come to your notice?
>
> Would it not be possible that they are telegraphing only what they want you to know? If this is so, Captain, don't play their cards for them by making me suffer.
>
> If I learn that it is thus, I shall perhaps be a more terrible enemy for the Germans than you could ever be. They are capable of this.

The amateur spy was still not prepared to accept that Kalle had made a fool of her with his *intoxication* messages about breaking the French code and so on, which she still claimed as successful intelligence on her part. But she had pierced the riddle of the Madrid-Berlin messages. What she did not know was that Ladoux and Goubet had not been fooled but had deliberately decided to ignore the facts in order to get a conviction. Only Bouchardon, to whom the letter was addressed, did not know that the Germans had used a broken cipher. Only he could save her. But there is no evidence, at least in the files, that he ever asked Ladoux or Goubet whether her theory could be right, and that the French were reading "only what they want you to know."

On June 10, Clunet sent this June 8 letter on with one of his own, in which he made a final abortive attempt to have her released on provisional liberty. He said her health was degenerating and that she now had to share a cell with a convict, which was improper for someone still awaiting trial. The convict was presumably an informer. She was removed.

The last of the visiting cards, or addresses or names written on scraps of paper, was reached when a "rogatory commission" called in Sergeant-Major Georges Louis of the 12th Armored Cavalry (*cuirassiers*).

She had remembered who he was. After her devastating last interview on the Austerlitz platform with Denvignes, the sergeant-major had stopped her and asked her to be his godmother. In both world wars, women, especially if they were young and pretty, were asked to adopt lonely soldiers by correspondence as "godmothers."

But the sergeant-major, now stationed at the aviation school at Cazeaux, near Bordeaux, couldn't remember how the lady had gotten his name and address. Told it could have been at the Austerlitz station just after New Year, he said that that had been when he had returned from leave in Paris and that "I had been drinking a little." Finally, he remembered enough to be able to assure the police that "she did not put to me any questions concerning, from near or from far, the national defense."

The last complete and secret interrogatory—the fourteenth, and the fifteenth *comparution*—took place on June 12. Bouchardon marched up and down in his small office, and his fingernails must by now have been down to the quick; he raised his voice as he tried once more to pry some agreement that she had actually rendered services for Kroemer's money, which he said again was too much to be given for nothing.

Mata Hari asked that they interview the "Marquis" de Marguérie, who was still living at 3 rue Balzac and who, she reminded them, had known her for fourteen years. During her three-week visit over Christmas of 1915, he had spent "most of his time" with her. He had put her on the train for home. He had also put her on the train for Vittel in 1916. He knew her better than anyone.

"I informed him of what took place between Captain Ladoux and I and he counseled me to accept. He will tell you that I was serious," she said.

She was asked how much money she had spent in France between June and November 1916. She calculated that she had spent about sixteen thousand francs, not including Kroemer's money, which she blithely claimed to have used to pay off "debts in Holland."

The next day, Henry Jean-Baptiste Joseph de Marguérie made a formal testimony. He gave his age as forty-eight and his profession as diplomat. He had met Mrs. MacLeod, as he called her, "around 1903" when he was *en poste* in The Hague. She had just left her husband. She was very intelligent, with musical and singing talents. She had wanted to be an artist in Paris. He had met her again the next year in the French capital, and again in 1907 or 1908 in Vienna, at which time she had had a German lover. Discretion being the better part of diplomatic valor, he presumably thought it would do neither of them any good if he described how he had stage-managed her entry into Paris salons and how she had subsequently fooled the Guimet Museum. He merely said he had seen her "a few times" in Paris before the war. He had had meetings with her "several times" during her brief 1915–1916 visit and had taken her to the train when she left for home. She had sent him a card from Lisbon. They had seen each other several times when she was trying to go to Vittel.

Had she told him about her meeting with Ladoux? Yes, she had told him of a request by "a gentleman with a black beard" who had asked her "to work for our government." To Marguérie, she had seemed to be the right person, because of her "international relations" and her "intelligence." She was anti-German. But he had told her that the question of a permit to go to Vittel was outside his competence.

On June 19, Bouchardon sent a registered letter to Clunet, informing him that the final "interrogatory and confrontation" would take place on the twenty-first and that he had a right to be present. This was to be essentially a formality, the main purpose being to give Clunet copies of the interrogatories, to enable him to prepare a case.

The same day, Mata Hari wrote once more to the army magistrate, noting that her recruitment by Ladoux had taken place not in a restaurant but in the ministry:

> Could I under these conditions doubt a French officer or retain the least doubt about the reality of the mission which he had given me?

She recalled that Ladoux had followed up his instructions by sending her at once to Maunoury at the Prefecture of Police (actually, at the commissariat in the rue Taitbout), and Maunoury had asked her if she wished to travel via Spain or Germany to go to Holland. If she were a German agent, would she not have chosen the more convenient route, through Germany? she asked yet again.

Now she was in love with Masloff, whom she wanted to marry. "Since he is a Russian officer, I obviously could only work for the Allies," she wrote. Ladoux had "lacked perspicacity" in handling her.

Once more, she tried hopelessly to tempt them with what she could do for the Allies by resuscitating the offer made to Ladoux the year before:

> I have been the mistress of the brother of the Duke of Cumberland. The latter has, as you know, married the daughter of [Kaiser] Wilhelm, and he [also] has had with me some intimate relationships. I know that his brother-in-law has made him swear that he will not claim the throne of Hanover, but he would only take this oath for himself, refusing to engage his descendants. Between he and the Crown Prince, there is a truly ferocious hatred; it was this hatred which I was proposing to exploit in the interests of France and in my own interest. You will see what a service I would have been able to render to you.
>
> I would have renewed relations with the Duke of Cumberland and I would then have done everything I could to detach him from Germany and put him on the side of the Entente. All that would have been needed would have been to promise him, if the Allies won, the throne of Hanover.

This idea, she said, had occurred to her in Ladoux's office, where "I saw the big picture" (*j'ai vu fort et grand*).

She was referring to the fact that in 1907, when she was thirty-one, she had been the mistress both of the young Duke Ernst-August, who was then nineteen and the future father of the late Queen Frederika of Greece, and also, more especially, of his twenty-seven-year-old brother, Georg-Wilhelm. (Hanover was a small German principality called an Electorate, ruled by an Elector; it had provided the ruling family of Britain, which changed the royal name from Hanover to Windsor during World War I. All monarchical rule was abolished in Germany after the war.)

Having described the fantasy million-franc coup she had planned, her rhetoric overtook her:

> All my life I have been a spontaneous person, I've never dragged my heels [*je n'ai jamais marché petit*]. I see big objectives and go straight to them.
>
> I proclaim it loudly, all my stays in France have been pure of any suspicious contact. I have never written letters concerning, from close or from far, espionage. I have only frequented decent people. I have never asked military questions.

Her lawyer in The Hague, Hijmans, had written on May 21 to the Dutch legation, asking where Mata Hari was. Van der Capellen had apparently not passed on the confidential information that he had received through the Dutch foreign minister the month before. News of Hijmans' query presumably reached her with the usual delays, because on June 22 she wrote to the consulate-general saying that "apparently no one in Holland knows what has happened to me, although I have written to my servant, Anna Lintjens."

What had also prompted this letter was the receipt of a bill addressed to her hotel by a Hague furrier, C. H. Kuhne. Her letter to the consulate-general continued: "Please write to lawyer Hijmans, 19 Nieuwe Uitleg, to inform him of what has happened to me."

Even in prison and under threat of execution, the wily Frisian was not about to pay a stuffed bill, however. She added:

> I cannot accept a bill in which I see nearly 500 florins too much, and of which 700 florins have already been paid, without consulting the receipts which I have from him; there are probably other sections of the bill which have been settled already. . . .
>
> Please ask my lawyer, Hijmans, to ask my old servant to come

to his office. She should see my lover, the Baron van der Capellen, and ask him to give a thousand florins to Kuhne, but without accepting the total in the bill sent, and tell him that Kuhne should leave me in peace and not send me letters, either at my house or here, to which I am unable to respond.

Please ask my lawyer if, at home, in my house at The Hague, everything is in order, with the rent and the taxes paid, so that I can at least be at ease on that subject. The misfortune which has happened to me is terrible, but I am innocent; everything will come out.

Still concerned that she might have been taken advantage of financially as well as judicially, she wrote again to the consulate-general on July 16, asking them to send Clunet some papers that she had left behind by mistake one day with a consul. These were a "letter on violet paper written in Dutch and signed 'Anna,'" to which Mata Hari said she had pinned her *Hollandia* ticket. Since the ship had taken her only as far as Falmouth, she wanted reimbursement for the rest of the trip, then a voyage of several days in a private cabin. The shipping line, Royal Dutch Lloyd, responded promptly. On July 24, the day the trial opened, Clunet received a check from them for 328 francs.

Others were thinking along similar lines. The last items in the files before the actual trial documents are an expense account from Commissioner Priolet for his taxi fare "and other costs" in connection with her arrest, totaling twenty-eight francs and forty-five centimes, and three accounts for even smaller sums from another inspector.

Almost the only sum that remained to be paid was a human life.

With the interrogation over, Mata Hari was once more back at her inkwell. On June 29, she wrote to Clunet asking him to ask Bouchardon if she could have one photo of Masloff—any one— from those seized. The request was apparently refused.

On June 30, she wrote to Lieutenant André Mornet, who was to be her prosecutor and who had now taken charge of the case from Bouchardon, asking to be able to get more money from Holland. This too was refused. The draft would have had to come from van der Capellen, and his response would have been embarrassing for the prosecution's case, since it would have been difficult not to question him as to whether he had sent the earlier drafts that were being attributed to Kroemer.

On July 2, she renewed this request and complained of humiliation and insults from the prison's male guards. The next day, she wrote to Mornet again, stressing the need for money from Holland to pay her lawyer. Actually, although she had selected him, Clunet had had himself named as appointed by the court, to protect himself from opprobrium in the current wave of "espionitis," and the later judgment refers to him as *avocat d'office*. He probably did not expect or want to be paid, but he may well have suggested that Mata Hari use "legal fees" as a stratagem for getting permission to bring funds from Holland.

On July 5, there was another letter for Mornet about the money, noting that she had other bills beside her legal ones to settle, including one for a photographer.

The next day, she sent a letter to the Dutch legation, asking them to write to Anna, who should send her the correspondence with the theatrical dressmaker who had seized her furs in Berlin. This would have been to buttress her argument about having been "swindled" by the Germans and having had a reason to accept Kroemer's twenty thousand francs. On the same day, she wrote to Mornet asking for permission to write to Anna. The request must have been refused, and the letter to the Dutch legation must not have been transmitted because it remains in the files.

In a second July 6 letter to the prosecutor, she complained about prison food and the vermin-infested cell and tried to appeal to his conscience: "I am crying all the time." She had now begun to vary her signature again, sometimes signing Zelle MacLeod, sometimes Zelle McLeod.

On the same day, still hoping to be able to write to Anna directly, she penned a separate letter to her servant, saying that in addition to the correspondence with the costumier she needed the receipt from an Amsterdam lawyer, Edward Phillips (whom van der Schalk had sent to Berlin to recover her blocked funds and jewelry), and her album of clips to reconstitute where she had been at what time. She also asked Anna to tell van der Capellen to send her eight thousand florins. This letter was returned to the files also.

The separate letters to Anna—one through the legation, one

direct—appear to have been a test of what she could or could not put into a communication to get it through. The first had asked only for the costumier correspondence; the second had gone a little further and had specifically asked for the baron to send money. A third missive (and second direct letter) to Anna that day said frankly that she had been in prison for five months accused of espionage. She explained that she had been unable to write. The money was needed from the baron to pay her legal and other bills, she said, noting that "when I shall be out of this prison, I will need treatment for several weeks." Anna should tell the baron that she had tried to return to Holland twice. She again specified that she needed eight thousand florins. This letter was, of course, not delivered.

On July 10, she wrote to Mornet again, complaining of his refusal to send on her letters to Anna and pleading her money problems. If she could not pay Clunet, she would defend herself! She suggested that Mornet order the sale of her gold cigarette case, which she estimated would bring about four hundred francs.

Later in the day, she sent yet another letter to the prosecutor. She had thought of a new source of finance. She noted that on January 16, 1917, she had sent Vadim de Masloff three thousand francs to settle a "debt of honor"—the phrase usually meant money lost at cards, for which there would be no paper proof, only the loser's conscience and "honor." He had promised to repay her with money from his father, whom she referred to here as a Russian brigadier general. Would Mornet please collect the sum? It appears to have been a step that she was reluctant to take, because she added: "It is your fault that I must claim the return of this money. *Never never* would I have done anything of the sort." We may recall, however, that Masloff had testified that she had in fact once tacitly reminded him of the debt. Mornet, of course, just added the letter to the dossier of her correspondence.

On July 19, a change of clothing finally arrived from her baggage at the hotel, so that she could at least be neatly attired for her trial. There were two blouses, a tailored costume of skirt and *jacquette*, a pair of *bottines* (shoes to the ankle), as well as her long-awaited pair of blue leather bedroom slippers.

10. *The Trial*

SHE HAD ENTERED a world of chiaroscuro, where everything was black or shadows and the rare lights were deceptive. It was the sort of world that existed well before Kafka gave his name to it and even for centuries before World War I.

In our own time, we have seen how the United States wanted a spurious "body count" in Vietnam that included women and children, to show that the war was being won, and a spurious estimate of enemy strength that excluded hundreds of thousands of civilian guerrillas, to show that the war was winnable. The Poincaré-Briand government in the France of 1916 had asked, in effect, for a "body count" of spies; all questionable foreigners became expendable. By obeying Ladoux's vague instructions, Mata Hari had committed "intelligence with the enemy," even though, strictly speaking, since she was Dutch, Germany was not her enemy. When bodies are needed, technical violations are enough. The use of the *intoxication* messages, the fabrication of others, the refusal to call or question key witnesses, particularly van der Capellen and Anna Lintjens, or to permit the defense to have the court president ask questions dealing with national security, ensured that a docile panel of mostly over-age soldiers would do what the nation expected of them.

The life and travails of Mata Hari paint a clear picture of the heroine. She was superficial, supercilious, arrogant, selfish, self-indulgent, and maddeningly impractical; but with all these vices—and having to wear false breasts the way some of her elderly lovers may have worn false teeth—she charmed men as infallibly as sugar and arsenic charms flies.

A reporter of our age—such journalism was not publishable then—would have exposed her false biographies instead of seeing them as "great copy," travestied her dancing, and related her hollow life as an elegant parasite in a corrupt society, including her habit of not paying bills. But such a reporter could have said as much about hundreds of other courtesans and *demi-mondaines*, and the reporters of the day were mostly as corrupt and superficial as the lady herself. Mata Hari was a creature of the Belle Epoque, for better or, usually, for worse.

At twenty-seven, after her miserable marriage, she had found herself facing a bleak future. MacLeod had been a dreadful husband, but by the standards of the day he was probably not exceptional; a more patient wife might have endured and perhaps even succeeded in improving him, as his third wife appears to have done. The story of their marriage was of two selfish people brought together by a practical-joke advertisement in a newspaper and locked together in the stifling and segregated intimacy of white colonial life, as awful then as it would remain for two or three generations, in Asia and Africa. Both wanted to let themselves be loved, rather than to love. MacLeod's only saving grace was his affection, albeit possessive, for his daughter. There is no evidence, not one single anecdote, that Mata Hari liked children, despite her occasional rumblings of guilt about Non.

Let us try to look at it from her side. Back in Holland, she could have become a bitter, lonely woman or she could have found a dull Dutch widower to marry her and pay the bills. Neither possibility conforms to her character at the time, although she might have settled for a Francophile like van der Capellen later on, had he not been married. More probably, one suspects, had she remained in Holland after returning from Indonesia, she would have ended up in the famous brothel quarter of Rotterdam, where some establishments must presumably have been more elegant than others.

Her achievements, in an age when there were few opportunities for women not prepared to accept "suitable" marriages or teaching or domestic service or the brothel, were not inconsiderable. She had become a stage and *demi-mondaine* celebrity. She was no more of a fraud than most stage artistes of her epoch in inventing a biography (or biographies) that would make her a theatrical novelty. And she became a courtesan in an age when the profession was not only respectable but even useful. This was an era when most of the wives of the aristocratic or upper-middle-class men

235

whom she accommodated had never had an orgasm and for whom sex had often become a chore. Divorce was frowned upon and rare. Even the most wronged and even battered wife would hardly consider it, knowing that the stigma would attach more to her than to her former spouse and fearing a great reduction in living standards for herself and her children.

If the husband could, preferably discreetly, find a mistress from whom he could return home contented and good-humored, the wife was usually even more satisfied than senior wives in polygamous societies, since she did not have to live with her rival. Writers like Coulson regarded Mata Hari as an overpaid prostitute, but she was really only a prostitute in the sense that an American secretary who marries her boss for the security he offers is a prostitute.

On the other hand, it is not difficult to understand that official, military France, in the dire situation faced by the country in 1916 and 1917, found this pretentious, over-aged, overweight, overpriced harlot of the now-disgraced Belle Epoque—a whole "culture" that had contributed to France's weakness—somewhat distasteful; while the British, with the largest prostitute population in industrial Europe, found her immoral, which was as irrelevant as it was hypocritical.

She was foolish, reckless, impulsive, and impetuous, as are most people who get into trouble, especially perhaps those who get into trouble for things they have not done. She was right in suggesting to Bouchardon that Ladoux had a petty mind compared to her own soaring fantasies and ambitions. ("I have always been spontaneous. . . . I see big.") Whether she would have proven to be a great spy is doubtful; but since this is the world of politics, a fool, then as now, can often find the gold seam in the rock, undeservedly. Had she actually reached Belgium and von Bissing, and Berlin and the Crown Prince, she would probably have been shot by the Germans in Germany eventually, instead of being shot by the French in France at German instigation.

What she had found herself in was a political situation in which she had to prove her innocence before a court that had virtually decided her guilt in advance. Her lifelong habit of fabulizing—one of her few characteristics that might have been a useful skill in a spy—had given anyone who wanted it a reason to disbelieve almost anything she said. Her sophisticated naïveté could be presented as subtly disguised intelligence.

Her chief adversaries, the poorly paid captains Ladoux and Bouchardon, were (probably genuinely) fascinated and appalled by her contempt for twenty thousand francs as the price of the puny tidbits of old French press and coffee-shop information she had passed on to Kalle. But for Mata Hari, all money was Monopoly money. She had expensive tastes. She lived in an age when women of mature mind knew that a man is more easily seduced by a sexily dressed woman, even one clothed from the ankles to the neck, than a naked one, who must rely on reality and leave nothing to the lover's imagination; and the roof over her head had always depended virtually entirely on seducing men, whether on the stage or in private life. To Ladoux and Bouchardon, she was an aggravating and dispensable creature from a neutral country ("neutral" is pejorative in wartime, just as it would later become "immoral," according to John Foster Dulles) that the French, in their vanity, saw as a bit of a "joke nation" peopled by dullards profiting from the conflict.

Uninstructed—indeed, insisting on "don't question my methods"—she had taken on the role of a double agent, making use of the fact that the Germans *wanted* her to help her bring off a profitable coup for the French. The objective, she had agreed all along, was money. If the Allies won the war because a woman in midlife crisis needed the cash to support a young lover, who would care? Certainly not historians.

Broadly speaking, the double agent is usually obliged to break certain laws of the country to which he or she is genuinely allegiant in order to carry out his or her task. No double agent can possibly pass solely false information to the country for which he or she is only pretending to work without swiftly losing credibility and probably life itself. Ladoux could reasonably complain that he had never told her what to say to the German military attaché in Madrid, to whom he had not known that she would be speaking; but the information she gave was of such ludicrous triviality that he would probably not have considered that it would be enough to carry the day.

If Ladoux had genuinely thought that she was a German spy, then he too would have been guilty of "intelligence with the enemy" when he confided in her that the French already knew about the submarine landings on the Moroccan coast, for instance. Today, a reporter who told the Soviet ambassador, at a reception, of a major Pentagon scandal that would only be public knowledge when his story appeared in his paper several hours later—in order to try to get the envoy to answer a few questions—would be similarly culpable, if the law were applied to the letter, since he would be passing on what was, for a few hours more, genuine intelligence. But any reporter who missed such an opportunity would be regarded by his peers as incompetent.

Mata Hari had told Kalle that she had "pretended" to work for the French, in order to get him to talk, and had sauced the dish by letting him "do what he wanted with me." Kalle, we can see, was obviously not fooled; he had given her a mixture of stale (submarine) and false (French code) information to make her think that he was fooled and to see if she would then go to the French, which of course she did. By the time she was planning to leave Madrid, he must have learned, while using the current code, that Kroemer had given her twenty thousand francs and that she had done nothing for it in return. (Providing that Eiffel Tower reception was good that day, French intelligence must almost certainly have learned it at this time as well, but Ladoux would have been reluctant to pass it to Bouchardon for use at the trial—as he would any information obtained involving the current code—until Mata Hari volunteered her own account. This would help to explain why Bouchardon appears to have been much more excited than Ladoux by her Kroemer story.)

Kalle then started up a false traffic in a broken code, asking for her to be paid ten thousand francs. Perhaps he sent an additional message in the current code, telling them to agree to less, or perhaps Berlin wisely decided that, since the only purpose of a further payment would be to help persuade the French to shoot their own agent, any payment would do, and three thousand francs would be enough. Obviously, for the subterfuge to be credible, something had to be paid for the gossip about Marie Bonaparte and Briand, and so on.

The hyped version of these messages produced by Bouchardon, and written by Ladoux, has Kalle referring to two missions in France; but Kalle presumably knew that Kroemer had only tried to recruit her in 1916, before her second wartime visit to Paris, and therefore he would not have made that mistake himself. That was Ladoux's *surenchère*—upping the bidding—to help clinch the case.

From Ladoux's point of view, arresting Mata Hari because of the messages in the broken code, and being careful not to take any action that would let the Germans know that their code in current use was broken also, would strengthen the German ignorance of this major French achievement. By arresting Mata Hari, but not arresting, at least not at once, a real spy that Kalle was sending into France—and whose mission would be referred to in the current code—Ladoux could falsely reassure the Germans that their present code was inviolate.

At the trial, much would be made of her telling Kalle that she had only "pretended" to work for the French (after all, being recruited by the "unsuspecting" French would surely help to justify her taking twenty thousand francs, even if she had not come up with any intelligence yet, and would explain her contacts with Denvignes) while having failed to tell Ladoux that she had been recruited by Kroemer. She had said that she had not confided in Ladoux because she wanted to announce her recruitment into German intelligence after getting back to Holland, making it her first coup for France—just as she had used her recruitment by Ladoux to try to impress Kalle. While there is no reason to disbelieve that this congenital dissimulator was telling the truth about wanting to withhold her achievement from Ladoux until the right time, there was a more obvious reason for her holding back on the bearded captain. It was that she knew that, prompted by the British, he had had her shadowed for six months in France, from May to November 1916, and had openly expressed suspicions about her. Had she told Ladoux about the Kroemer episode when accepting Ladoux's request that she spy for France "on speculation" (with no financial guarantee), he might have wanted to delay her exit visa pending further investigation. He might never have allowed her to go at all. She would have been blocked in Paris for the duration of the war—which might last, for all anyone knew, for a decade. She would have had no means of earning the money to pay for the Russian gigolo with whom she was infatuated, except by deceiving him on an assembly-line basis—which would hardly have worked, emotionally, and which she had resolved not to do, because the aging hussy was finally in love. She could not explain to Bouchardon that she had withheld the information for fear that Ladoux would investigate her further, because this would have been negatively interpreted; but this must surely have been more in her mind than the question as to whether this was the fine-tuned moment to impress Ladoux with the fact that she was already Germany's H 21.

Mata Hari was clearly indignant that the French would use the Kroemer episode against her, since she had volunteered the information in order to explain what she was doing—and to explain it very logically. But since the French had the key to the current German code, it is quite possible, as noted, that Ladoux and Goubet knew this much about her already, if Kalle had referred to it in his traffic in the normal code, not intended for French consumption, but available to them anyway.

She could not understand why this proof of her usefulness as a French spy—which was not a confession, but an admission of having held something back to impress Ladoux later—was being seen as negative. She seems to have expected it to win her freedom. The extensive investigation had turned up no evidence that she had ever spied for anyone in France. The two men whose job appears to have been to get a conviction at any cost were left with two rhetorical questions to put to the court: why would the Germans part with twenty thousand francs in advance, and how could she go to Kalle if she had done nothing for it? Only a court that asked no real questions would have convicted on so little.

For Ladoux and Bouchardon, however, there was the awkward question that she had not gone to Kalle on her first passage through Madrid, in November, and had only spoken to him when she found herself unexpectedly in the Spanish capital again the following month; and then, she had given him only information that was outdated, known, speculation, or rumor, and was clearly not worth twenty thousand francs, plus the 3,500 pesetas he added. It had been old and very inferior stuff when she had passed through Madrid in November and had become very cold leftovers by the time she spoke to Kalle the following month. Curiously, Mata Hari, who was resourceful in defending herself but clearly not resourceful enough, never tried to make the point that if she had convinced

Kalle that she had pretended to join French intelligence, that alone might have been worth twenty thousand francs. Obviously, Kalle knew from the start that he was dealing with an impostor—hence the broken-code messages. But that is another question, since Bouchardon was presumably never told that Kalle was using a redundant cipher.

Bouchardon would have to build the case for the prosecuting attorney, Lieutenant André Mornet, on the fact that she had voluntarily informed him that she had received twenty thousand francs from Kroemer and had admitted to getting a further 3,500 pesetas from Kalle. The prosecution could—and would—insist that this implied that the two drafts of five thousand francs from Holland in November 1916 and January 1917 came not from van der Capellen but from Kroemer, whom she had admitted to telling her servant about as a last-resort source for funds.

An undated, unsigned memo in the military justice files, which appears to be in Bouchardon's handwriting and was probably for Major Jullien, the head of the army's prosecution force, goes further and calls van der Capellen a "straw man" for "Krämer" and Mata Hari.

The memo states: "Every time the lady Zelle mentions in her letters the Baron van der Capellen it is necessary to read Krämer." An insertion in darker ink, possibly by Bouchardon but perhaps by Jullien or some other recipient, adds before the word "Krämer" the words *semble-t-il* (it would seem). But just as no proof was ever offered that Mata Hari wrote "the Baron" when she meant "the Consul," so no proof was ever presented for the astonishing hypothesis that the Dutch colonel was a traitor to Holland, a "straw man" who had loaned his identity to a German espionage operation—which would imply that even if the money came from him, it was actually money that the colonel took from the consul for the purpose.

The prosecution case breaks down on two massive points that neither Mata Hari, Clunet, the court, nor, in all probability, Mornet and Bouchardon, could know: that the Madrid-Berlin traffic was in a broken code that was clearly meant to be read by the French and was therefore *intoxication*, which her own confessed perfidy toward the Germans explained and indeed even justified—from the German point of view; and that the radio messages had been hyperbolized, expanded, and augmented with "messages" drafted by the Second Bureau. For an examining magistrate like Bouchardon to pretend that the false or hyperbolized messages were true, in order to startle a defendant and get a confession, was perfectly legitimate; there is no law that says that a French examining magistrate, or an American district attorney or police officer, must tell a suspect the truth in his or her efforts to get a confession; *but the hyperbolized and false radio messages were introduced into evidence*—a deception by the Second Bureau of both the defense and the prosecution.

Apart from the genuine distaste that Bouchardon and Ladoux obviously felt for Margaretha Zelle, convicting Mata Hari would help preserve the best French intelligence secret of the war. By going along with the *intoxication* messages about Mata Hari in the redundant code and not acting precipitately about intelligence acquired through the active code, the French could lull the enemy into a sense of false security about their present cipher. If Churchill, a generation later, could let Coventry be pulverized to preserve the advantage of such a massive secret as possessing the enemy code— and no one has seriously suggested that his painful decision was wrong—surely shooting a Dutch harlot with ideas above her station was justifiable to the French in 1917, who were then expecting their capital city to be besieged again by *les Boches* and who were anxious to preserve their greatest intelligence asset—their possession of the active German code? I am trying, of course, to put the most logical and acceptable justification on the murder of a rather raddled innocent and asking myself if, in the same situation, any reasonable person might not have given consideration to the thought that the crime was worth it to help save the country.

Neither Clunet nor the court was to ask for proof that the Kalle messages existed. Indeed, the present writer only assumes that Kalle actually sent the earliest ones that are in the files because they both explain and invalidate the prosecution case and make comprehensible the fact that the more lengthy, more incriminating and additional—spurious—messages were used by the prosecution. Moreover, Locard attests to the genuineness of the "Eiffel Tower" originals. The Second Bureau pretended to both Clunet and the court that the breaking of the German code was a "national defense" secret. Neither Clunet nor the court was therefore to be told that there were (at least) two codes and that the Germans knew that the one used to incriminate Mata Hari had been broken. To have revealed this would not only have proved that the traffic was *intoxication* but also that it was no longer a national defense secret. There is, it should be stressed again, no reason to believe that the two junior legal officers, Bouchardon and Mornet, knew that there were two codes involved and no reason to believe that the Germans ever learned, until the war was over, that *both* had been broken.

Clunet's *plaidoirie*—his address to the court for the defense— is not in the files, but we may assume that he laid heavy stress (as eyewitnesses have claimed) on her foreignness, which meant that Germany was not for her "the enemy" and that her freewheeling discussions with a German officer were therefore permissible. Foreigners are of course liable to the same laws as the French if they are arrested in France or extradited to there for offenses committed in France, but they cannot be held to requirements of loyalty to the French Republic. More important, we do not know if Clunet asked why the prosecution, after questioning seamstresses and drunken sergeant-majors, had not had the wit to obtain testimony or at least affidavits from Colonel van der Capellen and Anna Lintjens. The court president apparently never asked about this huge gap in the prosecution's case.

As we have noted, Clunet was not allowed to call the baron or his client's maid; he was not even allowed to tell these key witnesses that the case existed; this would have been passing on intelligence about the fate of a "German spy" to neutral citizens not cleared to know it. The only reason van der Capellen knew that an espionage case existed (and "Marguérite" never knew for sure that he knew) was because he had persuaded the Dutch foreign minister to instruct the Dutch legation in Paris to investigate.

Van der Capellen and Anna had no means of knowing that they themselves were involved in the evidence, that there was any debate about the two five-thousand-franc drafts, or that his or her evidence as to their origin might help "Madame"—that a few sentences from them and a notarized statement from an Amsterdam bank could blow André Mornet's case out of the water.

Even after her execution, van der Capellen had no means of knowing—any more than the French public did—on what grounds she had been convicted or to know that the drafts from Holland were used as evidence against her. Indeed, at this point—he was, after all, a career colonel—he was probably wondering whether Marguérite was not really a German spy, as a French court had decided, and whether this perhaps explained her unusually extended second trip to France. He had never heard of the Marquis de Beaufort and probably would not have wanted to. And as for Vadim de Masloff, the Squire of Butter . . .

While Mata Hari was in prison, the much-rumored spring offensive of which she had spoken to Kalle had in fact taken place. France recovered the Chemin des Dames but with staggering losses— a major reason for General Nivelle's replacement as chief of staff. The offensive did not achieve much else, and the Germans, as noted earlier, were to recapture most of the area the following year.

General von Bissing, the target of her abortive plan, and who had commanded the German forces in—and occupation of—Belgium since November 1914, had been replaced in April 1917 by General von Falkenhausen.

On March 10, 1917, the Russian garrison in Petrograd (renamed from St. Petersburg at the beginning of the war) had mutinied, calling for the overthrow of the monarchy. On March 15, the Czar Nicholas II had abdicated in favor of his son Michael, who had abdicated in his turn the following day. A provisional government was declared. Russia stayed in the war, but its troops were more and more demoralized and mutinous.

After her execution, the news from Russia became worse. On November 6, 1917 (October 24 under the old calendar, hence "October Revolution"), the Bolshevik Revolution took place. On November 28, the Russians were to offer the Central Powers "armistice and peace," and an armistice was signed on the Eastern Front on December 15. A trendy British playwright-novelist called W. Somerset Maugham was recruited by the Secret Service and shipped to Petrograd with crates of gold bars to buy off the Revolution and get Russia back into the war, but without success.

The only good news of the year had been America's entry into the conflict on April 6—an intervention that would prove decisive the following year.

*   *   *

Bouchardon had transmitted his voluminous papers and his summary of the case to the commissioner of the government—prosecuting attorney—Lieutenant André Mornet. Mornet was a seasoned and theatrical lawyer who was to become one of the best-known government attorneys of his generation. Whereas Bouchardon chewed his nails, Mornet eschewed protein altogether; he was a nondrinking, nonsmoking vegetarian.

The trial, which opened on July 24, was held in an upstairs courtroom at the Palace of Justice. Mata Hari was transferred the night before to the Conciergerie, a prison close by. She entered the court building from the basement with a gendarme escort and her lawyer, Clunet.

The fact that the famous dancer was to be tried for spying had been announced, and there was a substantial crowd both in the street and in the *Salle des pas perdus*, the vast antechamber where witnesses waited to be called. The press noted that she was wearing, not the two-piece that we know had arrived from her hotel five days before, but a blue dress, open at the neck, and a tricorn hat draped with a lace mantilla. The weather was hot—eighty-two degrees—but cooler inside the tall-ceilinged building. Bystanders saw the trio go up the broad staircase. Despite the weather, her gloved hands were folded in a fur muff.

A throng of reporters and public filled the room to capacity as she took her place in the dock, with her attorney at a table just in front of her. Facing her were Mornet; Sergeant-Major Rivière, the clerk; the president of the military tribunal, Lieutenant-Colonel Albert-Ernest Somprou, and his six assessors. Somprou, in his sixties, was an officer of the Republican Guard, a sort of paramilitary riot police under military discipline. The assessors were Major Fernand Joubert, aged fifty-three, of the 230th Regiment; Captain Lionel de Cayla, aged fifty-five, of the service corps; gendarmerie Captain Jean Chatin, aged fifty-six; Lieutenant Henri Deguesseau, aged fifty-seven, of the 237th regiment; Sublieutenant Joseph de Mercier de Malaval, of the 7th armored cavalry (*cuirassiers*), who is described as "young"; and Sergeant-Major Berthommé of the 12th artillery regiment.

Everyone, including the public, stood up as Somprou entered with his assessors; then all except the defendant sat. The files note that, as required, Somprou had on his desk the Code of Military Justice, the *Code d'instruction criminelle* (textbook for preparing a criminal case) and the *Code pénal ordinaire* (penal code), which prescribes maximum, minimum, and mandatory sentences.

The clerk asked her if she was Marguérite-Gertrude Zelle, using the French version of her name, and she said she was. (The official accusation describes her as "Zelle Marguérite-Gertrude, forty years old, born in Leeuwarden, divorced, a dancer" and lists her last address before her arrest as "12 boulevard des Capucines." This was actually one of the entrances of the Grand Hôtel, not the Elysée-Palace; presumably Bouchardon had put yet another flub into Mornet's brief.) Somprou asked the clerk to state the title of the case and Rivière said it was the French Republic against Marguérite-Gertrude Zelle. Mornet then requested, for reasons of national security, that the case be heard *in camera* and that the record of the proceedings be sealed. Somprou and his assessors retired to consider this, then returned and agreed to Mornet's demands. The press and public were ordered out, and guards were stationed in the corridors to keep everyone at least ten paces from the court and out of earshot. Many hung around, expecting a result that day. The courtly Somprou invited the defendant to sit down. The scene was set.

The national atmosphere in which the trial took place was dramatic, and Mornet, a thin, bearded figure, took full advantage of it. The Germans were not exactly at the gates of Paris, but the city had been declared a "retrenched camp." The battlefield carnage had by then become the greatest known in history, and remains so to this day. The Petrograd revolution in March had led to mutinies in the trenches, with French soldiers raising the red flag and refusing to serve a leadership adjudged corrupt and inefficient.

Tough African soldiers of the 2nd Colonial Infantry Division had been the first to revolt, in May, followed by the 9th Corps, which had fought with special valor at Verdun. Other units affected were the 58th, 109th, 111th, 258th, and 259th Infantry Divisions. Many soldiers on leave had deserted, although the punishment for that was death. Military historians say that about half of all French army units were plagued by desertions or by small-scale mutinies, usually refusals to "go up to the [front] line."

Everywhere, public and military morale was poor; there was widespread uncertainty as to whether America's entry into the war would make a serious difference, since the United States had little experience of fighting and most of its soldiers were hastily trained civilians—as of course were the other Allied soldiers, although they were by now battle-hardened. The Petrograd mutiny had considerably weakened the Russian support for the other Allies, and the October Revolution then brewing would, as noted, take Russia out of the war altogether, allowing the Central Powers to throw their full military weight against France. President Poincaré was pressing his campaign against "defeatism"; as victory on the battlefield was elusive, shooting as many spies as possible would at least show that the government and the military brass back in Paris were doing something to protect the soldiers at the Front. Twenty-nine politicians who had called for a negotiated peace with Germany had been lined up and shot as well. Countless foreigners had been arrested on suspicion of espionage. Over a thousand had been expelled. About five hundred had been charged with spying and, before the war was over, nearly three hundred would be executed. Mata Hari's was only one case among many. The campaign against "foreign spies" helpfully gave the impression that it was not the French who were responsible for all the battlefield defeats, but insidious strangers in their midst.

The prospect of shooting a woman was not exceptional. Mata Hari was not alone in that either. The French had already shot at least two women and were to shoot others. It was, after all, the Germans, in 1915, who had crossed that barrier with the English nurse Edith Cavell, arrested on the lesser charge of helping British and Belgian prisoners of war escape to the relative comfort of internment in Holland.

Somprou called on Mornet to present the case for the government. Mornet explained that the police had conducted a "discreet surveillance" of the accused, starting shortly after her arrival in Paris in May 1916. He laid heavy stress on the fact that most of the numerous men she frequented were officers.

She had asked for permission to go to Vittel for health reasons, although she had written to her lover in Holland, van der Capellen, saying that she was in excellent health. She had asked an old friend, Lieutenant Hallaure, to get her a health certificate saying she needed to take the waters. This had led to her contact with Captain Ladoux.

At Vittel, she had continued to frequent officers, including aviators from the nearby airfield at Contrexéville.

He made absolutely no mention of Vadim de Masloff. She herself, under questioning from Somprou (who alone could ask questions, including those suggested to him by Mornet and Clunet), gave two reasons for going to Vittel: Masloff and "the cure."

Surveillance had continued after her return to Paris, Mornet explained; there she had persisted in frequenting many officers. He recounted her attempted trip to Holland and her return to Spain from England. Then the Eiffel Tower had intercepted radio messages from Madrid; these messages had showed that she was Agent H 21 of the Cologne intelligence center. The then minister of war, General Lyautey, had ordered the military government of Paris to arrest her, and this had been done.

Mornet then read out the Kalle messages and the replies from Berlin. The first ones in the files, as noted, are the genuine ones, but it is reasonable to assume that the ones he read were the expanded or unauthentic ones used by Bouchardon in his interrogations, since Bouchardon had prepared Mornet's case for him.

Then the courtroom rhetoric began.

"The Zelle lady appeared to us as one of those international women—the word is her own—who have become so dangerous since the hostilities," Mornet said. "The ease with which she expresses herself in several languages, especially French, her numerous relations, her subtle ways [*souplesse de moyens*], her aplomb, her remarkable intelligence, her immorality, congenital or acquired, all contributed to make her suspect."

Mata Hari had offered herself "as a sort of Messalina, dragging a horde of admirers behind her chariot," the accuser cried. Eventually he got to the subject of the case, her dealings with Kalle.

"The Zelle lady had furnished von Kalle with information about the intentions of Princess George of Greece, about the political situation in Paris and the progress achieved by the party opposed to the Briand government, about France's domination by England and the fears inspired by this in a certain number of isolated French politicians. She spoke to him about a general offensive prepared on all fronts for the spring under the direction of England, the dropping of spies behind the lines by the aviator Védrines, the travel limitations imposed on our officers, the discovery by the French of German invisible ink. Collecting even the most individual information, she also revealed to the military attaché that the Belgian Allard, with whom she had traveled on the *Hollandia*, was a spy in the service of England."

Clunet presumably pointed out later that the Védrines story had come from Kalle, not from Mata Hari.

Mornet reported that "headquarters" had said that the information that she had given Kalle had contained "some truth." He made little mention of the information she had given to Ladoux and Denvignes but said that she had "successfully fooled" Denvignes. He poked fun at her "epistolary abundance." (What else does a prisoner in isolation, possessing a pen, do except write letters to whomever she hopes might read or listen?)

He drew attention to the fact that some of the information she brought from her conversation with Kalle was false, such as the report that the German consul-general in Barcelona was in charge of German intelligence in Spain. The true director, Mornet said, was Rueggeberg. He offered no proof, because this was "sensitive material." He said that the Barcelona story had been "passed on by the Germans before." He referred to the pricing of German spies, once again without proof, and said that the twenty thousand francs she had received from "Krämer" could only have been for substantial intelligence. He did not mention that the information about the Kroemer payment had been volunteered by Mata Hari herself.

He described Griebl as her true lover and made the Berlin police officer out to be a major figure in German intelligence. Needless to say, no proof was offered for this either. One of Mornet's advantages was that he could glibly say that anything was "known" to French intelligence, and neither the court nor Clunet could challenge him to prove how it was known.

"On two occasions," he said, "in December 1915 and June 1916, she penetrated the war site [*place de guerre*] of Paris with a mission to collect documents and information in the enemy's interest." Once again, no evidence of this was offered except presumably the falsified cable in which Kalle was made to tell Berlin something that, were it true, Berlin would have known already.

She had, Mornet said, "maintained intelligence with Germany in the person of Consul Krämer and the military attaché von Kalle." The proof that she was a spy, he noted, resided in the payments of twenty thousand francs, the two payments of five thousand francs, and the payment of 3,500 pesetas.

He concluded with a stirring reminder of soldiers dying at the Front by the hundreds of thousands, betrayed by spies. "The evil that this woman has done is unbelievable," he cried, with unconscious irony. "This is perhaps the greatest woman spy of the century."

The prosecution called five witnesses. Inspector Monier testified about his surveillance, noting the fact that she had frequented a large number of officers. Commissioner Priolet gave testimony about her arrest. Colonel Goubet and Captain Ladoux confirmed the points that Mornet had made. There is nothing in the files about what questions were asked of them by the court at Clunet's request, so that a researcher must rely on eyewitness accounts in books by Massard and others, and these tell us little. The fifth witness, Albert Ramilloy, a furrier who had come to the prosecution's notice after the *instruction* process was over, testified by affidavit. He said the accused had become his customer in 1907, and that in August 1908 she had come to him to ask him to cash "three" postdated checks given to her by Alfred Kiepert, described as a "landowner at Marienfeld, near Berlin." The dates cited for the checks would appear to be wrong, but the matter seems to be of no consequence.

The defense could neither cross-examine hostile witnesses nor question its own directly. The latter were called the following day.

Initially, Mata Hari had asked for Masloff to be called. But there is a letter in the files from her, addressed to "Lieutenant"—presumably Mornet—in which she changes her mind. The letter bears no date, only "Friday."

If Vadim appeared, she said, she knew that she would cry and "there would be nothing that you could do with me" because "he is the man I love the most in the world." She asked therefore that Masloff not be called.

She asked for Messimy, no longer describing him as the "Marquis de Messimy" but calling him a colonel, not knowing that he had been promoted general. She also asked for Denvignes; for the Captain Gerbaud of the general staff at Chambéry with whom she had dined at the Lyon station; for Dr. Boulimié, the chief doctor of the Vittel spa, who could testify that she actually did take the waters at Vittel and had needed a treatment; and for another Vittel doctor, Amblard, who had treated her during her prewar visit. She described the latter physician as "mobilized," meaning that he was serving with the army. The letter differs from all the others in being signed "Mata Hari," with the breves on the second *a* of Mata and on the *a* of Hari.

On July 14, she had written again to Mornet, asking that he produce in court the letters which she had sent to Ladoux (from Paris in September 1916, from Scotland Yard in December, from Madrid in December, and from Paris the following month), as well as the letter from Senator Junoy that she had passed on to Ladoux and her Madrid letter to Denvignes when he was on Christmas leave in Paris. All these, of course, supported her case that she had worked for French intelligence.

They were never produced. The French were prepared to follow due process a little better than the Germans had done with Edith Cavell, even to the point of picking up the defendant's boa feather from the cleaner's; but in the end it was to be a similarly ruthlessly conducted trial to Cavell's, with the result virtually decided in advance.

On July 17, she had written once more to Mornet with a revised witness list, headed by "Col. A. Messimy" and "Henri Rapférer, *aéronaute*." These could testify that she had done a little amateur intelligence work for France in Berlin in 1914 by writing to inform them of German plans to invade.

The others on the list were "Marquis H. de Marguérie; Marquis F. de Beaufort; Lt. Hallaure; Staff Captain Gerbaud, Chambéry; Lieutenant Mège, Ministry of War; Dr. Boulimié; Dr. Amblard." (Boulimié's name is wrongly spelled in some books as "Boulinier.")

On July 22, there was another letter to Mornet, complaining that the letters to Anna had not been transmitted, preventing her from producing the evidence about her troubles in Berlin at the outbreak of war, as well as her album of letters and clips to show where she had been at particular times. Why Clunet was not handling all these matters himself may testify either to his inadequacy or to his client's headstrong determination to manage her own case.

* * *

The most distinguished witness she got—but not in person—was her old flame General Adolphe-Pierre Messimy, the former minister of war who was now serving at the Front. A letter was read first from his wife, saying that her husband was "with the armies" and would therefore be unable to respond to the summons. Mrs. Messimy wrote that she knew nothing that could possibly connect Mata Hari with espionage and that her husband was "of the same opinion." (Massard, in his memoirs, invents a totally different letter in which she says she is sure her husband never knew "this person," and he says that Mata Hari laughed when it was read in court.)

Messimy, serving at the time in Sector 55, did however receive the summons and wrote himself to say that at no time had the accused ever discussed the war or military affairs with him. Mata Hari, ever the professional courtesan, asked that the signature not be read because "this gentleman is married," but Somprou said he was obliged to read the evidence fully.

Messimy's letter is not in the files because it was leaked to the press later. It is signed with an *M*, then a wavy line, then *y*. This led to speculation that it had been written by the minister of the interior—the minister in charge of the police and internal security—Léon Malvy. Clemenceau, who had become prime minister, brushed aside Malvy's denials that he had been the lover of a convicted German spy and banished him to Spain for five years. He was able to return to Paris after the war and persuaded Messimy, who by then had heard of Malvy's misfortune, to set the record straight. Malvy was reelected to the Assembly and became minister of the interior again in 1926. One day in the Assembly, an opposition deputy accused him of having been Mata Hari's lover, whereupon the poor man fainted.

Most of the books about Mata Hari contain descriptions of Vadim de Masloff on the witness stand. He is usually described as never looking in her direction and of testifying that all that existed between them was a passing affair to which he had never attached any importance, while she either stares at him in disbelief or cries. In fact, the Russian, then serving in Sector 189A, neither appeared nor sent written testimony. When she had originally asked for him, before changing her mind, his commanding officer had said he could not be spared from military duty. Captain-Major de Beaufort, the dashing Belgian marquis whom she had come to Paris to meet in 1916, also found the same pressing excuse for not responding. So did Lieutenant Hallaure.

René Masson claims that Mège appeared and that the cryptographer gave evidence on "polyalphabetic inversion" and "squared figures" (or ciphers); if asked the right questions, he might have proved a useful witness for the defense; since he was an officer, he was presumably in charge of the cipher service. Nevertheless, if Masson's account is to be believed, the issue of the type of code used by Kalle was not mentioned. There is no mention in the trial papers to show that he ever appeared at all, and it would seem unlikely that the prosecution would have wanted him to testify, for fear that Clunet might ask Somprou to put some probing questions. In his deposition, mentioned earlier, Mège, it will be recalled, was not asked about codes at all, only about Mata Hari's table conversation.

The one defense witness who loyally appeared for certain was Henry "Robert" de Marguérie. Unfortunately, neither the court nor—through the court president—the defense could ask this cipher expert from the foreign ministry about the cracking of the German codes. There is, of course, no reason why he should have known in which code the true Kalle messages were sent. Indeed, as with Mège at his deposition, Marguérie was apparently not asked about codes at all, or indeed what work he did at the ministry.

His testimony is not in the files, and we must rely on the memoirs of Ladoux and others for an account of his appearance. Ladoux and Massard say Marguérie testified that he had known the lady for fourteen years and had been her first lover when she had come to Paris in 1904. He recounted their three days together when she had first come back to Paris in 1915 and said neither of them had mentioned the war at all.

Mornet bristled with disbelief.

"Are you asking us to accept, sir, that you spent three days constantly in each other's company and not a word escaped your lips of the question which obsesses us all, the war?"

The elegant dandy was not ruffled.

"I am a very busy man, and I am obsessed with the war night

and day," he said. "For just that reason, it was a great relief to spend three days talking of philosophy, Indian art and love. It may sound unlikely to you, but it is the truth."

When the court president said he had no questions, Marguérie added a last defiant word: "Nothing has ever spoiled the good opinion that I have of this lady."

Most accounts then say he bowed, not to the court, but to the accused, before strutting away.

Three hours of the afternoon were taken up by Clunet's *plaidoirie*, his plea for the defense; of this, as mentioned, no trace remains in the files, and we are left with the suppositions traced earlier.

The hearings had lasted from eight-thirty A.M. to seven P.M. on the first day and had resumed at eight-thirty on the twenty-fifth. It was now early evening, and the judges withdrew to consider the charges. Outside in the street, the crowd waited for the result. The heat wave continued: it was now eighty-five degrees.

The prosecution made eight charges against Mata Hari. In translating them here, the present writer has replaced by an ellipsis a formal phrase that occurs in all of them, *en tous cas depuis temps de droit*, which roughly means that the time of the alleged offense does not fall outside a statute of limitations:

> 1. To have introduced herself into the war place [*place de guerre*] of Paris in December 1915 . . . to procure there documents or information in the interest of Germany, an enemy power.

This charge is based on the fabricated version of one of Kalle's messages, in which her two journeys to Paris are described as "missions." No evidence was presented to show that she actually tried to procure "documents or information," and the fabricated message does not have Kalle saying that anything was obtained in 1915.

> 2. In Holland . . . notably in the first semester of 1916, to have procured for Germany, an enemy power, notably in the person of Consul Krämer, documents or information capable of harming the operations of the army or compromising the security of places, posts or other military establishments.

This is essentially based on the information she volunteered that she had accepted money from Kroemer. No evidence was presented that she actually gave him sensitive information, and the prosecution did not claim that she had met with him until just before her departure in the summer of 1916. If she had procured such information during her visit of December 1915 to January 1916, she would hardly have waited several months before passing it on. Bouchardon and Mornet have insisted that "Krämer" would not have given her twenty thousand francs as an advance unless she had given proof of spying skills before. Mata Hari has said that, given her fame and lifestyle, he could hardly have offered her much less, and that she swindled him out of the money because Germany had swindled her out of her furs at the outbreak of war.

> 3. In Holland, in May 1916 . . . to have maintained intelligence with Germany, in the person of the aforesaid Krämer, with the intention of favoring the enterprises of the enemy.

This charge means that, when she spoke to Kroemer and accepted his money and his invisible ink, she *intended* to do something in return, even if she subsequently did not. It is a lesser, "fallback" charge, based on the prosecution's hypothesis.

> 4. To have introduced herself into the war place of Paris . . . to procure there documents or information in the interest of Germany, an enemy power.

This is another charge of "intent," and is based on the same fabricated Kalle message referring to her journeys as "missions."

> 5. In Paris, since May 16, 1916 . . . to have maintained intelligence with Germany, an enemy power, with the intention of favoring the enterprises of the aforesaid enemy.

No evidence was produced to support this charge, which the surveillance reports in Paris and Vittel negate. Had she "maintained intelligence" with Germany while in France, there would have been no need to repeat her information to Kalle in Madrid; even had there been, she would have gone to him during her first stopover in the Spanish capital, rather than a month later, when she was only in Madrid unexpectedly because of the misadventure at Falmouth, or she would have asked Ladoux to send her to Holland via Switzerland and Germany. The message sent from Berlin to Kalle, in the broken code meant for the French to read, is at least more realistic in complaining that her work in France had been unsatisfactory and authorizing only a small amount of expense money. In one of his interrogations, Bouchardon had said that there was no valid reason why she should use the Dutch diplomatic pouch to send her letters to Anna and van der Capellen, insinuating that her preference for this safer and more efficient method over the wartime mails was a method of getting "intelligence" to "Krämer"; but no evidence was presented to prove that this was true. Since the trial was *in camera*, and the trial papers sealed in advance, the fact that the French employees of the legation were all informers could have been revealed if, when steaming open her letters, anything incriminating, such as the use of invisible ink, had been found.

> 6. In Madrid, in December 1916 . . . to have maintained intelligence with Germany, an enemy power, in the person of the military attaché von Kalle, with the intention of favoring the enterprises of the enemy.

This charge stands or falls on whether the court accepts that her story of Briand and the Greek princess, her tidbits from the French press, and the popular rumor that the Allies would launch a general offensive when the mud dried out in the spring (the Germans, of course, shared the same rumor about their own army) was the sort of thing that was meant to "favor the enterprises of the enemy."

> 7. In the same circumstances of time and place . . . to have procured for Germany, an enemy power, in the person of the aforesaid von Kalle, documents or information capable of harming the operations of the army or compromising the security of places, posts or other military establishments, the said documents or information dealing notably with internal politics, the spring offensive, the discovery by the French of the secret of German invisible ink and the divulging of the name of an agent in the service of England.

The charge that she had passed on France's "discovery of the secret of German invisible ink" is neither in the Kalle *intoxication* message nor any of the fabricated ones. It may conceivably refer to one of the two messages that are missing in the "Dubail" set. Nor was evidence presented that the French had in fact made that discovery, or which of the many inks was involved. She admitted passing on the shipboard gossip that Allard was a British agent, even to various people in Vigo after she landed. Like the previous charge, much depended on whether the court found that any of the information she gave Kalle was of any value to Germany or was not just as useless as the *intoxication* information that Kalle gave her.

> 8. In Paris, in January 1917 . . . to have maintained intelligence with Germany, an enemy power, with the intention of favoring the enterprises of the aforesaid enemy.

No evidence was presented on this charge at all, only the Bouchardon–Mornet hypothesis that the last two drafts of five thousand francs from Holland came from Kroemer and not from van der Capellen, a point on which neither the latter nor Anna Lintjens was ever questioned. (The judgment was to specify that her crimes had been committed in "1915, 1916, 1917.")

The court, after only thirty to forty-five minutes of deliberation—accounts vary—found her guilty on all eight charges. Clearly, they must have accepted the fabricated versions of Kalle's *intoxication* messages as genuine. This in turn meant that they accepted that the payment of twenty thousand francs by Kroemer, the two five-thousand-franc drafts, and Kalle's 3,500 pesetas were payments for services rendered or to be rendered.

It was reported at the time that the verdicts were unanimous, but the trial papers reveal that one assessor voted "not guilty" on the heaviest charges—numbers two and seven—and on number five, which accused her of being in contact with German intelligence while in France in 1916 and 1917. Curiously, this assessor voted guilty, with his colleagues, on the weakest charge—the last, which specifically refers only to such contact in Paris in 1917.

None of the judges ever discussed the case afterward. It would have been a grave offense for them to have done so, and all were under military discipline. Waagenaar procured the names of the judges and set out to find the only one who might still be alive in the 1960s—the young sublieutenant, Joseph de Mercier de Malaval. He found he had died in 1945 and that he had never told the woman whom he had married after the war, and who survived him, that he had served on the Mata Hari panel.

Where the panel, including the dissenting assessor, was unanimous was on the sentence, which the clerk read out: "The Council

unanimously condemns the named person, Zelle, Marguérite, Gertrude, as mentioned above, to the punishment of death." She was
also ordered to pay the costs of the investigation and trial. Eyewitnesses have recounted that Clunet began to sob when he heard
the sentence, while Mata Hari stared ahead in disbelief.

Thunder crackled, as outside the court a thunderstorm finally
dispersed the crowd.

There are ample indications that Mata Hari was never a German
spy. Indeed, in a professional sense, she was never a spy at all, for
anyone. As she said in one of her interrogations: "A courtesan, I
admit it. A spy, never!" The notion that early recruitment in Berlin
explains her relationship with Griebl in 1914 is invalidated by his
willingness to appear with her around the time of the outbreak of
war. Her financial and other problems in Germany at that time
hardly point to an agent already recruited and about to go gallantly
to war for Germany. The thought that this self-indulgent woman,
living in high style with the likes of the Crown Prince, the Duke
of Cumberland, and the wealthy Kiepert, would have gone off to
a school for future women spies and studied there under grim and
disciplined German spymistresses hardly seems credible. In any
event, the notion that she was "recruited" before the war appears
to have been abandoned by the prosecution.

By the time she reached Kalle, had the Germans been checking
up on her after she accepted Kroemer's money, it is unlikely that
they would not have known about her love for Masloff, a victim
of German gassing who was threatened with total blindness. What
sort of help for the Germans could they expect from someone who
was now so emotionally involved against them? In any event, the
intoxication traffic makes it clear she did not fool Kalle.

No evidence was produced, despite the intense surveillance, that
she ever voluntarily contacted Germans until she found herself
unexpectedly back in Madrid on an abortive mission to prove to
Ladoux that she could use her neutral citizenship, fame, and seductive powers to penetrate the ranks of German decision-makers.
The notion that, while in France, she preferred to glean information
by sleeping with officers on leave rather than asking questions of
major figures like Messimy, Cambon, or Marguérie hardly makes

sense, especially since Ladoux encouraged her to go to the top—von Bissing—for information on the Germans.

If Kalle had sent additional messages in the current code, which was also (unbeknownst to the Germans) broken, and if these had been incriminating, Ladoux would have had a case—although a puzzling one, since the *intoxication* message would then be treason on Kalle's part against one of his own and would have been known to be so to Berlin. Why would Berlin realistically say that her work had been unsatisfactory, thus enabling them to use only a small sum of money to bait the French trap, if the purpose of the traffic were anything more than to get the French to arrest a woman who was trying, however amateurishly, to penetrate German intelligence after swindling Germany out of twenty thousand francs?

If she was a German spy who had only pretended to accept Ladoux's request that she work for France in order to penetrate French intelligence for the Germans, why did she refuse the apparent offer of French invisible ink, which the Germans might have wanted to analyze? Why should she refuse anything, if her objective was to impress Ladoux falsely? If she was not the total duffer at intelligence that she appears to have been, why would she write in clear and through the mails to inform Ladoux of what she naïvely thought was useful information obtained from Kalle?

To make its case, the prosecution had to read into the evidence the Madrid-Berlin messages, or purported Madrid-Berlin messages, deciphered and in French translation, thus conceding that France had broken a German code. But the originals were never produced; if it had been seen that some of the messages offered in evidence were longer than the originals, this would have pointed to falsification. By not testifying that the messages came in an earlier code, the prosecution was implying that France had broken the current or active German code, which was of course the case. To have admitted that the messages were in an earlier code that the Germans had replaced when they knew it had been broken, the prosecution could have usefully given the false impression that the active German code was inviolate, thus keeping a precious secret from all those in court with no need to know—the judges, Clunet, and Mata Hari, for instance. But this would have raised the point that the Madrid-Berlin messages were *intoxication* in the first place.

Getting the other side to execute its own agents was nothing new and may still go on. Bouchardon and Massard say in their memoirs—although this was not said at the trial—that Ladoux had in fact given Mata Hari the names of six people to contact in Belgium; five, they say, were French agents already "surfaced" by the Germans; the sixth was a genuine German agent. By including him in the list, Bouchardon says, Ladoux hoped—if Mata Hari betrayed the names or was careless about the list—to get the Germans to shoot the fellow because his name had appeared on an official list of French agents, implying that he was doublecrossing Berlin. If Ladoux had in fact given her these names, she would surely have said so as additional proof that Ladoux had definitely taken her on. If the list ever existed, it might be argued that it was not used as part of the case since it would suggest that Ladoux had been remiss, given his doubts about her. But Massard and Bouchardon's story, which would appear to be untrue, at least points up the fact that getting the enemy to shoot its own is not unusual.

Mata Hari says, in effect, that she took Kroemer's money and ran, since Germany owed her at least that much for her furs. Kalle's *intoxication* traffic bears this out, implying that he had unmasked her as a bumbling French agent trying to seduce secrets from him after already stealing money from the trusting Kroemer.

Marthe Richard had a list of all the spies who worked for Kalle and von Krohn (whom readers will recall was Mrs. Richard's lover and was senior to Kalle), and she affirms in her memoirs that Mata Hari was not one of them. Moreover, all Marthe Richard knew about "H 21's" presence in Madrid was her chambermaid's report of an "Englishwoman" in the hotel. All the memoirs of the German spymasters published after the war insist that she was never their spy, although they agree that Kroemer tried to recruit her. Had she really been a German spy, how could they not have claimed this famous and reputedly beautiful martyr for their own? Significantly, perhaps, they never destroyed or removed the dossier which this writer has read, and which proves her innocence, when they conquered Paris in 1940 and ruled the city for over four years.

Ladoux must have seen through Kalle's game. Why otherwise would the Germans have used the redundant code? But the order was out to catch and shoot spies, to help morale; so the Kalle traffic, gussied up with some imaginative additional messages, would add one more to the body count, and one who was only a despicable foreign courtesan in the first place.

The prisoner was taken back to the Conciergerie, then returned on the morrow to Saint-Lazare and her old cell, number twelve. Sister Léonide and Sister Marie were waiting to comfort her. The two prostitutes mentioned much earlier had now been moved into her cell to guard against suicide. Either Dr. Bizard or Dr. Bralez visited her daily, except on Sundays.

On July 28, the Dutch minister of foreign affairs instructed his envoy in Paris to try to get the sentence commuted to imprisonment. The only immediate reaction evident in the files is a memo of July 30 from the minister of war instructing the "government commissioner"—presumably Jullien—to look into the role of acting consul-general Bunge in Mata Hari's affairs.

On August 17, the tribunal of revision met to review the process. It was composed of Judge Couinaud and four other judges, three of them military (a colonel of the 82nd Regiment of heavy artillery, a gendarmerie major, and a Republican Guard major). The tribunal found that the trial had been conducted correctly and refused to order a retrial. Clunet was present for the hearing, but since he was not accredited to any courts of appeal, another lawyer went through the formality for him. Clunet informed the Dutch legation the same day and instructed another attorney to file a formal appeal. On August 31, The Hague again ordered the Paris legation to seek a less drastic penalty.

On September 2, Mata Hari herself wrote to the Dutch envoy in Paris, Ridder van Stuers, politely inferring that the trial had been a mockery but adding: "I have asked for the revision and the quashing of this judgment; however, since this means finding judicial errors, I do not expect to obtain satisfaction." The letter, which was not passed to the legation, indicates that Clunet had not yet had the courage to tell her about the tribunal of revision's decision.

The actual appeal was heard on September 27 and took only a few minutes. The lawyer whom Clunet had asked to take the case could not appear and sent a replacement, who said he would "accept the wisdom of the court"; but he also relayed Clunet's request to be able to address the panel himself. This was refused, and the appeal rejected. Clunet told the Dutch envoy on the twenty-eighth that the only hope was presidential clemency. This news was passed on to The Hague, and the envoy was told the following day by his government to beg for clemency from President Poincaré. The diplomat sent a hand-carried note to the Quai d'Orsay on October 1, asking the French foreign minister to transmit the request of "the Queen's government" to the Elysée. A letter from Mata Hari to the Dutch legation, dated September 1, similarly urging her government to do something, was returned to the file. Not above adding insult to injury, the returning note specifies that it was not delivered to the legation "because of the disobliging terms which she has used with regard to French justice."

Although the trial result had been announced, efforts were still afoot to keep its details secret. In late August, we find a spirited correspondence in the files between General Dubail and Major Jullien about whether Mata Hari could meet and exchange letters with a Dr. M. Milhaud, the lawyer appointed by the government to wind up her affairs, and under what conditions such contacts could take place. It was decided, curiously, that his letters to her were to be opened and read—presumably he had consented to this—but that hers would be protected by the lawyer-client tradition of secrecy. Dr. Milhaud had offered to turn over any letters that appeared "suspicious."

Early the next month, there is a similar exchange of letters before she is allowed to receive a dentist, Dr. Charavet.

On August 23, she had written again to Anna, saying that a painter called Otto had done a pastel portrait of her and that Anna should contact him and have him send the picture to "the Baron." She suggested that van der Capellen might pay Otto five hundred francs for his work. This letter was returned to the files, undelivered.

There was a similar undelivered fate for three more of her letters of the time. On September 10, she wrote to the Dutch consul-general, complaining of not being allowed to write to Anna. On September 15, there is another letter to Anna apparently testing the strictest limits of what she might be allowed to write, if anything. It was just a note to say that she hoped to see Anna and the baron soon. A September 18 letter to Anna said more boldly that her earlier letters had been held back by the French. All these missives went into the files.

She was allowed to receive a letter dated September 12 from a certain A. J. Kooij of Sneek, the Dutch town where she had lived with an uncle after her mother died. He described himself as a "publisher, printer, binder and manufacturer of packing paper" and he asked for her permission to edit and publish the memoirs she was believed to be writing. We do not know if she responded.

Laundry bills from her hotel and similar invoices were still coming in, and official bills to be paid from her estate were to follow after her execution, such as one that asked for 299 francs in medical fees, twenty-four francs for appeal court costs, twelve francs for "the costs of process and judgment," twenty-five centimes for her extract from the *casier judiciaire* (to show that she had no previous offenses), and forty centimes for "printing."

Her "epistolary abundance" scorned by Mornet clearly continued, with most letters being returned undelivered. There are twenty-one envelopes for undelivered letters in the files, including several addressed to "*Mejuffrou* Anna Lintjens."

The last thin hope for the convicted woman was the appeal for presidential clemency. Most books on Mata Hari have Clunet going personally to Poincaré, who is usually described as his old law-school classmate, and pleading for his client's life. Some even put Clunet on his knees. In fact, the only appeal for clemency was the diplomatic one in the name of the Queen of the Netherlands, but the Quai d'Orsay mistakenly sent the response to Clunet instead of to the legation. Clunet received Poincaré's rejection on Saturday, October 13, and had to wait two days for the legation to open on the Monday—a few hours after the execution. Clunet called at the legation on his way home from the killing ground. Given the early hour, he must have been the first visitor. That he did not call on the legate at his home on the Saturday probably reflects his intense reluctance to pass on bad news; after all, he did not tell Mata Hari either.

The reaction of Poincaré and his advisers was hardly surprising; this was not the time to pardon spies. A key figure in the refusal of clemency would have been Paul Painlevé, a provincial mathematics professor from Lille who had entered parliament in 1910 and become minister of war in March 1917. In September, a month before the execution, he had taken on the additional post of prime minister, to be replaced by Clemenceau in November. This academic, who had had an early interest in aviation and who had been, in 1908, Wilbur Wright's first French passenger, was a firm hawk and a protagonist of the policy of shooting French defeatists and foreign spies.

On the Sunday, October 14, Clunet received an unsigned copy of an order from the military justice bureau of the general staff of the military governor of Paris, setting the execution for the morrow. A similar copy exists in the files. It specifies that the execution will take place at the "firing range" of Vincennes. Perhaps a leak about this led to the press cars heading for the range the following day and arriving at the château too late to be admitted, or perhaps the press knew that executions normally took place at the range. Another order sent out that day on General Dubail's authority said the prisoner was entitled to "Protestant assistance." This was presumably not because officialdom foresaw that Arboux would baptize her the following morning but because the original arrest warrant had described her as being of Protestant obedience.

Clunet responded with a last-resort letter, now in the files, addressed to *Commandant* (Major). This was probably for Massard who, as Dubail's representative, would preside over the execution. This said (as noted in Chapter One) that there was a "rumor in the theatrical world" that Mata Hari was pregnant, and called for a medical examination.

The old lawyer also resourcefully suggested that, since she had been condemned as a spy for the Germans, France offer to exchange her for a captured French general called Marchand. There would, of course, have been no reason for the Germans to exchange their most senior prisoner of war for a nonspy, but in any event Clunet's proposal was not followed up.

The events of that Monday morning were described at the beginning of this book. Mata Hari died bravely and well and, one likes to think, in the style of a Hindu resigned to destiny. One may speculate that the absurdity of the investigation, the trial, and the verdict made her fate more acceptable to her. This scatterbrained and often impossible woman became a creature of dignity and intelligence as she confronted the riddle of death and rebirth, dying apparently more for what she was than for anything she did in relation to the war. Edith Cavell had swooned at the sight of the firing squad, and the German riflemen had had to stand over her inert figure and fire into it at point-blank range. Mata Hari gave her audience a more illuminating scene.

Significantly, perhaps, none of her demeanor after the "baptism"—in the cell, on the ride to Vincennes, and above all before the firing squad—suggests the behavior of a Christian, especially that of a just-converted Christian adult. She did not pray or cross herself or show any apparent concern about an "afterlife" in heaven, limbo, or hell. Her manner before the firing squad was essentially that of a Buddhist—she herself would have said a Hindu—accepting an end to what had become a miserable and illusory existence and hoping for a more tolerable reincarnation.

Cavalry sergeant (*maréchal des logis*) Petey of the 23rd Dragoon Regiment marched to the stake and fired the coup de grâce. From where he stood, Bouchardon thought it went through the ear, but most reports say the temple. An Army physician called Robillard, described as "first class *aide-major* doctor," assigned to the Beguin Hospital, unbuttoned the bodice of her dress and was about to put a stethoscope to her chest when he started back, his hands and arms covered in spurting blood, and exclaimed "A bullet through the heart!" From ten meters, all eleven bullets had hit the body somewhere.

Robillard signed a death certificate later, and he, a Lieutenant Choulot, and the clerk, Captain Thibaud, signed the papers saying the execution had been carried out. Choulot is described as an army judge.

The eleven Zouaves formed up in single file.

"Pour défiler—en avant—marche!"

A bugle sounded the French equivalent of "The Last Post," and the Zouaves were marched past the corpse and off the Caponnière. The Zouave who had fainted was borne away on a litter. Sergeants bawled, and the larger body of soldiers were then marched off to breakfast.

As the military began to be evacuated, Captain Thibaud, the chief of the military court clerks, stood in front of the corpse and asked: "Does nobody claim the body?" Usually this was done by a prisoner's family, represented by the defense counsel. Clunet, apparently beside himself with grief, said nothing. What family did he represent? But a tiny figure, protected from reproach by her nun's habit, walked up to the inert figure. It was Sister Marie, still sobbing quietly; she removed Mata Hari's wedding ring, apparently by prior agreement. She would wear it all her life.

A horsedrawn gun-carriage, rather like a dray, appeared. Two soldiers jumped off the flatbed and carried down an unstained whitewood coffin. Mata Hari was lifted inside, and two nails knocked in to keep the lid on. Then the soldiers lifted the coffin onto the dray, jumped aboard themselves, and took the only seating available—the casket itself. The driver snapped his reins and the clumsy vehicle moved slowly off. Since the body was now State property, the gun-carriage was escorted by a mounted gendarme.

There was a brief stop at a cemetery, where Arboux was waiting alone. The nuns must have dropped him off there on their way back to the prison. In those days, it would have been forbidden for them to be present at a Protestant ceremony, especially one performed according to the rites of such an obscure cult as the Baptists. The thought occurs to a writer that Mata Hari may have been convinced to accept a christening to ensure that at least there would be some last rite, if only according to something resembling the Dutch Reformed faith of her childhood, which she had given up to become a Hindu. It was, after all, improbable that the French State would pay for a funeral pyre and a Hindu priest. There was a war on, and a shortage of firewood.

The coffin was unloaded and Arboux said his piece. The coffin was then slid into an empty tomb for a few seconds, pulled out, and lifted back aboard the gun-carriage. Mata Hari, the soldiers, and the gendarme then set off at a horse's walking pace for the destination of unclaimed bodies of executed prisoners: the faculty of medicine of the University of Paris, where the students that day must surely have found it a more interesting cadaver than most— even if, given the circumstances, it is hard to conceive of what useful organs would have survived undamaged to serve the cause of science.

11. *The Sequel*

On October 19, four days after the execution, Captain Georges Ladoux was arrested. For spying. For Germany.

One of his agents, newspaper owner Pierre Lenoir, had been taken into custody and charged with going over to the enemy. He protested that his actions as a double agent had been misinterpreted, that the Germans must have set him up. This all has a familiar sound. Like Mata Hari, he was ordered to name his accomplices. She could name none. He named Ladoux.

Lenoir's accusation must have been more than cynicism—i.e., he was claiming to work for France, therefore Ladoux was his accomplice—or gallows humor, because the facts he produced were enough for the military government of Paris to take the extraordinary step of arresting the head of French counterespionage. The St.-Cyrian officer and protégé of General Joffre was released to house arrest after a few days and spent the rest of the war going through the same sort of interrogations as Mata Hari.

There was no question of fudging a case here. Shooting spies might be good for morale, but finding the second most senior figure in French intelligence to be a German agent would have had just the opposite effect. His arrest was kept secret.

On January 1, 1919, two months after the victory, the case was dropped. But apparently someone was not satisfied, because he was rearrested the following day and put through further interrogations. He was court-martialed and acquitted on May 8.

Both the Ladoux and Lenoir dossiers are still sealed, so, without knowledge to the contrary, it is only fair to assume that his acquittal was justified. Had he been arrested sooner, one can only hypothesize as to the stunning effect it would have had on Mata Hari's case—that her principal accuser had been thrown into jail, accused of being a German spy. Was his handling of the Mata Hari case a factor? Had his scrofulous behavior over the intercepts been discovered? Even arresting him a few days sooner might have led to a postponement of the execution until Ladoux's case was settled, nineteen months later, when the witch-hunt atmosphere of the war had passed. On the other hand, Ladoux's arrest did not help Lenoir, who was tried, found guilty, and shot.

We have to ask if Ladoux knew, through the breaking of the current code or through links to German intelligence, of Kroemer's attempt to recruit Mata Hari and of the fact that she had "swindled" Germany out of twenty thousand francs—in short, if he knew it before she revealed it to him but did not want the French to suspect that he was in touch with German intelligence. Did he get a message to Kalle? Presumably not; if he was part of a German plan to get rid of her, it would have been more effective—in terms of impressing Colonel Goubet more—if Kalle had used the current code for his messages to Berlin. And if Ladoux was a German spy, why did the Germans not know that their current code was broken? The writer is inclined to conclude that Ladoux, although apparently guilty of perjury, obstruction of justice, and complicity to murder in Mata Hari's case, was innocent of the charge that he spied for Germany.

After his acquittal, Ladoux stayed on in the army for four more years, finally reaching the rank of major in 1923 at the age of forty-eight. Then, with the promotion improving his pension and giving him a title he could wear for life, this strange and complicated man retired. He became for a while the economics editor of *Le Matin*.

France had always attracted visitors, but now a new phenomenon was appearing—*touristes*, arriving in organized groups, hence *le tourisme*. Ladoux, who must still have had useful contacts, became the inspector of resorts and spas for the new department of tourism. Perhaps he visited Vittel.

Pierre Bouchardon went on to a steady career as an examining magistrate in civil life, until his death in 1950.

When France fell in 1940, he remained loyal to the government of Marshal Philippe Pétain, which collaborated with the Germans. But as the fortunes of war began to change, he, like many others, resigned from government in time to be reappointed at the Liberation. He was the first examining magistrate whom Marshal Pétain faced when he was brought back from Germany and charged with treason.

By then, Bouchardon was seventy-four and had a white Vandyke beard. The eyes, once described as beady, under their arching brows, were now qualified as "mischievous" in the press. We do not know if he still chewed his nails while he interrogated.

He persuaded Pétain to do exactly what he had persuaded Mata Hari to do: to waive his right to have a lawyer present at the first *comparution*. Pétain had asked for a certain lawyer, who declined to take the case. The Marshal, then eighty-nine, was offered a lawyer designated by the authorities and turned him down. It was at this point that he agreed to go through the formality of a first "appearance and interrogatory" alone.

When Pétain finally acquired a major attorney, Jacques Isorni, his counsel fulminated that far more substantial questions had been asked than were justified at a *première comparution* and that his client's rights had been violated. No one wanted the most important postwar trial in France to be vitiated by anything, so Bouchardon was replaced.

Had this not happened, another coincidence with the Mata Hari trial would have occurred, because the prosecutor for whom the Pétain case was being prepared was none other than André Mornet.

The man who had been a humble lieutenant in World War I—when Pétain had been the general who had covered himself in glory by keeping the Germans from Verdun, becoming later a seven-star Marshal of France—was now the Republic's procurator-general, a title later changed to attorney-general. Mornet too had served Vichy for a while, then resigned in time to score heavily at the Liberation. He was still skinny and peppery, with a bilious temper and hooded eyes; like Bouchardon, he wore a dapper white beard.

Isorni put on one of the best performances of his career, claiming that someone had had to stand between the French and their occupiers and that Pétain had taken on an ungrateful task out of patriotism; but the case—although enormously different from Mata Hari's—was decided in advance. Mornet demanded and got the death penalty, later commuted by Charles de Gaulle to life internment on the windswept island of Yeu, off the Breton coast.

Questioned on one occasion on the Mata Hari case by a journalist, Mornet said he had had only a weak brief to go on—"not enough to flog a cat," as he put it.

Colonel Joseph-Cyrille Denvignes was apparently adjudged too incompetent for his sensitive field position in Madrid. He was called home and promoted general.

Paul Painlevé, who as Poincaré's prime minister must have recommended strongly against clemency for Mata Hari, remained in politics, becoming minister of war again in 1925 and retaining that post in most administrations until 1929. He introduced the peace-time draft in 1928 and started the work on the Maginot Line. He died in 1933 at the age of seventy.

Major Arnold Kalle stayed in Madrid for six years in all, then returned home. He continued to serve in government, becoming a *Ministerialdirektor* in 1928. He was still an army officer and only retired from the army, with the rank of general, in 1932, a year before Hitler came to power. He returned to his home village of Bieberich-am-Rhein. He was then fifty-nine.

The young naval lieutenant Wilhelm Canaris, whom most writers mistook for Mata Hari's "controller" and lover in Madrid but who never met her, became the head of all German intelligence in World War II; he joined the plot against Hitler, was caught, interrogated, and finally strangled with a piano wire.

Consul Kroemer, whose name the French never learned to spell, despite Mata Hari's wise advice, returned to live in Germany in 1919. He died in 1938.

Major Friedrich Gempp, notwithstanding the defeat and the decimation of Germany's army, became a lieutenant-colonel in 1920 and a full colonel in 1923, continuing to serve in intelligence. He retired as a brigadier general in 1927 at the age of fifty-four but returned to the *Abwehr* at the outbreak of war in 1939. In 1943, five weeks before his seventieth birthday, the handsome, monocled officer was promoted to major-general. According to German military records, a year after the war, on August 11, 1946, he was "abducted by the Russians," and is *seitdem vermisst*—missing ever since. (Curiously, these records show, Gempp's mother's maiden name was the unusual one, Rapferer, also borne by Mata Hari's *aéronaute* friend, who was presumably from Alsace-Lorraine. Were they related?)

Henry Hoedemaker, the creepy passenger who made Mata Hari's life miserable aboard the *Zeelandia*, told relatives after the war that he thought she had been arrested at Falmouth and subsequently arrested and convicted in France because of his negative reports on her from Madrid in the summer of 1916. He committed suicide in 1921.

John MacLeod's first reaction to the news of the execution, when informed by journalists in Arnhem, was: "Whatever she did, she didn't deserve that."

The retired major's second marriage, in 1907, to Elizabeth van der Mast, had—as noted earlier—ended in separation in 1912; his wife and younger daughter Norma, born in 1909, had departed from his life, leaving him alone with Non. In 1917, he divorced and on October 3, a few days before his first wife's execution, he married another woman, Grietje Meijer, then twenty-five, who had been the teenage Non's "nursemaid" since 1913. MacLeod was then sixty-two.

After the execution, MacLeod bombarded his foreign ministry and the Dutch legation in Paris with letters, trying to assure that his ex-spouse's estate should go to Non. An unsigned letter in the Mata Hari file, dated January 26, 1918, and emanating from the *procureur de la république*, asks the commissioner of the government (Jullien) to find out if Mata Hari left a will. Another letter, from Dr. Milhaud, the lawyer appointed by the government to handle her estate, says there was no will. MacLeod was finally informed that all her belongings had been auctioned on January 30, 1918, and had realized 14,251 francs and 65 centimes—in purchasing terms, with inflation, the equivalent of about five thousand dollars today, although much less then. This money had been seized to help pay the costs of her trial. MacLeod complained to the Dutch press that Non had been cheated.

He also noted that the papers had reported that Griet had written two or three letters before she died, of which one must have been for her daughter; he complained that nothing had arrived.

There is a letter in the dossier from Estachy, the prison director, to Jullien, saying the three letters she wrote just before her execution had been given to Pastor Arboux. Writing under the letterhead of the Consistorial Union of the Reformed Churches of Paris and the Department of the Seine (which, among other tasks, allocated Protestant chaplains to the prisons), Arboux informed Jullien that the three letters were for her daughter and "two persons among her personal relationships." He said explicitly that there was no will. The night before the execution, he related, Mata Hari had asked him: "Do you think it's for tomorrow? If so, I ought to write a will." He had, he recalled, told her that he knew nothing of execution plans, and he added that she never really seemed to believe that she would actually be executed.

By April 10, 1919, MacLeod was still asking for a death certificate, which Non would require if she wanted to marry before the age of twenty-one. One presumes that the Dutch legation finally procured this.

Like her mother, Non was dark, moody, and tall—five feet eleven inches—and, like Mata Hari, Non was trained as a kindergarten teacher. Like both her parents, she chose the colonial life. On August 10, 1919, she was due to depart to teach in the Dutch East Indies. Her new stepmother, only a few years older than Non, had helped her pack her trunks for the ship the night before, when the girl went to bed at eleven. She never woke up.

Her death was never explained. The popular story that she was tubercular seems implausible, given her decision to go to Indonesia, her father's approval, and the colonial government's acceptance of her. The report that she had had a cerebral hemorrhage—a fatal stroke—seems more likely. She was twenty-one.

She was buried in the graveyard at Worth-Rheden. Putting her full name on the gravestone would have almost required, given her youth, adding "Daughter of . . ." No doubt MacLeod, conscious that everyone in Holland knew the real name of Mata Hari, did not want his daughter's grave to attract curiosity-seekers, so the marker simply says "Our Non," and the dates of birth and death.

MacLeod became a father again on March 20, 1921, and called his new daughter Non. He died seven years later at the age of nearly seventy-three and was buried with his eldest daughter. To the stone were added the words "And Her Father," with his dates.

Eduard van der Capellen apparently stopped paying the rent for Mata Hari's house, because the two sisters who owned it had its contents auctioned over two days, on January 9 and 10, 1918. From 1923 until 1938, it was the residence of the Dutch actress Fie Carelsen, who played Mata Hari in a 1932 play.

Van der Capellen retired from the Dutch army in 1923, with the rank of major general.

Anna Lintjens retired to a village in the Limburg province of Holland. In 1931, at the age of seventy, she was very ill. Fearing death, she burned all of Mata Hari's papers in the kitchen stove so that they would not fall into greedy hands. She died a few years later.

Jean-Hélie Hallaure, who had been seventeen when he first met Margaretha Zelle at Molier's stables, was only twenty-six when he sent her on her fatal visit to Georges Ladoux's office. After the victory, this war-wounded son of a prosperous Norman *notaire* (nonbarrister lawyer) was given an allowance by his father and went to New York, where he married an American. The couple were to spend the rest of their lives in the village of Sainte-Marine (coincidentally, Marine is French for Marina, the name given to Mata Hari by her beloved Vadim) in the Finistère peninsula of Brittany. Hallaure died around 1960.

Jules-Martin Cambon, who was seventy-three when the war ended, was one of France's five delegates to the peace conference at Versailles two years later. He had by then retired from the foreign service, but he remained the elder statesman of French diplomacy and still has his name on streets and cafés in France—a very rare distinction for a civil servant.

He died at Vevey, a pleasant resort town on the Lake of Geneva, in Switzerland, in 1935, at the age of ninety.

Félix "Xavier" Rousseau did not die in 1914, after his misadventure with the law, as official France for some reason believed;

but, as his widow much later said of Mata Hari: "When she restored him to me, he was ruined." The champagne salesman eked out a modest existence and died in 1945, aged seventy-two.

Henry Jean-Baptiste Joseph de Marguérie remained at his sensitive post in the Quai d'Orsay, despite his loyal defense of someone condemned as a German spy. After the war, he took advantage of the return of Alsace-Lorraine to France to enter politics and was elected senator from the Moselle in 1920. He was only removed from the diplomatic list in 1922.

The well-tailored, humorous, sophisticated, lifelong bachelor survived through World War II and died in 1963, at the age of ninety-five.

Vladimir de Masloff's right eye was saved, and he went back to the front lines, where he reportedly was wounded again. At the end of the war, he married Olga Tardieu, the daughter of a Frenchman and his Russian wife.

With the revolution, the Czar's officers faced two choices: exile in France, which many took, often using their aristocratic training to become a new generation of butlers and chauffeurs—or taxidrivers—or returning home to fight for a restoration. Vadim and his bride returned to Russia, so their fate—or at least his—is not hard to guess.

Had he married Mata Hari and settled down to exile in the avénue Henri-Martin, however short a time the mismatch lasted, she would presumably have saved his life. If she could have saved her own, that is.

12. *The Mythology*

MATA HARI'S FAME as a spy, notwithstanding her extraordinarily brief and inconclusive embrace of the art, lies in the fact that she was famous already. As an exotic naked dancer, she was a household word, despite her faltering career on the boards, much as Mae West remains famous in America because she was naughty earlier than others. Mata Hari has become, undeservedly, the most notorious, the most well-known of all spies, with a name that has meaning to hundreds of millions all over the world, most of whom would not recognize the names of Rudolf Abel, Kim Philby, or General Oleg Penkovsky, because she was a headline name; just as Brigitte Bardot, if she were (perish the thought!) arrested tomorrow as a Soviet agent, would displace Mata Hari for the title, while probably reinvigorating the earlier legend by being dubbed "the new Mata Hari."

The legend far surpasses the woman. The main sequel to Mata Hari's secret trial and conviction and her relatively public execution was the mythology that grew up around this "greatest woman spy of World War I." And naturally, with the papers sealed, tidbits of information leaked and were altered and hyperbolized, getting further and further away from the truth—with the fraud often encouraged by those who had contributed to her perdition, which became the source of their own momentary fame as authors.

Ladoux and Bouchardon were not the only ones to embroider history. Edmond Locard, the canny cryptographer whose work, along with that of his colleagues, is the principle proof of her innocence, loyally did not conclude that there had been a complete miscarriage of justice when his own name appeared on a book thirty-seven years later, in 1954.

Locard, who had only his own keyhole perspective of the drama to go on and relied for the rest on the books of others, the rumor mill, and imagination, decided that her real lover was the German consul in Amsterdam, whom he portrays as a major figure in German intelligence who had recruited her in the toils of passion. He bases this on the fact that, apparently, he says, all her letters to van der Capellen—which he believes were letters to the consul—were "love letters."

He sees her as a lazy spy, doing nothing for the Germans in Vittel, where she was having an affair with a Russian called "Marov." He thinks the German she was dealing with in Madrid was Lieutenant Canaris, whom he promotes three ranks to naval captain and whom he says had the room next to hers at the Ritz Hotel. (The humble cryptographer had no "need to know" which code numbers referred to which German intelligence officers.)

Apparently unnoticed at the time—perhaps precisely because he does not denounce it as part of a miscarriage of justice—Locard, in his little-read *Mata Hari*, does reveal his own great secret. He writes:

"Canaris, a decidedly ugly fellow, sent Mata Hari, or rather Agent H 21, to France, signaling her departure by a radio-telegram whose cipher he knew the French general staff possessed. Canaris liquidated a costly mistress and an ineffective spy."

Since she had received only 3,500 pesetas from Kalle—and this would appear to be German government money, not Kalle's own—this hardly warrants Locard's image of her as an expensive mistress; and since she was leaving for France anyway, Kalle, it may be noted, had no problem in "getting rid" of her. Locard also theorizes that the Germans wanted the French to look bad by "doing an Edith Cavell."

Locard apparently spoke to Dr. Bralez, Dr. Bizard's assistant, for a physical portrait of the lady and received from the physician a brief discourse on facial anatomy. He quotes Bralez as saying Mata Hari was "beautiful but not pretty. There was something bestial in her lips, jaws and cheekbones."

Locard also printed what he claimed was the text of Mata Hari's last letter to Non, which seems much too long for the few moments she spent writing it. It is also signed curiously for a mother's letter, and the supposed epistolarian misspells her own name: "Margarida-Gertrud Zelle-MacLeod."

*   *   *

Major Emile Massard, who represented the military government of Paris at the execution, wrote a book, *Les espionnes à Paris* (*Women Spies in Paris*), in 1922.

The major confuses India with the Dutch East Indies and says the lady was raised in Burma. He refers to her constantly as "Mata," as though that was the name Mr. Hari had given his daughter. He says she was Jewish and that she asked for a milk bath in prison. He describes Kalle as von Krohn.

It was Massard who launched the famous legend that she received Priolet and his five inspectors stark naked and tried to settle the warrant then and there by inviting them all into a warm bed. Another legend that owes its origin to the imaginative major is that Clunet had comforted her at some point by saying that the firing squad had been bribed to fire blank cartridges. Historians might assume that Massard borrowed this baroque idea from the opera *Tosca*, then a Paris favorite.

Although Massard only claims that Clunet was telling her a white lie so she could get some sleep, the story naturally led to a further legend, in other books and articles, in which she is never actually shot at all. She was said to have rejected having her hands tied—attested to by all the eyewitnesses who wrote—because it is easier to simulate death lying facedown on the ground than while lying over from a post, a difficult posture for a stocky forty-one-year-old in a corset to maintain motionlessly for long.

This story, which required ignoring the coup de grâce—unless that was a blank cartridge job also—and the absence of a pool of blood, has her "body" left on the field to be rescued by a gallant lover called Pierre de Morissac (or Pierre de Mortissac; the name varies). The couple are later spotted—like Himmler in more recent times—in all sorts of places, including Wiesbaden (where Mata Hari spent her honeymoon with John).

Yet another version was that the plan existed but misfired (no pun intended) by being uncovered in time, and that the distraught Morissac gave up his playboy life and walked on foot through Spain to visit all the places where she had stayed (which become much more numerous than just Madrid and Vigo), thus carrying out a sort of "stations of the cross." Finally, he enters a Chartrist monastery in Pamplona. (This story surfaced again in 1948 when *The New York Herald Tribune* published a brief story saying that

Morissac, the "last lover of Mata Hari," was now living in a Spanish monastery.)

Massard, however, hints at *intoxication* messages by claiming that the Germans frequently betrayed their worst spies to the French to distract attention from their better ones. Contradictorily, he calls Mata Hari "the greatest woman spy of the war."

Monique Saint-Servan, whose *Mata Hari* appeared in 1959, makes von Krohn the lady's German contact in Madrid. He now gets the favored room next to the dancer's at the Ritz that Locard gave to Canaris, thus doing an injustice to Marthe Richard's authentic achievement. Kroemer, in Amsterdam, becomes "von Schaeffer."

Saint-Servan has the truth about Mata Hari's treachery emerging through a Ladoux agent called Miguel, who is a servant in the hotel, but not before Mata Hari has tried to seduce a French military attaché. This is no limping Colonel Denvignes, old before his time, but a young captain with blue eyes and a blond moustache called Sudreau—who is warned in time by Ladoux, tipped off by Miguel.

Saint-Servan believes Ladoux did give Mata Hari a list of names in Belgium; she identifies the spy for the Germans whom Ladoux wanted Berlin to suspect and shoot as Peter van Balley, whose address she gives as 54 rue de la Montagne des herbes potagères in Brussels. She says he was executed by the Germans on November 13, 1916. Allowing time for the formalities and trial, he must therefore have been arrested by the Germans before Mata Hari left France, even perhaps before she first met Ladoux. Whether Ladoux gave her Balley's name and address remains uncertain and even improbable; it would have been safe to do so, although perhaps unwise to tell Bouchardon and the military court. Saint-Servan appears to be accurate about the date of Balley's execution and presumably about his picturesque address.

Saint-Servan also believes the Pierre de Morissac legend and says Mata Hari only returned to Paris from Madrid because the lovelorn Morissac telegraphed her to come back. Morissac seems to be based, here, partially on Marguérie, since he is said to have known Mata Hari for "ten years," with perhaps a bit of Rousseau thrown in, since the lovers are said never to have married because of objections from Morissac's father, an elderly marquis. (Readers will recall that Rousseau's mother briefly objected to her son's passion.)

This particular writer attributed Mata Hari's initial trip to Paris to the generosity of the impoverished and parsimonious Adam Zelle, who sends his daughter to study dancing under a Russian master in the rue Mouffetard. The dark secret in Mata Hari's life is her poisoned son, whose death she has avenged by killing the Javanese maidservant. (In fairness to Miss Saint-Servan, this could well be based on a cathartic myth of the dancer's own; it sounds like her.)

Mata Hari's last letter, from prison, is of course to Morissac; and far from converting to Baptism in her final moments, she converts the young Dr. Bralez to Buddhism.

Another legend, created earlier by a German writer, was launched in France in 1970 by Danielle Hummert and Alex Roudère, in their *Mata Hari, danseuse, courtisane et espionne* (*Mata Hari, Dancer, Courtesan and Spy*). This is that, tired of the brutal and drunken MacLeod, she had had an affair with an Indonesian sultan, whom she meets while convalescing from her illness on the coffee plantation.

Naturally a child is conceived, and naturally she is a daughter— i.e., Mata Hari II. "Banda" is raised by the sultan but later falls in love with Peter van der Bergh, the deputy governor of the Dutch East Indies and a man "forty years her senior." He dies in 1935, leaving Banda all his money.

During World War II, Banda becomes an unwilling collaborator of the Japanese occupying army, then later a middle-aged fighter in the Indonesian resistance. But like her mother, whom she resembles, she can never get her loyalties straight, and she goes on to become a CIA agent in China and is finally shot by the Russians when she is captured in North Korea (where a Eurasian from Indonesia would be a little conspicuous) during the Korean War.

The author says the daughter to whom Mata Hari wrote moments before her execution was Banda. The other two letters, we learn, were for "Karl Breitenstein," a German diplomat (Kroemer?) and Mata Hari's "Uncle Paulus," to thank the old man for persuading Queen Wilhelmina to intervene with Poincaré to try to save the dancer's life.

This book accepts the tale that Mata Hari studied spying in

Lorrach in 1912 and says her lover in Madrid was Canaris, whom she had first become attached to in Berlin in 1907 (when Canaris was a seventeen-year-old orphan and still in the *gymnasium*). Her brief affair in Berlin in 1914 with Griebl becomes one with Kurt von Jagow, whose real first name was Traugott; von Jagow is described as head of all German espionage, the job held by Major Gempp. Actually, as we know, Traugott von Jagow was the head of the Berlin police and probably never met Mata Hari.

In Britain, E. Temple Thurston wrote *Portrait of a Spy*, which sets out to prove that Mata Hari was responsible for "hundreds of thousands" of Allied deaths. In France, Dr. Bizard contributed his *Souvenirs d'un médecin de Saint-Lazare* (*Souvenirs of a Women's Prison Doctor*) to the literature. In this, he claims, as noted earlier, that he first met Mata Hari while doing his monthly medical inspection in an elegant cathouse.

From Spain, the faithful Senator Emilio Junoy produced a book to prove her innocence. Also from beyond the Pyrenees, Blasco Ibanez came to her defense in *Mare Nostrum*. He seems to have been the only writer to have interviewed Clunet. All the Spaniards' romantic arguments were forcefully answered in Louis Dumur's *Les défaitistes* (*The Defeatists*).

Not all the books claim to be nonfiction. Charles-Henry Hirsch wrote an opera, *La danseuse rouge: La chèvre aux pieds d'or* in 1937. The title doesn't translate well: *The Red Dancer, or The Nanny-Goat with Golden Feet.*

In the scenario, a widower called Marc Brégyl, who is apparently Clunet, falls in love with a twenty-year-old Russian dancer called Toutcha when she appears with the Ballets Russes in Monte Carlo. In World War I, she is accused of spying for the Germans, and Brégyl, a lawyer, sings a long baritone *plaidoirie* in response to the *requisitoire* of a tenor representing Mornet. She is finally danced to the stake, where bass drums finish her off.

A well-written novel, *Pavane pour une espionne* (*Dirge for a Lady Spy*) was published by René Masson in 1965. Since this is fiction, a few liberties with the facts are forgivable. "Von Jagow" is now the German foreign minister; although recruiting her for Germany, he does not become her lover—an original touch. (Masson appears to have confused the police officer Traugott von Jagow with the politician Gottlieb von Jagow.)

The author has Vadim giving her a German helmet as a souvenir and she ends up using it as a candy jar. When Priolet comes calling with his arrest warrant, she invites him to help himself to the bonbons while she is dressing. This novel also has Mata Hari converting Bralez to Buddhism during long cozy cell evenings when she ruminates on her life.

In writing Clunet's *plaidoirie* for him, Masson perceptively has him asking whether it might not be possible that the Germans had set her up, saying "Suppose they knew that their dispatches were being intercepted?" Had Masson read Locard's book?

Guy de Bellet, in his 1970 biography *Mata Hari*, replaces Henry de Marguérie by someone called Philipe (*sic*) Berthelot, who is "director of the Quai d'Orsay" (the job, although not quite the right title, of Jules Cambon) and says he was the "right hand man of Aristide Briand" (who was prime minister, not foreign minister).

In this book, her friends and lovers call her "Mata." Bellet confuses the Cambon-Marguérie mixup further by reviving the Morissac story, changing the name to Mortissac. He rejects the *Tosca* plot but does have Mortissac finally mortifying his flesh in a Spanish monastery.

His *requisitoire* by Mornet contains such phrases as "France is fighting for her destiny, for victory. We would betray the most noble of our sons if we spared this avid tart [*demi-mondaine*] simply because she knows the right people."

Clunet comes off better, arguing absence of proof and points of law.

Five years earlier, Kurt Singer, in his 1965 book *Mata Hari*, had devised the legend of Mata Hari's affair with the sultan, which he places as having started on the night the two children were poisoned, thus making her guilt at leaving the infants in the care of the maid more traumatic. The distraught MacLeod, the reasons for whose own absence at the time are not hard to guess, flogs his wife when he finds out what has happened.

It is during her dalliances with the sultan that she learns Javanese dancing. Singer brings Banda into the world, as he does Breiten-stein and the role of von Jagow, although he has Mata Hari finally being lured into German intelligence by Canaris in 1912 (when Canaris was twenty-two). "Von Jagow," actually, appears to be Griebl.

Singer puts her specific dates at Lorrach as being November 1912 through February 1913, when she was dancing in Paris. He ex-plains her short visit to Austria as concerned with setting up a German spy network in that country (an ally of Germany's) and her trip to Egypt (which was in 1908) as laying the groundwork for German efforts in Morocco (in 1916). He even has her setting up networks in Italy and Britain and, at the outbreak of war, in Holland.

According to Singer, she got the plans for the tank (a British invention) from a lovesick British general. Her Russian lover is "Marov." In Spain, he confuses her with Clara Benedix and has her dancing the flamenco in Barcelona. He confuses Kalle with von Krohn.

Sir Brian Thomson becomes head of the Criminal Investigation Department at Scotland Yard. Instead of returning her to Spain, he allows her to proceed to Holland, and later becomes Winston Churchill's bodyguard. (Churchill became prime minister in 1940, by which time Sir Basil, if still with us, would have been seventy-eight.)

At the trial, there are ten charges instead of eight, and Cambon testifies instead of Marguérie. He accepts the *Tosca*-plot-that-failed story, which he thinks explains Mata Hari's appearance of courage before the firing squad. Pierre de Mortissac is now a count.

His biography of Banda appears to have been followed faithfully by Hummert and Roudère, with her finally meeting her fate some-where north of the Imjin River.

A fiercely polemical anti–Mata Hari book was written by a com-patriot of hers, Charles S. Heymans, whose *La vraie Mata Hari* (*The Real Mata Hari*) appeared in 1930. Heymans was the Paris corre-spondent of the *Bataviaansch Nieuwsblad*, a Dutch East Indies news-paper.

Heymans met John MacLeod shortly before his death; he is the only apologist in the literature for this "fine old officer," and he relies heavily on the ex-husband's bilious version for an account of Mata Hari's early life. This includes her supporting herself by part-time prostitution after MacLeod deserted her in Amsterdam, and taking the infant Non along with her when she does so.

The long, shrill diatribe accepts all the legends about her role as a major spy, responsible for hundreds of thousands of deaths. Heymans improves on Massard's story by having her receive Priolet and his inspectors in her *robe de chambre*, then taking it off before offering her gentlemen callers bonbons from the German helmet. He recounts that Clunet and "Mortissac" plotted a *Tosca* scenario and expected it to happen and that both were horrified when she actually died.

Major Thomas Coulson's *Mata Hari*, published a few years after the victory, is also a diatribe. It appears to contain more outright inventions and more exuberant mendacity than any other book ever published about the lady. She is almost always somewhere other than where she actually was in life, thus making it possible for her to be doing whatever the major fantasizes.

There are so many wrong names that at least some of Coulson's sources would appear to be French. He seems to have been the first to make Kroemer "von Schaeffer." The notorious Fräulein Schragmüller, who ran the spy school at Lorrach, to which Coulson naturally assigns Mata Hari, becomes Frau von Heinrichsen. He confuses Kalle with von Krohn and Cambon with Marguérie. Masloff is "Marov," and she cuts short her idyll with him in Vittel to dash back to Paris to report to the Germans that the French are about to launch an offensive. The dark-haired Russian officer is blond and he is "completely blind"—which perhaps explains, for the author, his attraction to Mata Hari.

These are peccadillos. The dancer's demonic genius is responsible for several major German victories, going back to the Chemin des Dames débâcle in 1914, when she was in Holland. The Second Bureau, praise be, finally latches on to this extraordinary spy after they discover that one of her letters to her daughter in Holland is written in code. And so on, for 312 pages.

An original effort, and apparently the most recent French book on *Mata Hari*, is Michel Leblanc's *L'ennemie de Mata Hari* (*Mata*

Hari's Rival), which appeared in 1974. This is based on interviews that Leblanc had with a retired French police commissioner, Paul Collart, then aged ninety, whom the writer found living in an old people's home at Sclos-de-contes in the South of France.

Collart claimed to Leblanc that Mata Hari was under surveillance in Spain from late 1915 because of a British tip. Collart and his Spanish-born wife Roda were both then in French intelligence in Madrid, and worked with Marthe Richard.

Collart argued that the Germans tried to recruit Mata Hari but that she never did anything for them; he says Dr. Schragmüller had called her "a dud shell." All this sounds like the truth.

The one curious new feature in the book is that Collart insists that Mata Hari had a child (Mata Hari III?) by the Crown Prince of Germany and that the little girl was adopted by someone called Ilse Lidenoffen, who raised the infant at the expense of her royal father. Collart said the child's name had been changed to Elisa Dubois.

The most recent novel is a readable yarn by Dan Sherman called *The Man Who Loved Mata Hari*, published in New York in 1985. In this book, she meets Masloff in Paris in 1904, when he would have been seven, which perhaps explains why he has just failed his exams at Oxford. Sir Brian Thomson becomes head of Scotland Yard. A fictitious British painter replaces both Marguérie and Morrissac, trying to rescue her from prison in spite of her love for a ruthless German spymaster and ending up traumatized in Spain. Much of the book is based on Waagenaar, including the supposition that she did not get a fair trial.

For the record, in 1930 the authorized work on Germany's World War I spying appeared in Berlin. It was the *Geschichte des Weltkriegs und Nachkriegsspionage* (*History of World War and Postwar Espionage*), edited by Hans Henning, Baron Grote. This contains a chapter on Germany's women spies by Wulf Bley, in which he says: "The dancer Mata Hari was executed, although she was absolutely innocent. She was only a great paramour [*Lebedame*]." Dr. Schragmüller, who is described as heading Major Gempp's IIIC Bureau in Antwerp, is quoted as saying: "All H 21's information for Germany was false. She was never one of ours."

Gempp himself, in an article published on January 31, 1929, in the *Kölnische Zeitung*, states that Mata Hari "never did anything for German intelligence." He repeated this in another newspaper article five months later.

Neither the book nor the articles say anything about Kalle's *intoxication* messages or their role in her fate.

In 1932, a certain Colonel Lacroix, then head of military justice in France, took advantage of his position to read the sealed Mata Hari dossier. He could not, under law, reveal what he had learned, but he did tell a French reporter, Paul Allard, that he had found "no palpable, tangible . . . proofs of her guilt." The present writer can only agree.

Index

871089

DATE		